Beyond Crisis

KAIROS

In ancient Greek philosophy, *kairos* signifies the right time or the "moment of transition." We believe that we live in such a transitional period. The most important task of social science in time of transformation is to transform itself into a force of liberation. Kairos, an editorial imprint of the Anthropology and Social Change department housed in the California Institute of Integral Studies, publishes groundbreaking works in critical social sciences, including anthropology, sociology, geography, theory of education, political ecology, political theory, and history.

Series editor: Andrej Grubačić

Recent and featured Kairos books:

Practical Utopia: Strategies for a Desirable Society by Michael Albert

In, Against, and Beyond Capitalism: The San Francisco Lectures by John Holloway

Anthropocene or Capitalocene? Nature, History, and the Crisis of Capitalism edited by Jason W. Moore

We Are the Crisis of Capital: A John Holloway Reader by John Holloway

Archive That, Comrade! Left Legacies and the Counter Culture of Remembrance by Phil Cohen

Re-enchanting the World: Feminism and the Politics of the Commons by Silvia Federici

Autonomy Is in Our Hearts: Zapatista Autonomous Government through the Lens of the Tsotsil Language by Dylan Eldredge Fitzwater

The Battle for the Mountain of the Kurds: Self-Determination and Ethnic Cleansing in the Afrin Region of Rojava by Thomas Schmidinger

Beyond the Periphery of the Skin: Rethinking, Remaking, and Reclaiming the Body in Contemporary Capitalism by Silvia Federici

Building Free Life: Dialogues with Öcalan edited by International Initiative

For more information visit **www.pmpress.org/blog/kairos/**

Beyond Crisis

After the Collapse of Institutional Hope in Greece, What?

Edited by John Holloway, Katerina Nasioka, and Panagiotis Doulos

Translations from the Greek by Anna-Maeve Holloway

Beyond Crisis: After the Collapse of Institutional Hope in Greece, What?
Edited by John Holloway, Katerina Nasioka, and Panagiotis Doulos
© 2020 PM Press.
First published as: *Πέρα από την Κρίση. Μετά την κατάρρευση της θεσμικής ελπίδας, τι* (*Pera apo tin Krisi. Metá tin katárrevsi tis thesmikis elpidas, ti?*). Athens: Futura, 2017.

PM Press gratefully acknowledges the support of the Instituto de Ciencias Sociales y Humaniades "Alfonso Vélez Pliego," Benemérita Universidad Autónoma de Puebla in the production of this book.

ISBN: 978-1-62963-515-6
Library of Congress Control Number: 2017964736

Cover by John Yates / www.stealworks.com
Interior design by briandesign

10 9 8 7 6 5 4 3 2 1

PM Press
PO Box 23912
Oakland, CA 94623
www.pmpress.org

Printed in the USA.

Contents

Preface

Disillusion. Yet . . .

Disillusioned anger stalks the world and threatens to destroy us all.

Syriza lost the election at the beginning of July 2019. Of course it did. Its fall opened the way to the return of the right-wing New Democracy Party, now with a more aggressive program than ever.

Left (or left-ish) governments have a huge responsibility. It is not just that they disappoint us, it is much more than that. They pick up people's hope and anger and channel it into defeat and disillusion. That disillusion does not kill the anger, but it pushes it in a different direction, and that new direction is often terrifying, taking politics and state violence into realms that were barely conceivable ten or twenty years ago. In the United States Obama disappointed and opened the way to the barbarous, war-mongering fool, Trump. In Brazil, Lula (and later Dilma) disappointed and let come into power the unimaginably awful Bolsonaro. And now Tsipras, after all his promises of a radical Government of Hope, has destroyed those hopes with his reversal of policies after the referendum of July 2015 and has opened the door to the regenerated New Democracy.

This is not the old game of alternating between "left" and "right" governments, which used to be understood as the hallmark of a healthy democracy. Since 2008 the game has changed. The huge upsurge of anger in all the world that resulted from the collapse of the financial system and, much more, from the attempts to rescue the financial system gives a new sharpness to political conflict. The anger has flowed against the established power structures but in different ways. Some anger has swung toward the left, calling for radical change in the system, but some swings toward the right, calling for strong leaders, strong national boundaries, exclusion of ethnic minorities, more control, more authority, more "racial purity." The institutional Left may succeed in channeling the first type of anger into electoral victory and hope for meaningful change, as Syriza did. But the institutional Left is bound to the state and to the reproduction of capital, so, inevitably, it betrays the hopes it promised to fulfill, it breeds disillusion. It is easy then for the disillusioned anger to just go home and close its eyes or to swing to the right and support nationalist-authoritarian solutions. And those solutions cause untold misery in the present and take us a step closer to human extinction, possibly in the near future.

Disillusion stems from the institutional Left. Yet . . . If we only blame the Left for not completing the role "it is made for," we give no answer to the present waning of anticapitalist struggles, the social demobilization, and the re-emergence of the Right's "law and order" doctrine all around the world. We just rephrase the question. This book, from its very beginning, aims to go further than the currency of Syriza, to go beyond rephrasing the question. Our argument is that to be true to the hope and anger that fills so many of us, we must break from the suffocating logic of the institutional Left, from left parties and fairer distribution and better social services and a different balance between locality and center. It is a deeper change that we need if we are to defeat the disillusioned anger that threatens to destroy us all.

What can we do? The eternal question—but there is no eternity for human existence, just a probably shortening time of life on earth. What can we do? Read the book and send us your answers.

John Holloway, Katerina Nasioka, and Panagiotis Doulos
Athens and Puebla, July 2019

Introduction

John Holloway, Katerina Nasioka, and Panagiotis Doulos

"Hope is on the way." And now hope has gone away, leaving a trail of disappointment and depression. The crisis is here. The storm is here. And it has broken out in full force.

Is this all? Was that really hope that left? Or was it illusion, making way for true hope? Or should we just come to terms with depression?

"Hope is on the way." This is the slogan with which Syriza won the Greek elections on January 25, 2015. The result was rupture with the two-party system (PASOK–New Democracy) that had dominated Greek political life since the fall of the dictatorship in 1974. Syriza's rise to power was supposed to bring a new type of politics—and not just "new policies"—emerging from a radical situation. Indeed, for a period of time and with very few losses compared to other left-wing governments, it managed to conserve a militant rhetoric. And, thus, the government of Syriza, led by Alexis Tsipras, became the "sweetheart" of the global Left. With Greece in the world's spotlight, intellectuals flocked to the country to express their political support to the Government of Hope. Then came the July referendum, the massive No, and the hurrahs. And after that, devastation; the collapse of hope.

But let us go a bit further back in time, before the institutional date of the elections of January 25, 2015; let us travel to the explosive, anti-institutional date of December 6, 2008. On that day, Alexis Grigoropoulos is shot down by a uniformed police officer (another death in the body count of democracy). The revolt that breaks out changes the experience of resistance in Greece forever. It opens up a huge cycle of questions and practices on how to change things, how to take our lives in our hands—but, above all, on what we want this life to be like when we have it in our hands. Rage against the wretchedness of capital, of money, of the state, of patriarchy, of the institutions, of political representation and assimilated social roles. It all explodes just as the world begins to panic over the outbreak of the world crisis triggered by the bankruptcy of banking giant Lehman Brothers. The images of the crash had been broadcast across the entire planet a few months earlier, on September 15, 2008. Those who claimed the 2008 revolt in Greece was an "isolated" local incident breaking the link that connected it to capital's global onslaught are the same who now speak of the "Greek experiment."

In the years that followed, a cycle of struggles—or, rather, various cycles of more or less intense struggles—opened and closed in Greece (forty-two general strikes from 2010 to 2015 and thirty-one massive protest events during the 2010–2012 period, as Leonidas Oikonomakis mentions in his chapter). The announcement of harsh economic measures and Greece's appeal to the common support mechanism of the IMF and the EU made thousands of enraged people take to the streets. The following dates are very few, just a small taste of the increasing social indignation expressed by Greek society in recent years. On May 5, 2010, the massive national strike that followed the announcement of the first packages of austerity measures (the first memorandum) is marked by the death of three people in the death trap of the Marfin Bank, in the bank's headquarters on Stadiou Avenue in central Athens. On June 28–29, 2011, massive protests at the center of Athens during the voting of the Midterm Program, clashes in and around Syntagma Square, and efforts to seal off the parliament building are met with heavy police repression (almost 2,200 units of teargas and stun grenades were used in two days, according to the national press). On February 12, 2012, during a march against the passing of the second memorandum, Athens goes up in flames, clashes with the police rise to the intensity of a mini-December, ninety-three buildings in the town center are damaged, seventy-six people are taken to hospital, and at least another eighty are arrested. Still, all measures are approved by the Greek parliament. Rage gives way to despair.

During the same period, continuous elections led to a succession of short-lived governments that reflected the impasse and agony of the political-economic establishment, which tried to break resistance on the streets and channel it toward a path of compromise: the ballot. The alternation of repression and electoral hope was the binomial of coercion aiming at social decompression and the demobilization of militant action (the equivalent to what happened with the Kirchner governments in Argentina but also in other Latin American countries and around the world). The promise of returning to the "good old days" of the "kind state" of the "Left of capital" would make even Keynes laugh from his grave, but it did not fall on deaf ears. From the 2009 elections to Syriza's electoral victory in 2015, the party's ratings skyrocketed from 4.9 percent to 36.34 percent. Meanwhile, the country had seen its private debt transformed into public debt (the famous "bailout"), which led the country's "ship" into the IMF harbor and caused the resignation of the PASOK government in the face of the social reaction following the vote for the first memorandum; the 2010 three-party government led by Lucas Papademos that voted for the second memorandum (in February 2012); the May 6, 2012, elections, in which Syriza came in second with 16.78 percent of the vote, while New Democracy, the country's major political force, with 18.85 percent of the vote, was unable to form a government; the repeat elections of June 17, 2012, which once again led to the victory of the Right and of New Democracy (29.7 percent) and to the formation of a government (with PASOK and Democratic Left), while Syriza emerged as a powerful opposition (26.9 percent), and the once-mighty PASOK, representing the political center, took a plunge from 43.92 percent to 12.3 percent in 2009. This is also when the far-right Golden Dawn party, a recognized neofascist organization with a long history of murderous assaults and racist actions against immigrants, entered parliament. This was also just before Syriza's electoral victory, when the crisis led to a convergence between right-wing and left-wing patriotisms/nationalisms against foreign intervention and supervision, as Dimitra Kotouza discusses in her chapter.

Then Syriza won the 2015 elections. Its campaign promises included the return of the basic salary to prememorandum levels, the restoration of collective contracts, and the protection of the social state. These proposals shaped the "radical discourse" of the "first left-wing government." The rhetoric was presented as both realistic and rational, in line with the "European spirit"; that meant that a "compromise with honor" with the "Institutions" could be attained through negotiation. The negotiations turned into a spectacle. For months, we witnessed a deluge of headlines and incidents, which culminated during the referendum of July 5. Although the result of the referendum was "no to the continuation of the austerity programs"—against all prognostics and the massive propaganda spearheaded by the mainstream media—the Syriza government voted for the third memorandum in a final agreement on July 13, 2015. The dogma of "there is no alternative" found new expression when the Government of Hope came up against the Wall of Reality. The shattering of systemic hope gave way to massive depression.

And now what? Where to? How do we pick up the pieces? What can be salvaged from the destroyed scenery? On the one hand, there is the enormous, glaring defeat of the institutional Left: the allegedly more radical parties of the new "Left" in Western Europe (Podemos, Die Linke, the Labour Party under Corbyn, the Pirates, etc.) increased their power or won elections (in Greece they even won a referendum with the enthusiastic support of the people) and then, in the case of Greece, went on to implement Europe's most reactionary and repressive policies. True devastation. The state is no longer the counterweight that keeps the rope of exploitation tight. The rope has broken and the worker is in free fall, plunging into poverty and misery, topped with a strong dose of repression. No one feels part of the institutions of solidarity anymore; institutions that were, until recently, the cornerstone of the demands of the labor movement.

The failure of the institutional Left to put the institutions of mediation between the economy and politics, between wealth production and human life reproduction, back on their feet tells a simple truth: this mediation was erected on quicksand. The heartbreaking voices of the supporters of Syriza, now calling to the people to understand the necessity of the "honorable but painful compromise" that will supposedly salvage fragments from the social state's fallen castle, show to what extent these same voices have scorned the realism revealed by reality. They also show how much they have disdained the historical role of social democracy as a mediator between labor as cost and as investment, between the worker as a producer of surplus value and as a partner. This is a transaction that is no longer profitable for capital and has therefore been abandoned. The *welfare state* could not save capitalism. Neither can the *neoliberal state*. This is not hard to understand. No referendum can annul the decisions of the stock markets, and no state can contain the crisis of financial capitalism within its national borders. Amazon workers in Scotland sleep in tents because they cannot afford to commute, just like thousands of immigrants in Greece, thousands of US citizens who have lost their homes, and all those who live in the shantytowns in the world's contemporary metropoles.

But this is not the time for the anarchist or autonomist movement to jump for joy and say, "We told you so. We told you there can be no radical change through the state." This is no time for rejoicing, precisely because Syriza's failure conceals another failure. What happened to the wave of social struggles, the explosion of creation-and-destruction, after 2008? It did go on for a few years, with its ups and downs, but where is it now?

Indeed, the resistance-and-revolt that unfolded during December 2008 and in its aftermath was not small in size or in radicalness. For a significant number of those who participated, these were practices that jumped off the pages of revolutionary history: clashes, massive popular participation, assemblies of thousands of people in the squares, collective processes of self-organization that managed to engage a broad social spectrum and turned Greece into the epicenter of social unrest. Yet they were not capable of producing even a small (reformist) victory. In this, Greece is nothing special; there is nothing unique in the case of Greece to explain what actually happens all around the world: the *state of exception* is the norm. Capital rules. The austerity measures that the Eurozone governments insist on to show the Greek people they must bow before Lord Money continue to be implemented.

The electoral rise of Syriza during the months and years that preceded the 2015 elections can be partly interpreted as a response to the limits of antistate movements. The interstice created between the intensifying neoliberal onslaught and the weakened anticapitalist resistance was precisely the "space" that Syriza's electoral "hope" came to fill. Double devastation. Not only the cataclysmic devastation of the institutional Left but also the failure of the extra-institutional Left, of the anarchist and autonomist sphere, to effectively challenge the rule of money. All endeavors launched were subdued by the violence of money or repression, and others faced (and continue to face) constant decimation, difficulties, contradictions, and internal conflicts. Along with them, other plans dropped like flies: what form or direction the anticapitalist struggle should assume; how it should be organized; what the organization or its charter should be like; how the collective subject would come together, or who this subject would be (or is). There is now an empty space in the place until recently occupied by the connective element of the unified subject, which until now appeared to be some kind of political program: social organization is running breathlessly, trying to keep up with the frantic rhythm dictated by the unifying force of money. Money rules with great arrogance. Capital rules, and it is destroying humanity. Now it is we who must destroy capital.

So how do we pick up the pieces? What direction should we follow from now on? How do we understand what happened, and how do we learn from it? This is the book's main concern. The challenge, therefore, is to think *beyond the crisis*, to think from the starting point of rage, pain, bitterness, the refutation of illusion and even of the experience of these years. What happened and is still happening in Greece is not far from what is going on around the world: the painful and often violent attacks on the conditions of subsistence (for human and nonhuman life forms) are legitimized in the name of debt. Greece is, simply, a particularly dramatic example of a broader conflict that has become more intense since the 2008 crash and is likely to become more acute as long as capital continues to be the dominant form of social organization. Attack, resistance, revolt at times, repression always, often defeat, the escalation of indignation and rage, and everywhere the same questions emerge: How do we get out of here? How do we break the depression looming above us like a toxic cloud? How do we break the system that is destroying us?

To think *beyond the crisis* is to exit the paralysis caused by the image of the crisis as a "biblical disaster" that is dictated by the "divine" commands of the stock markets and their representatives. It is to perceive crisis not as the "apocalypse" but as a historically defined condition with a critical content. To do this, we must stop thinking in nouns and start thinking in verbs. So it is not about *capital controls*, but rather that capital *controls*, capital *imposes* limitations; it is not about *measures of fiscal adjustment* (or *consolidation*), but rather "*adjust* your activity more, there in Greece, to the demands of the expansion of (future) produced value." In other words, the expansion of value appears as an unquestionable universal stake, while the "remedy" for the crisis dons the guise of the sacrifice that is imposed in order to satisfy the capitalist machine. Thus, contemporary commands leave a bad, authoritarian taste, mediated, however, by the mystical character of political realism. The commands of the moralists of the bourgeoisie are not in the least random: "You have been living beyond your means all these years. Now 'dance' to the rhythms of the economy, become competitive, above all do not protest, this is your fate, there is no other way. In other words: shut up and work." According to latest OECD data (2014), Greece ranks fourth in the world for working hours, behind Mexico, Costa Rica, and South Korea.

The analyses that try to understand the Greek debt crisis on the basis of the particularities of the euro or the political domination of one state over another (of Germany over Greece, for example) seem incapable of thinking *beyond* the transformations of capitalist domination. In a sense, capitalism itself remains untouched, and the problem is relegated to its separate expressions—imperialism, neoliberalism, socialism, and so on. The various perspectives of rejecting these forms acquire the spirit of a promise with a discount. The narrative of "Germany is the problem"— which focuses on its hegemonic character within a European Union in which Greece appears as a "debt colony"—leads to the return of nationalist discourses at the heart of anticapitalist critique. This way, it is the epiphenomenon and the consumption of nationalist ideals that become significant. The portrayal of Greece as a guinea pig trapped in the dreams of Northern Europe essentially shifts the problem toward an easily digested narrative that focuses on the political deficit, on the "deficit of democracy." We believe this is very dangerous, as it can very easily perpetuate a perception of the world (and of what is going on) as a clash between nations and reinforce the nationalism that is growing around us ever so menacingly. The rise of nationalist discourses is embodied in the sharp increase of far-right political tendencies that, in turn, sell a half-hope with devastating consequences. The promise of generalized terror becomes visible in the world (USA, Europe, Latin America) with the imposition of control, population administration, detention centers, and the spreading of massive fear. Hope remains half-hope, an impactful commodity to serve election promises that do not question capitalist barbarity and the multiple forms it acquires.

Our concerns are different. We do not speak of the restructuring of European states or of the particularities of the euro. Our questions are of a different type: After all this experience, how do we get out of here? The storm is getting stronger, the attack more intense, the misery deeper, and proletarization-without-labor is on the rise. But the hope of overturning the system that destroys us is not coming any closer just because the situation is getting worse. Hope is born out of struggle, out of revolt-and-resistance. That is where we invent different ways of *doing* that break normality, the unified logic of capital that controls and dominates. Not One Way, No One Logic, many different ones. This is a very different "plan," one that shone in the bright night sky of December 2008. This is what this book intends to do. It does not aim at giving answers but at "opening up a dialogue" in terms of democratic *consensus*. And that is why it does not express a single, unified political stance. The book's chapters disagree with each other on many points; they even enter into conflict with one another. But this is also the way in which they mutually complement the issues, questions, and self-critical discussions that are ever more urgent today for anticapitalist struggle.

The book begins with the chapter by Theodoros Karyotis, who analyzes the process of construction of the three main "plans"/imaginaries against austerity and the crisis, as well as their interaction: the dominant "Plan A" for reform and redistribution within Europe and the Eurozone expressed by Syriza before and after the elections that brought the party to power; "Plan B" for leaving the Eurozone and performing a national productive reconstitution, championed by a section of the Left that was initially part of Syriza and later broke off; and, finally, "Plan C," the open and contradictory experience of grassroots movements that revolved around the construction of the commons as an alternative not only for the inversion of the crisis but also for the creation of embryonic forms of an anticapitalist world.

The next chapter moves along the same lines. Leonidas Oikonomakis attempts an analytical critique of the politics of left-wing governments and their role as wave-breakers of radical, prefigurative social struggles. The shared experience of Greece, Spain, and numerous countries in Latin America highlights the collapse of "institutional hope," which nevertheless had important repercussions for the alternative endeavors that were developing at an experimental stage after the 2008 outbreak of the local crisis.

Then comes the analysis by John Holloway, who focuses on the crisis, capital, and the case of Greece from an antagonistic perspective. Rejecting half-hopes, the chapter mainly refers to a crucial dilemma (crucial for the very existence of human and nonhuman life forms today): if we are the crisis of capital, we can be something *beyond* that too. If capital is our destruction, we can be the destruction of capital. The experience of the (debt) crisis in Greece and the game of musical chairs that is being played ever more frantically, ever more terrifyingly, in our world clearly shows that there is no middle road between humanity and capital, that there are no euphemisms and intermediate categories, that we must forget half-hope. The problem does not lie in the different expressions of barbarity, of the continuously increasing onslaught of capital. The problem is capital itself. And the challenge is to break it, to break the rule of money, to say no to capital.

The next two chapters offer critiques of the forms of the state and democracy. In his chapter, Giorgos Sotiropoulos begins by critically analyzing the recent social struggles in Greece after 2011. His starting point is that democracy seems to have been performing a double function for decades. On the one hand, it has operated as a legitimizing concept for the liberal-capitalist societies of the "West." On the other, it has acted as a critical concept against the oligarchic tendencies of the same social formations. These two antagonistic democratic proposals—democracy as a system of governance and democracy as a social movement—came up against each other in the recent anti-austerity struggles and, in fact, clashed as two separate democratic models, as "representative" democracy and "direct" democracy. Yet the analysis of capital goes beyond criticizing Syriza's "betrayal" or the "democratic delusions" of the masses and reflects on the virtues, the limits, and the paradoxes of the historical project of democracy.

The subsequent chapter, written by Panagiotis Doulos, examines the relation between the "strong state," democracy, and austerity policies during the Greek debt crisis. The Greek crisis reveals the profound link between austerity policies and state policies for the repression and disciplining of the working bodies. Furthermore, the case of the Greek crisis is symptomatic of the limits of representative democracy and of the autonomy of the capitalist state as they manifest themselves through the experience of the referendum and the Syriza governance. So, if we can speak of the end of illusions today, what follows?

The following chapters offer a critical examination of the contradictions between the discourses and practices of anticapitalist movements. Panagiotis Drakos explains in his chapter why the Greek crisis and capitalist readjustment at the global level force us to reexamine the notion of imperialism, as well as the insufficiency of traditional (state-centered) anti-imperialist theories. In today's reformed field of social struggle, the rule of capital not only tends to unify the models of class domination but also condenses the analytical tools of liberating social theory. Through an anarchist interpretative approach, the chapter examines the notions of imperialism and internationalism in the light of neoliberal modernity.

The chapter by Dimitra Kotouza revolves around the process of unification of anticapitalist resistance (more specifically, of resistance against crisis and austerity) along traditional, nation-centered, racialized, and populist political lines. The author links the crucial question, "Whose lives matter the most?" to a critique against nationalism and antifascism with regard to the struggles of immigrants to acquire a voice or, simply, to survive. She highlights how national discourses emerge even in the movements that oppose fascism, the contradictions that appeared within the discourses and practices of those movements during the Greek crisis, and how difficult it is to break the representation and separation of the immigrant as a "foreigner" and a "threat" within a highly xenophobic, racist, and ultranationalist European reality.

In the book's last chapter, Katerina Nasioka attempts a critical approach to the revolutionary subject in crisis. The social clashes of recent years in Greece and around the world have left a powerful mark: disappointment, the collapse of illusions, the awakening of ghosts of the past. The crisis has led revolutionary theory to different analyses on the category of class. In many cases, class is abandoned as a concept that is incapable of describing today's transformed reality, as well as the possibility of an anticapitalist perspective. The failure of the labor movement as a positive, hegemonic subject often appears in terms of the defeat or disappearance of the proletariat as a class that fights capitalism. Are we, then, facing the end of class, or is this a new form of class struggle that lies ahead of us? Putting aside any effort to define the revolutionary subject, the text analyzes how and why the today's proletariat tends to become a photograph in the negative, a movement of self-denial of class definition, opening up (or maybe not) new perspectives of radical change.

Think beyond the crisis. Think of hope as denial, as a type of "celebration" against the melancholy of capitulating to capital. Think of the destruction of capital. This is what the book is mostly about.

We would like to warmly thank all those who contributed, in many different ways, to the creation of this book, from writing, translating, and editing, to designing and publishing. For their specific support in creating this English edition, we would like to thank the Instituto de Ciencias Sociales y Humanidades "Alfonso Vélez Pliego" of the Benemérita Universidad Autónoma de Puebla (BUAP) in Puebla, Mexico, and PM Press in Oakland, California. And our heroic translator, Anna-Maeve Holloway, who, after translating half of the book into Greek, translated the other half into English.

John Holloway, Katerina Nasioka, and Panagiotis Doulos
January 2017, Athens–Puebla

ONE

Beyond Hope: Prospects for the Commons in Austerity-Stricken Greece

Theodoros Karyotis

Since 2009, Greece has become a laboratory for the implementation of neoliberal austerity policies but has also seen fierce resistance and a surge of creative alternatives. In the ensuing years of strife, "hope" has been the notion around which political movements attempted to rally their supporters against the neoliberal restructuring. "Hope" in the Blochean sense of evoking the "not-yet" through prefigurative politics (Dinerstein 2014: 59) but also "hope" as an empty signifier (Laclau 2000: 56, 84), a catchall term to unify all different aspirations for overcoming the crisis under the common hegemonic project of Syriza (Katsambekis 2015: 158).

This chapter aims to outline the central political imaginaries of overcoming austerity that arose in this period—"Plan A," reform and redistribution; "Plan B," national economic reconstruction outside the Eurozone; "Plan C," a bottom-up reorganization of politics and economy around the commons—and the interplay between the three in the context of anti-austerity politics. It especially focuses on the abandonment of "Plan A" by the political forces that expressed it and the challenges faced by adherents of the third imaginary ("Plan C") in subverting the capitalist market and in addressing the question of power and the state.

Austerity and Its Discontents
The "Greek Crisis" as a Result of a Shift in the Mode of Capitalist Accumulation

The so-called Greek crisis started in 2009—when the newly elected PASOK (Panhellenic Socialist Movement) government readjusted upward the figure of the fiscal deficit and invited an intervention by the International Monetary Fund to prevent a default—that continues to this day. In the European mass media, two different images of the crisis and its impact on the Greek population were presented. At first, the crisis was largely attributed to the supposed lazy and corrupt character of Greeks (Douzinas 2013: 1)—a depiction that was later extended to other Mediterranean peoples. But after the Greeks voted in a purportedly anti-austerity government in 2015 and rejected austerity policies in a referendum, for a large part of the European public opinion, the Greeks were turned from perpetrators into victims, tormented by an inflexible and arrogant European elite led by the German government. What both of these depictions fail to take into account is that what we call the "Greek crisis" is the outcome of a shift toward a regime of accumulation that, having bled dry the countries of the Global South for several decades, is now being imported into Europe, starting with the weakest links in the chain. In that respect, it is neither "Greek"—since this is the model that in one form or another all European countries are expected to conform to, as attested to by the recent developments in France—nor is it a "crisis" in the sense of an extraordinary event. Instead, it represents a new normal that threatens to shake the foundations of social coexistence in the capitalist center as well. Nevertheless, Greece has been a privileged spot for observing how this paradigm shift plays out within the boundaries of the nation-state.

Processes of violent separation of populations from their means of subsistence have famously been described by Marx as a regime of "primitive accumulation" characterizing the early stages of capitalism (Marx 1990: 873–76), although it has been argued that this is an inherent and permanent characteristic of capitalism (De Angelis 2001; Bonefeld 2001). Indeed, David Harvey (2004) offers an updated account of the process in describing the strategy of "accumulation by dispossession" by which capitalism has been trying to confront its crises of overaccumulation since the 1970s.

The main components of this strategy can be readily identified in the Greek case, where a sovereign debt crisis has been used as a pretext for a massive operation of wealth transfer from the popular classes to the local and international capitalist class: The "bailout" program that was initiated in 2010 was designed to prevent a default of the Greek state to the European banks that had funneled huge amounts of capital to peripheral states in the previous decade, looking for higher profits (Milios and Sotiropoulos 2010: 233). By the terms of the bailout, the private debt of the banks was transferred over to European sovereign states in exchange for a drastic restructuring of the Greek economy that would have an "extractive" effect on two levels: On the one hand, the restructuring forced the fire-sale privatization of all state assets, including public infrastructure, such as ports, airports, water, and energy companies, where often the same powerful business interests acted as instigators, advisors, and purchasers in the privatization process (Trumbo and Peters 2016). On the other hand, it created a recessionary spiral that would pauperize the lower and middle classes (Papatheodorou 2014: 192), destroy the small and medium-sized businesses that used to constitute the productive backbone of Greece, and oblige the Greek people to give up their "family jewels," including eventually their homes, to opportunistic financial institutions. Overall, the bailout program constitutes a massive exercise in social engineering; its effects on everyday people's lives are only comparable to those in wartime situations or during the Great Depression of the 1930s (Krugman 2015).

Since capitalism is rapidly abandoning productive activity in the countries of the capitalist center and moving toward dispossession (through rent, tax, debt, privatization, etc.), on the one hand, and financialization, on the other, as means of value extraction, high unemployment has become the new norm. This does away with the conception of a stable lifetime occupation, with the related benefits of health care, pension schemes, holiday pay, and labor rights—which previous generations had to varying extents taken for granted—giving way to an immense growth of unemployed and precarious "surplus populations" with no economic and social rights and no access to the means of their own reproduction (Denning 2010). Moreover, the rearrangement of labor relations according to the terms of the "structural adjustment" means that those workers who have remained in waged relations have lost overnight the labor rights that were conquered by decades of class strife. The reduction of pensions and wages serves to compress even more the already-meager income of Greek families.

The transformation of the state is not limited to the privatization of public assets and the dismantling of universal health and welfare. The Greek state, having borrowed great amounts of money created arbitrarily by the lending international banks themselves—according to the fractional reserve system (McLeay et al. 2014)—and having channeled a lot of this money to oligarchic interests, to the clientelist networks of the PASOK and New Democracy parties for reelection purposes, and to exorbitant defense spending (Fouskas 2012) is now transformed into a mechanism of extraction of wealth from the popular classes in the name of paying back this very debt. Examples of this are the horizontal abolition of the nontaxable income limit in 2013 or the indiscriminate tax on house ownership that became known as *haratsi* (for its reminiscence of an Ottoman-era poll tax of the same name).

To consummate the consolidation of the neoliberal state, a big apparatus of repression was put in place to contain the anger of the population, including an unaccountable police force penetrated by the extreme Right (Papanicolaou and Papageorgiou 2016), brutal crowd control techniques, increased surveillance and censorship, judicial persecution of social struggles, and systematic framing, beating, and torture of activists by the forces of order (Dalakoglou 2013; Xenakis 2012: 445).

Rather than representing "collateral damage" or the unfortunate side effects of austerity policies, these phenomena demonstrate that the so-called austerity is little more than an orchestrated plan of wealth redistribution in favor of the ruling classes. In other words, the austerity program was designed to bring about a recession, which "cleared away inadequately-valorizing capitals, small enterprises, civil rights, workers' rights, trade union rights and parts of the public sector—whatever was necessary" (Milios and Rozworski 2015).

Responses to the Neoliberal Onslaught

The dominant narrative for overcoming the debt crisis—the one that proposed the dismantling of the public sector and the extinction of labor rights as a means of stimulating growth and attracting investment—resonated perfectly with the neoliberal discourse incessantly repeated by the corporate media in the last couple of decades, with the blessing of a series of governments. The strategy of blaming the victim has been effective, and a large part of the population has sat quietly through the attack, convinced by the media that they had to suffer to atone for their collective sins. Another common reaction has been entrenchment in xenophobic and reactionary identities.

Antagonistic narratives emerged eventually, however, being consolidated as coherent imaginaries of breaking free from austerity and neoliberal restructuring around 2011, around the same time as the eruption of the Movement of the Squares in late May.

The roots of the recent history of resistance in Greece can be traced back to the December 2008 uprising, where following the cold-blooded assassination of a teenager by the police in central Athens, thousands of marginalized urban youth took to the streets, transforming the urban landscape, giving rise to new participatory structures of coexistence, and forging militant subjectivities and collectives that last to this day (Nasioka 2014; Douzinas 2013).

The cycle of protest that started in 2010 against the first "bailout package" and ended with a renewal of the political elites in 2015 is a phenomenon that eludes a fixed description or characterization. In one form or another, a great part of the Greek population participated in the general strikes, multitudinous blockades of the parliament, occupations of government buildings, groups of civil disobedience, local antiprivatization initiatives, and of course the stellar Movement of the Squares in May and June 2011, which later was dispersed into a multitude of neighborhood assemblies.

This, however, did not constitute a coherent movement with fixed aims and organizational form, but a magma of struggles and militant subjectivities with diverse and even conflicting approaches to resistance and social change. The social disruption occasioned by the crisis and the obvious inability of the system to reproduce itself in the previous terms engendered a widespread rejection of the political system and the consensus built around the political parties, trade unions, and the institutions of the 1974 democratic transition.

Previously marginal electoral forces—most prominently Syriza and ANEL (Independent Greeks)—began to invest in this sentiment of anomy and to build hegemonic projects by presenting themselves as the political expression of social struggles. At the same time, a new imaginary gained ground that, in line with the worldwide protests of the Arab Spring, the *indignados*, and later Occupy, celebrated the multitude and diversity of struggles and gave emphasis to horizontality, self-management, and direct participation.

Commentators such as Douzinas (2013) and Kioupkiolis (2014) identify as a central element of the Movement of the Squares the concurrent and overlapping processes of a hegemonic construction of "the people" against the status quo, on the one hand, and the constitution of a "multitude" of diverse identities and struggles, on the other. These processes of hegemonic constitution and heterogeneous multiplicity were in motion throughout the years of intense resistance against austerity, as is attested to by the telling but inadequate distinction between an "upper" Syntagma

Square, where protesters were limited to inveighing against the parliament, and a "lower" Syntagma Square, where participants would wait their turn to take the podium to collectively debate, deliberate, and come to decisions (Prentoulis and Thomassen 2014).

Three Imaginaries of Social Transformation

Three main imaginaries, three different responses to austerity and the devaluation of people's lives, progressively crystalized as distinct but often overlapping projects within the wider wave of resistance. For the sake of discussion, I will codify them here as "Plans" A, B, and C, being, however, conscious that the word "plan" implies a coherence and a programmatic directionality that is for the most part absent in these cases.[1] The more fitting term "imaginary" draws attention to the fact that subjects "dream up" the social whole they want to arrive at before they set out to attempt to change the world. Hence, what I describe below are sets of ideas and values that inform the action of transformative political and social movements.

Plan A: An Imaginary of Reform and Redistribution

The first imaginary was expressed politically in the majoritarian project of the governmental alliance between Syriza and ANEL. It is an imaginary of reform and modernization of the Greek political and economic system without challenging the underlying institutional power arrangement. It combines a nostalgia for the golden years of European capitalist expansion—where the state played the role of mediator in class and social conflict and put in place the mechanisms of redistribution that are now being rapidly dismantled by the neoliberal assault—with a drive to modernize and rationalize the largely "feudal" Greek capitalism, making the economy competitive and attractive to investors, while reaffirming the country's allegiance to the project of European integration.

It is important to note that the "first ever left government" was not a result of a leftward shift in the Greek electoral body—rather, it was the outcome of a swift, calculated transformation of the Syriza party, which by 2013 had exchanged its radical discourse for a catchall populist anti-austerity rhetoric in a bid to occupy the space of social democracy left vacant when PASOK adopted a hard-line pro-austerity stance (Katsambekis 2015: 156). "Slowly the main focus shifted from wealth redistribution, taxing the rich, building up a social economy, and so on toward more supposedly neutral terms like growth, productive reconstruction, combating the humanitarian crisis, etc. that portrayed the society and the economy as something where we all share the same interests and where we aren't divided along class lines" (Kayserilioğlu and Milios 2016). This is to say that Syriza constructed its hegemony by building on a preexisting imaginary of a "fair capitalism," where the state safeguards rights and regulates the economy.

Not only did the working classes, which traditionally voted for PASOK, overwhelmingly vote for Syriza in the elections of 2014 and 2015, but also, most importantly, a great part of the disenchanted apparatchiks of PASOK also joined the ranks of Syriza. "Pasokification," a term gaining ground internationally to describe the collapse of social democracy due to its inability to provide an alternative to neoliberal austerity (Bailey 2016: 8), acquires here a whole new meaning: the rapid transfiguration of a left-wing transformative force into a centrist administrator of state power—a process that has its parallel in Spain and the Podemos party (Alonso Rocafort 2015; Mejía 2015).

In the light of its first two years in power, we can now safely conclude that the hegemonic project came at a great cost for Syriza: it gradually morphed from an anti-austerity coalition rooted in social struggles into its polar opposite: a systemic party that enforces the terms of neoliberal restructuring. The step from posing as a force that can save capitalism from itself to accepting the inevitability of capitalism's ongoing transformation was a small one—all it took was the predictable blackmail on behalf of the European neoliberal institutions to turn the Syriza-led government into a very effective instrument of neoliberal imposition. The enforcement of the third memorandum and its associated reforms has created a universal sentiment of discontent in Greek society: for example, the 2016 pension reform, which obliged small-scale farmers and precarious self-employed workers to pay social security contributions well beyond their means, sparked the most determined anti-austerity mobilization in years (Sotiris 2016); this was followed in 2017 by further wage and pension cuts and an increase in taxes and contributions for low-income workers (Vatikiotis 2017). Indeed, it is not far-fetched to argue that reforms of this scope and extent would have been impossible under the previous fragile and discredited Samaras government. It took a new, seemingly progressive government, with great reserves of political capital, to carry out this task.

Syriza's rise to power also came at a great cost for the social movements that have been in various forms resisting austerity since 2010: in its bid to become a hegemonic power, the Syriza party became involved in many social struggles, posing as a representative and champion of social resistances. But its effect was that of demobilization and complacency, since it promised a political solution to conflicts and channeled the desire for social change back into the institutional avenue, thus effectively ending the political system's crisis of legitimation. Not only did this create rifts within the social movements, but in practice Syriza also ignored, marginalized, or antagonized its erstwhile allies once it came to power (Karyotis 2015).

It could be argued that this danger is inherent in hegemonic politics. Laclau (2000) posits that hegemonic construction necessarily involves one force among the "chain of equivalence" of social struggles rising to become its leader and representative. But we should not assume that this is a consensual process: it presupposes an "unevenness of power" that allows the hegemonic force to embark on a process of "universalization" that necessarily suppresses and marginalizes particular truths, practices, and demands. In the Greek case, this process has marginalized anti-capitalist imaginaries in favor of a conception of a just capitalism—the impossibility of which was made apparent soon after said hegemonic force arrived in power.

This impossibility has laid bare for all to see the Left's "crisis of imagination," that is, its "total inability to even conceive of a world beyond capitalism" (Roos 2015b: 83). Time and again, the Left's responses to the systemic crises of the past decade exude nostalgia for the good old days of the Keynesian welfare state, full employment, and the state as the arbiter of social and class conflict. The European Left's neo-Keynesianism easily overlooks the fact that Keynesian policies were not the brainchild of illuminated and benevolent governments but a product of a class compromise that followed many bloody revolutions and two world wars; indisputably the conditions for a return to the "golden days" of peaceful Keynesian class cooperation are not available today, for a host of reasons.

The two main levers of capital in its ongoing process of "accumulation by dispossession" are the state and the financial system (Harvey 2004: 74). Although the state in its raw form is little more than a mechanism of domination, the pressures of the social revolutions of the previous century allowed its utilization under Keynesian patterns of relations between labor and capital as a mechanism of check on capital expansion and of redistribution in favor of the popular classes (Holloway 1996). Without question, this was a spatially and temporally limited arrangement designed to appease the restless working classes of the capitalist center, to guarantee their consensus and contain their power to rise against the capitalist mode of production, as well as to solve the crisis of effective demand of the early twentieth century.

The impossibility of implementing Keynesian policies in the twenty-first century is attested by two developments in the capitalist order: on the one hand, the move toward a rentier, financialized, and extractive mode of accumulation does away with the need for a well-off middle class as an agent of effective demand. This, in turn, eliminates the necessity to maintain social peace and consensus through a generous redistribution of surpluses. Fear and debt are the new disciplining instruments (Hardt and Negri 2012; Lazzarato 2012). On the other hand, the growth of the sovereign debt of all countries—"developed" or otherwise—means that the first lever of capitalist "accumulation by dispossession" (the state) is permanently subsumed to the second (the financial system) and thus cannot be used as a bulwark against the expansion of capital. In plain terms, the policies of indebted states are not dependent on the will of individual governments but are dictated by the lobbies of "creditors" under the threat of bankruptcy, and thus they are not subject to change according to the ebb and flow of electoral politics.

In other words, in its present form, the state as a redistributive tool is only capable of "upward" redistribution, through overtaxing, debt, privatization, or expropriation tout court. Different governments can negotiate the degree or intensity by which the lower and middle classes are bled dry, but they cannot challenge the essential extractive character of the state.

In light of this, Syriza's claim to engage in "negotiations" with the powers that be and have society's best interests at heart is simply a fig leaf to cover the party's inescapable fate of being the enforcer and guarantor of neoliberal policies of dispossession. Not only has there been an intensification of austerity policies, but also, most importantly, the net effect of the Syriza-led government is to convince the population that there really is no alternative to neoliberal restructuring, with a subsequent regression of the wide social struggles against austerity of the previous years into piecemeal efforts to negotiate individual or sectoral concessions, in view of the inevitability of the generalized attack on people's livelihoods.

Plan B: An Imaginary of National Economic Reconstruction outside the Eurozone

The second response, which has its political expression in the parties that flank Syriza from the left—including Popular Unity, the political formation that resulted from Syriza's split in September 2015—envisions a return to an imagined national sovereignty outside the Eurozone and an economic reconstruction on a national basis, with the state having a protagonistic role in the orchestration and financing of economic activity. A reactionary variant of this imaginary can be found in the ideology of the extreme Right.

Reasonably enough, the Greek Left argues that the main structural problem of Greek capitalism is that it has given up monetary and fiscal control to European organizations, which don't have its best interests at heart but implement policies according to the needs of the export-driven economies of the European center.

Popular Unity, in particular, is claiming to salvage the original programmatic commitments of Syriza, insisting nevertheless on breaking with the European common currency. A prominent party member, economics professor Costas Lapavitsas, argues that the most reasonable alternative to austerity would be a radical break with the Eurozone accompanied by "cessation of payments and restructuring of debt. Banks would have to be nationalised and public control extended over utilities, transport, energy and telecommunications.... This option requires a decisive shift in the balance of political power in favour of labour" (Lapavitsas et al. 2010: 3). Similar approaches are offered by other Greek Left formations.

The main issue with these varied and often contradictory approaches is their statism: they posit social change as a matter of simply applying the "correct" governmental policies where Syriza was not bold enough. Although it is evident that the lack of an autonomous monetary policy and the extreme hostility of the European Central Bank to the Greek government's designs are decisive factors in the subjugation of the Greek state to the desires of its creditors, the vision of an independent, productive, and competitive Greece outside the Eurozone would by no means be a panacea for the social ills brought about by capitalist restructuring.

Most importantly, this vision overlooks that the state's foremost mission is to ensure growth, attract investment, make the economy competitive, monetize the commons; if it doesn't achieve these goals, it is considered a "failed state." Without doubt, "competitiveness" in the global economy is synonymous to the compression of the income of workers vis-à-vis capital, the relaxation of environmental and labor regulations, and a consequent attack on nature and the commons.

Even though the left-of-Syriza Left is prepared to opt for rupture where Syriza chose continuity, it fails to challenge the underlying assumptions of a "return to growth," an extractive economy, and the infinite expansion of production, consumption, and credit.

This is not to say that the question of the currency is irrelevant or that Greece is better off within the Eurozone, but rather that we should be skeptical about the view that social change can merely be the outcome of the application of one or another economic policy at the top level.

Plan C: An Imaginary of Political and Social Reorganization around the Commons

The third response is the proposal of a constellation of grassroots alternatives that proliferated in Greece especially between 2010 and 2013, before the electoral rise of Syriza put an end to the legitimation crisis that had been a fertile ground for social experimentation. It advocates for a social reorganization around the commons (Roos 2015a). It proposes horizontal political decision-making at the local level, cooperative and solidarity-based economic endeavors, collective forms of ownership and management of resources, as well as direct democracy in the community and in the workplace against the culture of political representation.

The pressing social needs resulting from the economic collapse that followed the first memorandum accelerated the emergence of a diverse network of self-managed collectives that intervened in various aspects of production and reproduction (agriculture, manufacturing, distribution, commerce, defense of common resources, entertainment, health care, education). Born as a reaction to the hegemonic narrative that promoted atomized subjectivities and individualistic responses to the crisis, these endeavors have an explicit educational objective, aiming to forge militant subjectivities with a capacity for autonomous thought and collective action (Lieros 2012; Varkarolis 2012). Although they emerged as a response to the dismantling of the redistributive structures of the welfare state, they reject the uneven power relations of the state form, operating instead on the principle of reciprocity and carefully defending their autonomy of action against state actors, parties, and private businesses (Petropoulou 2013: 74), most of the times resisting bureaucratization and insisting on operating informally (Rakopoulos 2015). The central trait of these grassroots endeavors is a radical conception of democracy that elevates the horizontal assembly to the definitive organizational form and instrument of decision-making. As Sitrin (2012: 61) put it in regard to the similar movement arising out of the 2001 Argentinian crisis, "it is only with the desire for, and walk towards, open participation and nonhierarchy that people are able to create themselves and their communities anew; where the future desired can be prefigured in the present."

Undoubtedly these are attempts at fostering popular resilience against the conditions of increasing precarity. It is important, however, to go beyond the media depiction of these initiatives as a "social self-defense against the crisis," and view them as "politicized responses to austerity" that "encompass a present . . . much wider than the immediate consequences of hardship and address a future much further than one relating to the problems recession has brought to Greek households" (Rakopoulos 2015), that is, as a prefigurative component of a strategy of wholesale social transformation that exceeds the horizon of the "crisis." By counterposing the instances of popular power to the existing institutions, which are patently incapable of ensuring social welfare, if not openly indifferent to it, organized society does not only demand a return to the precrisis age but also actively proposes a social arrangement that seeks to overcome the system that generates these crises altogether. "Commoning initiatives are more than dikes against the neoliberal assault on our livelihood. They are the seeds, the embryonic form of an alternative mode of production in the make" (Caffentzis and Federici 2014: i95).

Examples of these initiatives include a wide network of solidarity clinics operated in a horizontal manner by volunteers to provide primary health care to the millions of citizens and noncitizens left without medical coverage by the imposition of neoliberal restructuring in the public health system (Petropoulou 2013: 77–78); solidarity economy networks that promote a new relationship with food, from its cultivation all the way to its distribution and consumption (Rakopoulos 2014); collectively managed social centers that act as liberated spaces from which to reconstruct a new autonomous sociality (Kioupkiolis and Karyotis 2015); and a multitude of workers' collectives that operate via processes of direct democracy, equality of remuneration, and social dispensation of any surpluses, thus constituting a hands-on critique of existing labor relations and the ontology of the capitalist firm (Kokkinidis 2015). A special place among these endeavors is reserved for the worker-recuperated factory of Vio.Me, which lies at the intersection of labor conflicts and alternative economic endeavors (Kioupkiolis and Karyotis 2015: 315–18; Azzellini 2015: 80–82). By occupying the means of production, by producing a new range of products under direct workers control, by mobilizing a wide movement of solidarity, and by demanding through militant action the legal recognition of its activity, Vio.Me attempts to expand the horizon of workers' struggles beyond the half-hearted defensive efforts of bureaucratic trade unions and test the limits of institutional tolerance of bottom-up alternatives.

Although many left-wing parties would be willing to welcome these bottom-up endeavors as long as they are part of a comprehensive program of state reform, for many participants these initiatives would in themselves represent "the embryos of a new world, the interstitial movements from which a new society could grow," in the words of Holloway (2010: 11). They envision social change not as the result of the application of one or the other policy from the top down, but rather as "a multiplicity of interstitial movements running from the particular." They represent an "antipolitics of dignity" against a culture of political representation that tends to disempower those it claims to represent. "Dignity is the immediate affirmation of negated subjectivity, the assertion, against a world that treats us as objects and denies our capacity to determine our own lives, that we are subjects capable and worthy of deciding for ourselves" (Holloway 2010: 39).

This emerging type of autonomous politics can occupy the center stage in moments of crises of legitimation of the political system. Dinerstein (2014: 33–48) provides us with an opportune schema to make sense of autonomy's motion. She proposes four "modes" by which autonomous politics engage with the existing state of affairs and enable social change: A mode of *negating* the existing state of social relations, through denunciation, insubordination, rejection of identities; a mode of *creating* prefigurative "concrete utopias" through social self-determination, in an attempt to realize the not-yet-existing in the now; a mode of *contradicting*, in which movements come up against the attempts of the dominant order to repress and appropriate them, as well as against their own internal limits and contradictions; and a mode of *exceeding*, in which the oscillation between rebellion and integration leaves behind a "surplus" of forms, values, and practices informed by solidarity and cooperation.

Self-Management of the Commons as a Way out of Austerity—and Capitalism

Although not all of the aforementioned endeavors utilize the vocabulary of the commons in their self-description, I consider the discourse of the commons one of the most potent analytical tools to construe the activity and objectives of grassroots initiatives, demonstrate their revolutionary potential, and explore their challenges and contradictions.

I depart from a radical definition of the commons as "autonomous spaces from which to reclaim control over our life and the conditions of our reproduction, and to provide resources on the basis of sharing and equal access, but also as bases from which to counter the processes of enclosure and increasingly disentangle our lives from the market and the state" (Caffentzis and Federici 2014: i101).

Commons-based endeavors intervene not in the narrow field of commodity production, but in that of biopolitical production, that is "indivisibly, the production of objects, subjects and relationships that encompasses social life in its entirety" (Kotsakis 2012: 49). In this respect, the commons is not limited to a shared "resource," but it extends to the collective processes by which we reproduce our lives; hence, it is more appropriate to speak of "commoning" as a process than of the "commons" as a thing. The dual nature of the commons as an object and as a process and the emphasis on collective management and open access makes the commons discourse a powerful tool for deconstructing the false dichotomy between the market and the state, which, according to Ugo Mattei, are not opposed, as modern economic thought suggests, but are "structurally linked in a relationship of mutual symbiosis," "inserted into a fundamental structure: the rule of the subject . . . over an object" (Mattei 2014: 39–40).

Of course, it would be premature to assert that commons movements represent a serious threat to the capitalist mode of production, or even that they have acquired enough self-consciousness to constitute a credible alternative. In Greece and abroad, grassroots and commons endeavors are hindered by issues of viability, scale, institutionalization, and coordination. Nevertheless, by emphasizing collective agency and proposing community as a new collective actor, by positioning themselves against the state and the capitalist market, commons alternatives offer a glimpse of a postcapitalist future and an articulate response to the Left's "crisis of imagination." They represent an auspicious—if only somewhat preliminary—reply to the great conundrum of the twentieth century, how to advance at once equality and freedom in the context of a large-scale process of social transformation.

This is why in the third part of this chapter I am going to look into the limitations and contradictions of the "actually existing" grassroots commons endeavors and address some of the main criticisms from the viewpoint of practice and the advancement of commoning as it relates to both the Greek context and the post-2011 political landscape worldwide.

Commons for Capitalism

It might look like a great paradox that the grassroots endeavors and commoning initiatives that I present here as a potentially anticapitalist force are touted and promoted by the most unlikely of sponsors, such as the World Bank and the European Union, both staunch advocates of neoliberal globalization. For instance, under the header of "social economy," the European Commission promotes the activity of cooperatives and associations with the explicit aim of contributing "to the EU's employment, social cohesion, regional and rural development" (European Commission 2016).

Nevertheless, it should not come as a surprise that capitalism needs some kind of commoning for its perpetuation. Indeed, the Industrial Revolution itself, as well as the ensuing transformations of capitalism, have been grounded on intensive—gendered as a rule—care work at home, outside of the sphere of exchange, by which labor power was reproduced physically and culturally (De Angelis 2012: 184). Although toward the mid-twentieth century the welfare state assumed some of the tasks of reproduction (such as health care, social insurance, education), the current restructuring dictates a reduction of the costs of social reproduction and the refashioning of the state into a mechanism of containment of the rage of excluded populations.

Thus, the promotion by capitalist institutions of a certain kind of "tame" and "harmless" commons is an indirect admission that the logic of capital, carried to an extreme and penetrating all spheres of social life, becomes an obstacle even to capital accumulation itself (Caffentzis and Federici 2014: 197). A certain kind of "economy of the poor" (Ruggeri 2014: 45) is encouraged when it can guarantee social reproduction and prevent social eruptions of the disadvantaged that could rattle the dominant order of things. In Greece, with the arrival of Syriza to power, this contradiction has reached a new level, as the Syriza-led government continues with the aggressive policies of dispossession, on the one hand, and, on the other, openly supports grassroots initiatives that aim to contain the humanitarian crisis, for example by promoting favorable legislation or by mobilizing a party-funded and directed structure, Solidarity4All, to exercise social policy through self-managed initiatives. It is evident in this case that the vision of the commons employed by the governing party is that of a "safety net" that will mitigate the most extreme repercussions of Greek capitalism, which the same government is trying to modernize and rationalize, not overcome.

Nevertheless, the fact that capitalism requires a certain amount of welfare provision by society itself should not lead us to a wholesale rejection of self-management and the commons, as do left-wing parties that insist on a state-centric approach to social change.[2] This is because this kind of argument fails to perceive that the proliferation of the commons is a double-edged sword for capitalism: a certain configuration of the commons can help capital out of its social reproduction crisis, but too much of it or too antagonistic a kind of commons is a direct threat to the value production mechanisms of capital, as it can empower workers and communities and "create a social basis for alternative ways of articulating social production, independent from capital" (De Angelis 2012b). Hence, rather than a priori co-opted spaces, the commons are a battleground, where two competing forms of value creation are struggling for predominance.

Another related significant objection is that to the extent that commoning endeavors involve commodity production the capitalist law of value penetrates the activity and imposes its logic.[3] Workers of radical cooperatives, for example, might have equality and democracy within the production unit, but the market operates as an external "boss," determining what is going to be produced and how, as well as the intensity of labor and the remuneration of workers. This leads to phenomena of self-exploitation, since the extraction of value by capital in this case is not done directly through mechanisms of appropriation of surplus value but indirectly through rent and tax or through the outsourcing of functions of capitalist businesses to seemingly "liberated" cooperative and self-employed workers.[4]

The Struggle for and through the Commons

To navigate the above criticisms, commons thinkers have often tried to differentiate between "anticapitalist" commons, on the one hand, and "distorted" or "commodity-producing" commons, on the other (Caffentzis and Federici 2014; De Angelis 2009). Certainly, this distinction is crucial to understanding that the significance of the commons stretches beyond their utilization as a safety net for social containment or as collective systems of management of natural resources geared toward the market.

Nevertheless, in societies where the market is the dominant mechanism of social reproduction, any attempt to draw a line between pure and adulterated commons is futile: necessarily all our commons are "hybrid" or "transitional" forms. To the extent that the social and physical existence of commoners is mediated by commodity exchange, if the commons are to take root at all in a world dominated by capital, a particular arrangement should be made that permits the coexistence—even in an antagonistic relation—of these two value creation systems. As De Angelis (2012b: 12) admits, "in a situation in which capital and commons are both pervasive systems that organise the social, it is clear that often a solution will imply a particular deal between these two, that is, a particular form of their structural coupling."

This is why the useful distinction between anticapitalist and capitalist commons should not be interpreted as a call to abandon the "distorted" commons to capital while we concentrate on the creation of pure, noncommodified commons. Rather, an agonistic stance within the existing fields of dispute of the commons is necessary,[5] one that actively seeks to intensify the subjectivity and community-building aspects of communing—utilizing commoning as a means of creation of communities of struggle.

To think that one can immediately and unambiguously place oneself outside of the domain of the law of value—such as some versions of the "communization" theory seem to suggest[6]—would be an exercise in self-deception. More often than not this attempt will end up in disappointment and the realization that we are unable to reproduce our existence outside of the world of the commodity. This is not only because the capitalist law of value permeates all social relationships, but also because the modern capitalist subject—even the one that wants to overcome capitalism—is constituted on the basis of the law of value through centuries of socialization.

Certainly, the requirements of the capitalist market are prone to "infect" any commoning endeavors with considerations that are alien to them: profitability, cost efficiency, competitiveness, and so on. But it is easy to overlook the fact that the "infection" can be bidirectional: "advancement of commons implies sooner or later a collision with other social systems governing them, the challenge to existing local rules, of capitalist ways to measure and give value to social action, its value practices, and other networked structures" (De Angelis 2012b: 13).

To say that commoning ventures that involve commodity production are not "real" commons would be correct if we posited the labor-capital contradiction as the dominant contradiction that inheres in the capitalist mode of production. But that would be to underestimate the countless other contradictions we are immersed in—following Harvey (2014), we could mention among them uneven power relations, uneven geographic development, private property, private appropriation of the fruits of our labor, gendered and racial divisions of labor, disparities of wealth, aliena-tion, and the economy's impact on the environment and the climate.[7] That would also be to underestimate the capacity of commoning endeavors to address and remedy these contradictions; it would be to reduce the mul-tifold activity of commoning to merely one aspect of it.

Commoning, however, implies a continuing struggle against capital in all the aforementioned fields. Exploring the political dimension of commoning should not boil down to a technical task of identifying what pertains to the commons and what to capital; rather, it should entail a constant attempt at identifying lines of flight within existing practices. "Whenever the value-struggle between the two different ways of giving value to human activity reaches a structural limit—and there is no social space left for capital or the commons to develop without contesting each other—a *frontline* is established. Reaching this frontline is, from the situ-ation of commons, the opportunity to mobilize against the capitalist logic, or to capitulate to it, depending upon a given situation of social powers" (De Angelis 2012: 186).

Even if capital is permanently adapting to the commoners' attempts to subvert it, appropriating and utilizing their structures for its own needs, there is no zero-sum game between the processes of resistance and appropriation: an "excess" is constantly produced, which gradually transforms social relations and prepares the ground on which future commoning endeavors will flourish.

The Question of Power

If in this essay the commons imaginary ("Plan C") enjoys coverage dis-proportionate to its actual political weight and popularity, it is because it addresses an issue that is essential to social change, that is, the construction of subjectivities and the propagation of values. The other two imaginaries described ("Plan A" and "Plan B") are top-heavy, operating on the assumption that power is just something that flows downward; the mere conquest of power at the top is enough to bring forth new social relations, structures, and values.

What they fail to take into account is that neoliberalism is not merely a political project but also a sociocultural one; as such, it was not only imposed—although, of course, violent imposition has had a central role—but it was adopted voluntarily by a great part of the population. This point is very important: liberalism, which at its core rests on the idea that there can be political equality without economic equality, fought a long and hard war—for people's minds among other things—against "actually existing" socialism, which promised both political and economic equality but delivered neither; the former eventually came out a winner in the 1990s. In its current mutation we call neoliberalism, the liberal project retains freedom as its buzzword, even if the term is now devoid of any real meaning and limited to "freedom of choice" among different products or to markets that are "free" of any intervention that might adapt them to human needs. The upshot is that as a cultural trend neoliberalism was adopted as an improvement over the previous situation (Fordism), invested in a social imaginary of "freedom," "flexibility," and "individuality," through its celebration of individual responsibility, initiative, and innovation. In short, neoliberalism has created a new anthropological type: entrepreneurial, competitive, efficient, profit-seeking. This was not just a side effect, but rather it was the core project of neoliberalism. Margaret Thatcher stated it bluntly at the time: "Economics are the method; the object is to change the heart and soul" (Thatcher 1981).

My argument is that commons movements take into account that the real battle is not for one policy over another; rather, it is a sociocultural battle between two imaginaries of social advancement, one of which emphasizes competition, individualism, and private initiative, while the other emphasizes cooperation, collective agency, and the commons. The fact that statecraft and economic policy are increasingly viewed not as political fields but as technical affairs best left to an "objective" administration by technocrats is only an outcome of the sociocultural predominance of the *Homo economicus*. In short, as elections and the alternation of governments in power are nowadays largely ceremonial and have no significant political effect, it is the social power of neoliberalism that needs to be contested, through the construction of values and subjects and the creation of social bonds and actual counterpower within society.

But this is not to say that the political can simply be dissolved within the social. The ordeal of the social movements in Greece serves as a harrowing reminder that power cannot be "conquered" at the top level, that it cannot be "abolished"—but neither can it be ignored.

We cannot, by any stretch of the imagination, argue that a disparate assortment of grassroots initiatives can offer answers to the pressing issues that society at large confronts. The effort to open up new political spaces, to build power from the bottom up, to form a coherent and self-conscious counterpower is long overdue in Greece. Failure to do so is detrimental to the project of social change, as it allows accumulated forces, knowledge, and experience to dissipate in times of demobilization, and it channels people's desire for social change back to the clearly ineffectual parliamentary avenue. In this respect, it is desirable that the movement of the commons constitutes itself as a self-conscious, even if diverse and decentralized, political actor. That is to say, it is desirable that the "imaginary" of the commons gives birth to a plan: "Plan C."

To this end, the political failures and weaknesses of the commons initiatives—such as isolationism and partiality—could possibly be remedied by what Kioupkiolis (2014) terms a "hegemony of the multitude," a process by which the autonomous experiences reaffirm their particularity while feeling part of a common project. "That is, the logic of difference should be supplemented with a logic of equivalence which unfolds around a common identity" (Kioupkiolis 2014: 161).

At the same time, it is the local level, rather than the national political scene, that can successfully be contested by grassroots movements. This is their natural field of intervention, but it also helps make politics a concrete engagement with life affairs again, rather than an abstract field best left to professionals, bureaucrats, and experts. As Murray Bookchin (1999) put it, the aim of such movements should not be to "exercise sudden and massive control by representatives and their bureaucratic agents over the existing economy; [but rather] to reopen a public sphere in flat opposition to statism, one that allows for maximum democracy in the literal sense of the term, and to create in embryonic form the institutions that can give power to a people generally."

This is not to say that municipal politics is an uncomplicated sphere unfettered by the dominance of capital or reactionary politics; inasmuch as local government is structured as a "miniature state," any attempts of progressive forces to conquer it can be equally frustrating, as recent experiences in Madrid and Barcelona help demonstrate. The "citizen platforms" Ahora Madrid and Barcelona en Comú, genuinely rooted in the social movements that emerged after 2011, were conceived as mechanisms of bringing the politics of the squares into the institutions and of overcoming the distinction between horizontal and vertical politics. Nevertheless, once in power, they were faced with the essential nature of the state—even in its municipal incarnation—as a guarantor of the reproduction of capital. Municipal governments led by the "citizens' platforms" have had a very hard time bringing the horizontal politics of the squares to the institutional sphere; on the contrary, they were often absorbed into a "governmentalism" that has alienated their social movement base (Espinoza Pino 2016) and has impeded the implementation of even the minimal points of their program, such as a moratorium on the foreclosures of the homes of families affected by the financial/housing crisis. For their timid public discourse, their continuation of policies of previous administrations, their lack of transparency, as well as for other arbitrary acts against the disadvantaged classes, such as intensifying the persecution of street vendors in the case of Barcelona, they have been criticized by scholars (Espinoza Zepeda 2016), social movements (Picazo 2016; Martínez López 2016; Sabaté 2016), and the radical Left (Espigares 2016).

Even if it would be a mistake to condemn on ideological grounds every effort on behalf of the forces of society to electorally penetrate or infiltrate the institutions, experience so far indicates that once they assume the form and the logic of the state, they can become powers of demobilization and appeasement, or even outright imposition. As Espinoza Pino (2016) points out, "governmentalism"—as an "infantile disease" of any left-wing or social movement-based organization that comes to power—has three main components: first, the primacy of "management" over politics; second, the conception of the public institution as a neutral space, where leaders are expected to govern "for everyone" and avoid thorny issues and conflict; and, third, the consolidation of a group of prominent figures who form the nucleus of a new political elite. Thus the conception of politics as a separate sphere with objective and value-neutral rules—which is nothing more than an ideological mantle to conceal the essentially classist and repressive nature of the state—displaces the embodied, passionate, contentious grassroots politics that gave rise to these political movements in the first place.

In the present cycle of mobilization, we have no examples of a successful "dynamic relationship" between, on the one hand, the movement as "constituent power" that mobilizes the "collective creative capacity" of society and, on the other, the political party, which by steering the public institutions guarantees the material conditions for society's self-determination (Azzellini 2016). Rather, we have experienced social movements as unable to maintain a critical independence from the electoral forces that claim to represent them, and those electoral forces losing sight of the horizon of social transformation and getting assimilated within the prevalent political culture. Through the experiences of social movements with power, particularly in Greece and Spain, many important questions have been asked regarding power and the state, but only a handful of useful answers have been given.

It would be safe to conclude that the end goal of grassroots movements cannot simply be the construction of a platform for contesting the elections. But this option should not be proscribed a priori; there may be cases where the movement decides that participation in electoral politics can afford it some tactical advantage. Furthermore, to be cautious about getting entangled in the dynamics of institutional politics in no case means a reluctance to organize, cooperate, compromise, scale up, reach out to society, or participate energetically in the public dialogue; there is no merit in partiality, marginality, or ideological purity. In any case, the end goal of grassroots movements is the transformation of politics through the promotion of wide participation in collective processes of self-management in wide areas of life, from material production to welfare and from education to entertainment, and ultimately the awakening of a new kind of grassroots militant citizenship that will claim power over everyday social and political life alike.

In Lieu of a Conclusion: The Current State of Affairs

In Greece, a very eventful 2015—complete with negotiations, a referendum, a prolonged confrontation with the powers that be, and a country constantly on the brink of "Grexit"—was succeeded by a pretty uneventful 2016, when hope had given way to resignation and the "banality of austerity" was accepted as a fact of life by the majority of the population.

The September 2015 elections, which resulted in the repetition of the Syriza-ANEL governmental coalition, served as a legitimation of Syriza's neoliberal turn. The "first government of the Left" has all but abandoned its imaginary of welfare and redistribution and has wholeheartedly adopted the discourse of previous governments of the inevitability of austerity and the longing for a return to growth through the attraction of foreign investment.

With Syriza having thus alienated its electoral base, a return of the right wing to power may be imminent. Although capitalist hegemony has been recomposed, this is a fragile state of affairs, since the rift created by classist austerity policies is only getting deeper, as indicated by the skyrocketing of electoral abstention to 45 percent in the latest elections— a figure previously unheard of in a country where voting is mandatory.

What is left of the Greek Left, still shocked by the mutation of its flagship party and by the inability of splinter group Popular Unity to enter the parliament, is given to introversion and half-hearted attempts at "reconstitution" of the political space.

The social movements, once the protagonists of fierce anti-austerity battles and of thousands of alternatives, barely protest at the moment, weakened by a general social resignation that has pushed the population back to their private lives. Even the bitter betrayals of flagship social struggles by the Syriza government are not surprising to anybody anymore.

Thessaloniki's water company, which had its privatization halted by a wide social movement that was supported—and even hegemonized—by Syriza, is now under privatization again, with many of the prominent previous members of the antiprivatization platform now promoting privatization, having become government MPs and bureaucrats. The environmentally hazardous gold mine in Halkidiki, which had awakened fierce resistance by the locals, has had its permits renewed by the government in office, and the antimining movement has been subdued with the combination of criminalization of protest—450 people in a population of 20,000 are now under legal persecution—and disorientation through promises for a political solution that were never fulfilled. The occupied factory of Vio.Me, the flagship of self-managed endeavors in Greece, is threatened by a legal process of liquidation, despite the promises of a series of governments to legalize its activity.

Returning to Dinerstein's schema, the social movements in Greece are now entangled in the mode of contradiction: through carrot-and-stick policies, the dominant order has managed to appropriate some of the initiatives of the previous years and repress many of the rest. But grassroots movements did not just reach an external limit but also an internal one, especially in regard to their ambiguous relation to the capitalist market and their perplexity vis-à-vis political power.

But the cycle of dissent and subordination is never a zero-sum game; there is an "overflow" of practices, values, and organizational forms that remain and form the substrate of the following cycle of mobilization.

A significant component of this "excess" is manifested as an advance in the public dialogue, traditionally dominated by the threadbare debate between the state and private initiative: a new discourse is emerging that uses the exciting new vocabulary of the commons and has begun putting emphasis on society's own capacity to collectively self-organize, rather than invoking the guardianship of the state or the market's invisible hand as a way out of social ills. This new discourse has slipped through the cracks of the dominant mediascape and is slowly building a legacy of ideas, values, and possibilities of action for the movements to come. In this sense, even if Greece is beyond "hope" as a hegemonic project, it firmly retains hope as an organizing principle.

Notes

1   Nevertheless, the schematization of different "plans" is very common in recent literature (Parkins 2015; Roos 2015a; De Angelis 2013, 2017). We should draw special attention to the schematization made by Massimo De Angelis, as it differs slightly to the one offered in this chapter. De Angelis (2013) talks of plans as "sense horizons around which different social forces coagulate . . . in order to deal with [capitalism's] impasse." He posits neoliberalism and neo-Keynesianism as capitals' Plans A and B, respectively, on a global scale. On the contrary, in this paper, the schematization is not of capitals' global strategies but of the imaginaries of "flight" that arose in response to restructuring and austerity. Nevertheless, De Angelis's description of "Plan C" around the commons coincides to a great extent with the use of the term here.

2   See, for example, the treatment of the Vio.Me-recuperated factory by the Ideological Committee of the Central Macedonia Branch of the Communist Party of Greece (2013).

3   Marx's law of value describes the way in which, in the capitalist market, the exchange value of products is linked to socially necessary labor time. In simple terms, it is the process by which markets self-regulate, rendering the production of one or the other product more or less profitable and dictating the intensification of labor to maintain competitiveness. Essentially, it is the process by which the market appears to take on a life of its own, regardless of human needs or desires; hence, it is a central element in our sense of alienation within capitalism.

4   It is interesting to note that in Argentina or Brazil, in the absence of capital and access to the market, worker-recuperated companies are often forced to

produce in the liberated factory as "subcontractors" of a capitalist enterprise that provides the raw materials and distributes the product to the market, thus obtaining the lion's share of the benefits. The reverse phenomenon is also frequent: a capitalist enterprise lays off the workers of an entire section and creates an employer-controlled "cooperative" in which the laid-off workers are hired anew. This sham "cooperative" is used by the original company as a "contractor," where the same workers work under worse conditions, without being entitled to any benefits or labor rights (Ruggeri 2014: 25, 40). The use of fraudulent cooperatives to circumvent labor legislation and promote precarity even affects countries with a strong cooperative tradition, such as Italy.

5   Chantal Mouffe has analyzed the term "agonistic" in her work "For an Agonistic Model of Democracy" in *Political Theory in Transition*, ed. Noël O'Sullivan (London: Routledge, 2000), 113–30.

6   See, for example, Astarian (2011), for a vision of a society based on production without productivity and the circulation of products without exchange, which will purportedly abolish both exchange value and use value.

7   In the words of David Harvey (2014: 68–69): "While the capital-labour contradiction is unquestionably a central and foundational contradiction of capital, it is not—even from the standpoint of capital alone—a primary contradiction to which all other contradictions are in some sense subservient.... Its tangible manifestations are mediated and tangled up through the filters of other forms of social distinction, such as race, ethnicity, gender and religious affiliation so as to make the actual politics of struggle within capitalism a far more complicated affair than would appear to be the case from the standpoint of the labour-capital relation alone.... But its overemphasis and its treatment as if it operates autonomously and independently of the other contradictions of capital have, I believe, been damaging to a full-blooded revolutionary search for an alternative to capital and, hence, to capitalism."

References

Alonso Rocafort, Víctor. "Centralidad, desmesura y esperanza." *El Diario*, April 17, 2015, http://www.eldiario.es/zonacritica/Centralidad-desmesura-esperanza_6_378372188.html.

Astarian, Bruno. "Crisis Activity and Communisation." *Hic Salta—Communisation*, 2010. http://www.hicsalta-communisation.com/english/crisis-activity-and-communisation.

Azzellini, Dario. "Constituent and Constituted Power: Reading Social Transformation in Latin America." In *Popular Sovereignty and Constituent Power in Latin America*, edited by Emelio Betances and Carlos Figueroa Ibarra, 15–39. New York: Palgrave Macmillan, 2016.

———. "Contemporary Crises and Workers' Control." In *An Alternative Labour History: Worker Control and Workplace Democracy*, edited by Dario Azzellini, 67–99. London: Zed Books, 2015.

Bailey, David J. "The End of the European Left? Social Democracy, Hope, Disillusion, and Europe." *Near Futures Online* 1, "Europe at a Crossroads," March

2016. http://nearfuturesonline.org/the-end-of-the-european-left-social-democracy-hope-disillusion-and-europe/.

Bonefeld, Werner. "The Permanence of Primitive Accumulation: Commodity Fetishism and Social Constitution." *Commoner* no. 2 (September 2001). http://www.commoner.org.uk/02bonefeld.pdf.

Bookchin, Murray. *The Murray Bookchin Reader.* Edited by Janet Biehl. Montreal: Black Rose Books, 1999.

Braudel, Fernand. *Civilization and Capitalism 15th–18th Century, II: The Wheels of Commerce.* London: Collins, 1984.

Caffentzis, George, and Silvia Federici. "Commons against and beyond Capitalism." *Community Development Journal* 49, suppl. 1 (January 2014): i92–i105.

Dalakoglou, Dimitris. "Neo-Nazism and Neoliberalism: A Few Comments on Violence in Athens at the Time of Crisis." *WorkingUSA* 16, no. 2 (June 2013): 283–92.

De Angelis, Massimo. "Crises, Movements and Commons." *Borderlands E-Journal: New Spaces in the Humanities* 11, no. 2 (2012b). http://www.borderlands.net.au/vol11no2_2012/deangelis_crises.htm.

———. "Crisis, Capital and Cooptation." In *The Wealth of the Commons: A World beyond Market & State,* edited by David Bollier and Silke Helfrich, 184–91. Amherst: Levellers Press, 2012a.

———. "Crisis, Commons and Social Movements." Paper presented at the International Studies Association Conference, *The Politics of International Diffusion: Regional and Global Dimensions,* April 3–6, 2013, San Francisco, 2013.

———. "Marx and Primitive Accumulation: The Continuous Character of Capital's Enclosures." *Commoner* no. 2 (September 2001): 1–22.

———. *Omnia Sunt Communia: On the Commons and the Transformation to Postcapitalism.* London: Zed Books, 2017.

———. "The Tragedy of the Capitalist Commons." *Turbulence* 5 (2009): 32–33.

Denning, Michael. "Wageless Life." *New Left Review* 66 (November–December 2010). http://newleftreview.org/II/66/michael-denning-wageless-life.

Dinerstein, Ana Cecilia. *The Politics of Autonomy in Latin America: The Art of Organising Hope.* London: Palgrave Macmillan, 2014.

Douzinas, Costas. *Philosophy and Resistance in the Crisis: Greece and the Future of Europe.* Cambridge: Polity Press, 2013.

Espigares, Evaristo. "El gobierno de Ada Colau: de las promesas a la realidad." Corriente Roja, April 4, 2016. http://www.corrienteroja.net/el-gobierno-de-ada-colau-de-las-promesas-a-la-realidad/.

Espinosa Zepeda, Horacio. "El mercadillo rebelde de Barcelona. Prácticas antidisciplinarias en la ciudad mercancía," *Quaderns-e, Institut Catala d'Antropologia* 22, no. 1 (2017): 67–87.

Espinoza Pino, Mario. "Construir movimiento municipalista (algunas hipótesis)." *Periodico Diagonal,* June 20, 2016. https://www.diagonalperiodico.net/blogs/funda/construir-movimiento-municipalista-algunas-hipotesis.html.

European Commission. "Social Economy in the EU," 2016. http://ec.europa.eu/growth/sectors/social-economy/index_en.htm.

Fouskas, Vassilis K. "Insight Greece: The Origins of the Present Crisis." *Insight Turkey* 14, no. 2 (Spring 2012): 27–36. https://www.insightturkey.com/author/vassilis-k-fouskas/insight-greece-the-origins-of-the-present-crisis.

Hardt, Michael, and Antonio Negri. *Declaration*. New York: Argo-Navis Author Services, 2012.

Harvey, David. "The 'New' Imperialism: Accumulation by Dispossession." *Socialist Register* 40 (2004): 63–87. http://socialistregister.com/index.php/srv/article/view/5811.

Harvey, David. *Seventeen Contradictions and the End of Capitalism*. London: Profile Books, 2014.

Holloway, John. "The Abyss Opens: The Rise and Fall of Keynesianism." In *Global Capital, National State and the Politics of Money*, edited by Werner Bonefeld and John Holloway, 7–34. London: Palgrave Macmillan, 1996.

———. *Crack Capitalism*. London: Pluto Press, 2010.

Ideological Committee of the Central Macedonia Branch of the Communist Party of Greece. "Regarding the So-Called Self-Management of Factories: The Case of Viome." [In Greek.] Κομμουνιστική Επιθεώρηση [Communist review] no. 5 (2013). http://www.komep.gr/2013-teyxos-5/gia-th-legomenh-aytodiaxeirish-ton-ergostasion-h-periptosh-ths-biome.

Karyotis, Theodoros. "Chronicles of a Defeat Foretold." *ROAR Magazine* no. 0, "Building Power," (2015): 32–63. https://roarmag.org/magazine/syriza-movements-power-commons/.

Katsambekis, Giorgos. "The Rise of the Greek Radical Left to Power: Notes on Syriza's Discourse and Strategy." *Línea Sur* no. 9 (2015): 152–61.

Kayserilioğlu, Alp, and Jannis Milios. "Austerity Unbroken." *Jacobin*, January 25, 2016. https://www.jacobinmag.com/2016/01/greece-syriza-tsipras-varoufakis-austerity-eurozone/.

Kioupkiolis, Alexandros. "A Hegemony of the Multitude: Muddling the Lines." In *Radical Democracy and Collective Movements Today: The Biopolitics of the Multitude versus the Hegemony of the People*, edited by Alexandros Kioupkiolis and Giorgos Katsambekis, 149–68. Surrey: Ashgate, 2014.

———, and Theodoros Karyotis. "Self-Managing the Commons in Contemporary Greece." In *An Alternative Labour History: Worker Control and Workplace Democracy*, edited by Dario Azzellini, 298–328. London: Zed Books, 2015.

Kokkinidis, George. "Spaces of Possibilities: Workers' Self-Management in Greece." *Organization* 22, no. 6 (January 2014): 847–71. https://www.researchgate.net/publication/273215070_Spaces_of_Possibilities_Workers'_Self-Management_in_Greece.

Kotsakis, Dimitris. *Three Texts Plus One* [in Greek]. Athens: Ekdosis ton Sinadelfon, 2012.

Krugman, Paul. "Europe's Impossible Dream." *New York Times*, July 20, 2015. http://www.nytimes.com/2015/07/20/opinion/paul-krugman-europes-impossible-dream.html.

Laclau, Ernesto. "Structure, History and the Political." In *Contingency, Hegemony, Universality: Contemporary Dialogues on the Left*, edited by Judith Butler, Ernesto Laclau, and Slavoj Žižek, 182–212. London: Verso, 2000.

Lapavitsas, Costas, Annina Kaltenbrunner, Duncan Lindo, J. Michell, Juan Pablo Painceira, Eugenia Pires, Jeff Powell, Alexis Stenfors, and Nuno Teles. "Eurozone Crisis: Beggar Thyself and Thy Neighbor." *Journal of Balkan and Near Eastern Studies* 12, no. 4 (2010): 321–73.

Lazzarato, Maurizio. *The Making of the Indebted Man: An Essay on the Neoliberal Condition.* Translated by Joshua David Jordan. New York: Semiotext(e), 2012.

Lieros, Giorgos. *An Actually Existing New World* [in Greek]. Athens: Ekdoseis ton Sinadelfon, 2012.

Martínez López, Gladys. "Críticas y división interna llevan a Ahora Madrid a posponer el reglamento de vivienda municipal." *Periodico Diagonal,* April 21, 2016. https://www.diagonalperiodico.net/global/30117-criticas-y-division-interna-llevan-ahora-madrid-posponer-reglamento-vivienda-municipal.

Marx, Karl. *Capital,* vol. I. Translated by Ben Fowkes. London: Penguin Classics, 1990.

Mattei, Ugo. "First Thoughts for a Phenomenology of the Commons." In *The Wealth of the Commons: A World beyond Market & State,* edited by David Bollier and Silke Helfrich, 39–44. Amherst, MA: Levellers Press, 2014.

McLeay, Michael, Amar Radia, and Ryland Thomas. "Money Creation in the Modern Economy." *Bank of England Quarterly Bulletin:* Q1 (2014). http://www.bankofengland.co.uk/publications/Documents/quarterlybulletin/2014/qb14q1prereleasemoneycreation.pdf.

Mejía, Pepe. "Nubarrones en el horizonte de Podemos." *Kaosenlared,* August 9, 2015. http://kaosenlared.net/nubarrones-en-el-horizonte-de-podemos/

Milios, John, and Michal Rozworski. "Ending the Humanitarian Crisis." *Jacobin Magazine,* July 21, 2015. https://www.jacobinmag.com/2015/07/tsipras-euro-merkel-debt-grexit/.

———, and Dimitris P. Sotiropoulos. "Crisis of Greece or Crisis of the Euro? A View from the European 'Periphery.'" *Journal of Balkan and Near Eastern Studies* 12, no. 3 (September 2010): 223–40.

Nasioka, Katerina. "Adventures of a Desert Rose: Athens in the 21st Century, a City in a State of Insurgence." [In Greek.] *Κομπρεσέρ,* May 27, 2014. https://kompreser.espivblogs.net/2014/05/27/athina-louloudi-exegersi/.

Papanicolaou, Georgios, and Ioannis Papageorgiou. "The Police and the Far Right in Greece: A Case Study of Police Voting Behaviour in Athens." *Crime, Law and Social Change* 66, no. 4 (November 2016): 397–419.

Papatheodorou, Christos. "Economic Crisis, Poverty and Deprivation in Greece." In *Greek Capitalism in Crisis: Marxist Analyses,* edited by Stavros Mavroudeas, 179–95. London: Routledge, 2014.

Parkins, Keith. "Plan C for Advancing the Commons Transition in Greece." *Medium,* July 27, 2015. https://medium.com/dark-mountain/plan-c-for-advancing-the-commons-transition-in-greece-8b18eef21e23.

Petropoulou, Christy. "'Alternative Networks of Collectivities' and 'Solidarity-Cooperative Economy' in Greek Cities: Exploring Their Theoretical Origins." *Journal of Regional Socio-Economic Issues* 3, no. 2 (June 2013): 61–85.

Picazo, Sergi. "Cinc Crítiques Que Es Podrien Fer Des de L'esquerra Al Govern de Barcelona En Comú." *Critic*, February 25, 2016. http://www.elcritic.cat/blogs/sergipicazo/2016/02/25/barcelona-en-comu-davant-del-mirall/.

Prentoulis, Marina, and Lasse Thomassen. "Autonomy and Hegemony in the Squares: The 2011 Protests in Greece and Spain." In *Radical Democracy and Collective Movements Today: The Biopolitics of the Multitude versus the Hegemony of the People*, edited by Alexandros Kioupkiolis and Giorgos Katsambekis, 213–34. Surrey: Ashgate, 2014.

Rakopoulos, Theodoros. "The Crisis Seen from below, within, and against: From Solidarity Economy to Food Distribution Cooperatives in Greece." *Dialectical Anthropology* 38, no. 2 (June 2014): 189–207.

———. "Solidarity's Tensions: Informality, Sociality, and the Greek Crisis." *Social Analysis* 59, no. 3 (December 2015): 85–104.

Roos, Jerome. "Greece Needs a Plan C: For the Commons and Communal Solidarity." *ROAR Magazine* website, July 4, 2015a. https://roarmag.org/essays/greece-plan-c-commons-solidarity/.

———. "Towards a New Anti-Capitalist Politics." *ROAR Magazine* no. 0 "Building Power," (2015): 80–115. https://roarmag.org/magazine/anti-capitalist-politics-21st-century/.

Ruggeri, Andrés. *¿Que son las empresas recuperadas?* Buenos Aires: Continente, 2014.

Sabaté, Arsen. "Ada Colau Endurece La Persecución Hacia Los 'Manteros' En Barcelona." *Izquierda Diario*, July 28, 2016. http://www.izquierdadiario.es/Ada-Colau-endurece-la-persecucion-hacia-los-manteros-en-Barcelona?id_rubrique=2653.

Sitrin, Marina. *Everyday Revolutions: Horizontalism and Autonomy in Argentina*. London: Zed Books, 2012.

Sotiris, Panagiotis. "The Dream That Became a Nightmare." *Jacobin*, February 10, 2016. https://www.jacobinmag.com/2016/02/greece-syriza-alexis-tsipras-varoufakis-austerity-farmer-blockade-protests.

Thatcher, Margaret. "Mrs. Thatcher: The First Two Years." *Sunday Times*, May 3, 1981. http://www.margaretthatcher.org/document/104475.

Trumbo Vila, Sol, and Matthijs Peters. *The Privatising Industry in Europe*. Report by the Transnational Institute, 2016. https://www.tni.org/files/publication-downloads/tni_privatising_industry_in_europe.pdf.

Varkarolis, Orestis. *Creative Resistances and Counterpower: Endeavours and Debates of the Radical Movement in the 21st Century* [in Greek]. Athens: Pagkaki, 2012.

Vatikiotis, Leonidas. "Memorandum—Steamroller for the Greek People," May 24, 2017. https://leonidasvatikiotis.wordpress.com/2017/05/24/memorandum-steamroller-for-the-greek-people/.

Xenakis, Sappho. "A New Dawn? Change and Continuity in Political Violence in Greece." *Terrorism and Political Violence* 24, no. 3 (2012): 437–64.

TWO

The Government of Hope, the Hope of Government, and the Role of Elections as Wave-Breakers of Radical Prefigurative Political Processes

Leonidas Oikonomakis

In "Shooting an Elephant" (1936), George Orwell narrates the story of a white police officer in British Burma[1] who, when an elephant goes on rampage and kills a local, asks for an elephant rifle in order to shoot the "beast." The locals bring him the rifle and, even though he would personally prefer not to shoot the elephant, feeling the pressure of the crowd he finally does what he is expected to: he shoots the animal, basically just "to avoid looking like a fool" in the eyes of the locals.

"[The white man] wears a mask, and his face grows to fit in it," says Orwell. "I had got to shoot the elephant. I had committed myself to doing it when I sent for the rifle," because "a sahib has got to act like a sahib" after all.[2]

In Greece, however, during the years of her self-destructive dance with the Troika (2010–2015), things unfolded in a very different manner. The "officer" Alexis Tsipras also promised the natives to "kill the Troika-beast" on their behalf, and he also did ask for and received an "elephant-rifle" (victory in the January election and the referendum of July 2015) to be able to do so. Yet he never shot the elephant. His face did not grow to fit in the mask he chose to wear, and he did not live up to the expectations of the "natives." As a result, he himself, together with him the institutional Left that he represents, ended up "looking like a fool," not only in the eyes of the Greek citizens who trusted him, but also in the eyes of the international community that was observing. But that was not the only effect the election of Syriza had on the Greek political landscape.

In this chapter I argue that the moment that elections were called in 2012, an extremely interesting—yet understudied—process unfolded in

Greece, which has to do with the functioning of the elections as an event, and the effect it had on the radical social transformations that were flourishing in the country until then. At that point the Greek Left—and some grassroots movements as well—decided to back the effort of an institutional left-wing party in an electoral struggle for social change. The proclamation of elections led to a massive reduction of social mobilization and the split of grassroots movements (those who would back Syriza and those who would not) and gradually brought about the abandonment—or at least the massive weakening—of radical horizontal transformative social processes that were being experimented with until then. In short, it brought back the *state* and the *party* as the main agents of change in the people's political imaginary.

In addition, after the election of the self-proclaimed "first government of the Left,"[3] we observe a "honeymoon period" with the movements, and when that ended the party—now government—intended to manage dissent through a strategy of "partial carrots and moderate sticks" (Trejo 2012: 46). This process did not take place only in Greece but also in other countries where similar social processes were at play: in Argentina in 2001–2003 and in Bolivia in 2000–2005, for example. That's a social phenomenon and a political functioning of the elections as an event in the process of radical social transformation that certainly deserves additional attention from sociologists and political scientists alike.

Greece's Self-Destructive Dance with the Troika

"Symbolism" comes from a Greek word. According to the *Merriam-Webster* dictionary it refers to "the art or practice of using symbols, especially by investing things with symbolic meaning or by expressing the invisible or intangible by means of visible or sensuous representations." Former Greek prime minister Giorgos Papandreou—or his advisors—used symbolism to announce the beginning of the country's self-destructive dance with the Troika of lenders in April 2010. He appeared on national TV—before it was closed down by Nea Dimokratia (New Democracy) and PASOK, only to be reopened some years later on by Syriza and Anexartitoi Ellines (Independent Greeks)—in front of the scenic port on the island of Kastelorizo to announce:

> We have all inherited—the Greek government and people—a ship that is sinking. . . . It is a national and urgent necessity to turn to

the mechanism that we have created together with our peers in the European Union for assistance . . . and our peers will offer us the leeward port in order to rebuild our ship with strong and reliable materials." (*To Vima*, April 23, 2010)

Never before had such bad news been announced from such a beautiful place, but the symbolism was clear: the "mechanism" Papandreou was talking about would offer Greece a "leeward port," like the one of Kastelorizo in the image, to reconstruct itself. He didn't say it at the time, but he was talking about the Troika: the IMF, the European Central Bank, and the European Commission. At the time, the country's public debt was at 120 percent of GDP, the unemployment rate at 12 percent, and the youth unemployment rate at around 30 percent; suicide rates were an unfamiliar concept.

The IMF and World Bank are certainly not well known for doing a good job when they meddle with national economies, and for this reason in 2009 Papandreou precluded the possibility of these institutions becoming involved in the Greek situation, saying he would reject that option for Greece in the event that PASOK would win the elections. In April 2010, however, things had already changed for Papandreou, and on May 5 Greece announced the signing of the first Memorandum of Understanding with the Troika. It involved massive cuts in welfare spending, the privatizations of the country's assets, and massive layoffs in the public sector, as well as heavy salary and pension reductions.

As was expected, Greek society reacted: it is very probable that Greece holds the world record in general strikes in the past five years (forty-two), while Kousis counts thirty-one big protest events (with the participation of 5,000–500,000 people) between February 2010 and December 2012 (Kousis 2013). It all culminated in the occupation of Syntagma Square on May 25, 2011, only ten days after the occupation of Puerta del Sol in Madrid and the #15M had begun. The occupation of Syntagma Square lasted for seventy-two days,[4] which makes it probably the longest of the Squares of the Real Democracy Movement (Roos and Oikonomakis 2014; Oikonomakis and Roos 2013). Five years later, with the country having followed the Troika's dictates, public debt reached 175 percent of GDP, unemployment was at 24.4 percent, youth unemployment rates had skyrocketed to 52 percent, and suicide rates had increased by 35 percent (Rachiotis et al. 2015)—but the data available concern just the first two years of the crisis.

The Squares

In retrospect, 2011 was probably the most critical juncture in the last five years. The popularity of the political system was at its lowest, representative democracy was seen as exactly the opposite of what its name suggests, and the Greek political parties had reached the nadir of their popularity (Teperoglou and Tsatsanis 2014). According to the Public Issue (2011), one of the main polling agencies in Greece, by the end of the year 82 percent of the Greek people had a negative opinion of PASOK, 72 percent of LAOS, 67 percent of New Democracy, 66 percent of KKE, with the most "popular" Greek party being Syriza, of which a *mere* 61 percent of the Greeks had a negative opinion. The Movement of the Squares seriously challenged the legitimacy of neoliberalism as an economic system, of *representative democracy* as a political one, and of the *party* as an organizational form, putting forward—or at least putting on the agenda—direct democracy, horizontality, and self-organization, as well as nationalization of the country's assets.

A few months later, Syriza would come very close to winning the national elections with 26.9 percent of the vote, just 2.9 percent behind New Democracy, a feat it would achieve a few years later, in 2015. Some theorists, like Paolo Gerbaudo (2016), for example, have connected the success of Syriza with the Movement of the Squares (which he wrongly calls *aganaktismenoi*):[5] "The electoral surge of Syriza in Greece that eventually brought it to power was largely propelled by the strength of the *aganaktismenoi* movement."

It is a common argument that completely lacks a solid base; there is no evidence whatsoever behind it. From what we actually know and what can be proven from the Syntagma Popular Assembly records (2011), the movement showed absolute mistrust for representative democracy and the existing political system as a whole, as well as for the political party—including Syriza—as an organizational form. And that feeling was not only prevalent among the participants of the Movement of the Squares; as we can see from the aforementioned poll results it was a rather common feeling in the country at the time. But while Gerbaudo's connection between the Movement of the Squares and the rise of Syriza lacks the necessary evidence, his—and others'—question is indeed legitimate: How did we go from a complete disregard of political parties, including Syriza (61 percent having a negative opinion of it), in December 2011 to second place in the national elections, only 2.9 percent behind the leading party? And then again to a victory in January 2015?

I argue that what contributed to this impressive U-turn was not the sudden belief in existing institutions, but rather the absence of alternative structures, which the Movement of the Squares failed to create—and, to be fair, did not have the time to create—before its disappearance. At the same time, another thing that contributed to the quick abandonment of the prefigurative dimension of the movement was the sudden calling of the elections, which forced both movement activists and Greek society as a whole to take a position on the governance of existing institutions, disrupting the process of creating new, not-yet-existing ones.

Elections as Wave-Breakers of Radical Prefigurative Processes

Periklis Korovesis, Greek author and former Syriza deputy, who was imprisoned and tortured by the Colonels' Junta, gave an interesting interview in the left-wing newspaper *Efimerida ton Syntakton*, in which he argued that "the elections have always been [about] the self-regulation of the system, and never [about] its overturn" (Κοροβέσης [Korovesis] 2015). When it comes to the experience of the 2011 Movement of the Squares, I would agree that this was exactly what happened. The mechanism is simple: the current political and economic system was seriously challenged, and the need to prefigure a new one was becoming stronger and stronger, but once elections were called people had to choose between participating in an existing structure or prefiguring a not-yet-existing one. As the experience of Greece has shown (one could also add Spain 2011–2015, Bolivia 2000–2005, and Argentina 2001–2003), it is more probable that the majority of the people will choose the already existing structure, the *constituted* power, to put it in Hardt and Negri's terms, instead of the *constituent* one (Hardt and Negri 2000, 2004). At the same time, as is commonplace in similar experiences (see Latin America's "pink tide" for example), once a left-wing, previously underdog party is perceived to be a serious challenger for the seat of government, street mobilization normally declines to a minimum, and when the party wins the elections what follows is a—shorter or longer—"honeymoon period" between the grassroots movements and the newly elected government (Zibechi 2009, 2010, 2012; Gutiérrez Aguilar 2008; Mayorga 2012).

Even though there is not enough evidence to prove that elections are (and in the case of Greece 2012, were) called purposefully in order to avoid the overturn of an "old" system and the emergence of a "new" one, there is enough evidence to suggest that once elections are called prefigurative

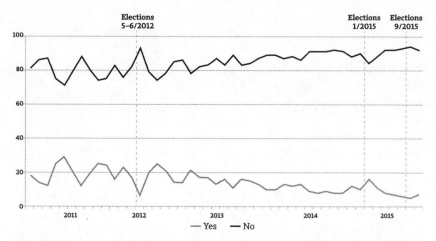

Participation in Social Mobilizations over the Last Month: March 2011–November 2015
Source: Public Issue, Political Barometer Chronics

politics are interrupted, social mobilization drops (della Porta, Fernández, Kouki, and Mosca 2017), and movements are generally split: some of their members participate in the elections in one form or another, while others prefer not to. In short, even if elections are not intended to be "the cheese in the trap," they eventually end up playing that role. According to the graphic above, produced by Public Issue Political Barometer Chronics in 2015, it is clear that participation in social mobilizations reached its peak in 2011, as well as just before and just after the 2012 elections that Syriza lost by a small margin, only to start a downward trend after that—when it was obvious that Syriza was a serious electoral contender—reaching its nadir after the party's electoral victory in January 2015.

That's not exceptional. Martín Portos (2016) created a database in which he illustrates the longitudinal dynamics of the 2007–2015 cycle of protest in Spain. He argues that the declining phase of protest events coincides with the founding of Podemos in January 2014. He continues:

> Along with the strength and popularity that Podemos gained in the first few months of the year and during the campaign for the European election in 2014, there was a reverse trend in the levels of anti-austerity mobilization, like a sort of zero-sum game. Only one mass event took place ever since, the *Marcha del Cambio*, coordinated by Podemos in January 2015 (which gathered 300,000 participants according to the organizers). (Portos 2016: 22)

45

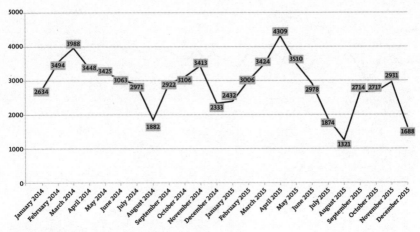

Announced Demonstrations, 2014–2015
Source: Spanish Interior Ministry combined data

In the chart above we can also see that a few months after the founding of Podemos in January 2014, the number of announced protests started dropping as well, especially before the May 2014 European elections in which the party made its first appearance. Protests gradually rose again until the May 2015 municipal elections in which Podemos did not directly participate, only to start dropping immediately thereafter when national elections were announced. It reached its nadir just before the December 2015 general elections in which Podemos received 20.65 percent of the vote. Yesenia Barragan, in an article published on *teleSUR* in February 2015, wrote:

> Furthermore, while some have enthusiastically talked about the rise of Podemos … as their potential savior, many activists working on the ground have talked about how Podemos has contributed significantly to a demobilization of genuinely horizontal organizing and popular resistance out in the streets. In Santiago de Compostela, for example, I spoke to a woman named Maria, who is a leader in the anti-eviction movement there, who said that the number of supporters coming out to anti-eviction actions has reduced considerably with the rise of Podemos on the left. "Don't worry about it," many have told her, "Podemos will fix the problem." In this uncertain, challenging time, where on the one hand these repressive laws are scaring people off the streets, and on the other hand, where parties like Podemos are not only attempting to capitalize on the

widespread fatigue that several years of constant marches and demonstrations have produced, but also actively promoting the notion that social ills can be cured through the ballot, it is imperative to recognize the many forms that repression and demobilization can take. (Barragan 2015)

This is the same argument that Guillermo Trejo makes in his book on popular movements in autocracies (Trejo 2012). He argues that in election—and more importantly in nonelection—years, opposition parties are very likely to offer their institutional and financial support to grassroots movements (they can serve as their "institutional voice," finance them, use the media to which they have access to promote their causes, etc.), but once they are actually elected they tend to take a more moderate stance and to distance themselves from the movements. He writes:

> To the extent that electoral victories often entail the adoption of moderate, multi-class and multiethnic political compromises, partisan leaders will at some point face powerful incentives to moderate the actions of their social movement allies and their niche demands, discourage public demonstrations, and drop from their platforms radical demands and identities that may alienate the median voter. These electoral incentives will eventually turn opposition parties into an important force for demobilization and institutionalization of protracted cycles of independent protest. Access to patronage, candidacies, and public resources will be a powerful incentive for social movement leaders and activists to follow party leaders in institutionalizing protest. (Trejo 2012: 44)

That's the strategy of (partial) carrots and (moderate) sticks according to Trejo, in which the newly elected government attempts to (partially) satisfy—some of—the movements' demands, co-opt those leaders that can be co-opted, and use nonlethal repressive power against the movements who do not cooperate. Of course, Trejo refers to opposition parties in autocracies, but the mechanism is not so different in democracies. Raúl Zibechi (2009) uses the same argument to summarize the experience of the pink tide governments in Latin America, especially in Argentina:

> In the first stage after the "progressive" governments took power, the subordination of social movements to their respective governments

predominated, resulting in demobilization, divisions, and the fragmentation of initiatives. Only small groups maintained open confrontation, while the majority collaborated with the state in return for subsidies and other material benefits, including positions in state agencies and institutions. Another large part of the original collectives simply dissolved.... [In Argentina,] most of the piquetero movement was co-opted by the state through social programs and the designation of leaders of the movement for government positions. The human rights movement, and in particular the Mothers' Association of the Plaza de Mayo (Asociación Madres de Plaza de Mayo)... has moved toward a more official role and begun to defend government policies. In addition, a section of the neighborhood associations have disappeared.

We observe the same mechanisms if we examine the Syriza case. After 2011 and throughout 2012, when it became obvious that, with the general dissatisfaction of the overall population with traditional political parties, Syriza had a chance in the upcoming elections, the party started intensifying the parliamentary, logistical, and media support it was offering to several grassroots movements that were mobilizing in the country at the time: the movement against the gold mine in Halkidiki, the movement against the privatization of water in Athens and Thessaloniki, the workers at ERT (the national broadcaster), the cleaning ladies who had been fired from the Ministry of Finance, and the worker-occupied factory of Vio. Me, just to give a few examples. Several Syriza MPs offered institutional support to the aforementioned movements and initiatives by posing questions in parliament, participating in their mobilizations, and providing visibility through the Syriza-controlled media. Theodoros Karyotis, a sociologist and activist involved in several of those initiatives throughout the crisis years, wrote recently in a relevant article for ROAR Magazine:

> Throughout the years of resistance to the neoliberal assault, two conceptions of politics played out within the social movements: on the one hand, politics as "the art of the possible," related to the growing influence of SYRIZA in social struggles; on the other hand, politics as an exercise of radical imagination and experimentation, put forward by the commons-based alternative.... By its nature, SYRIZA is much more understanding of the type of struggles that

envision a stronger state as the mediator of social antagonisms. This has resulted in the curtailing of demands that did not fit into a coherent program of state management—including most projects that revolve around popular self-management of the commons. Starting in 2012, the meteoric electoral rise of SYRIZA put an end to the crisis of legitimation, since it produced a long awaited institutional response to the crisis. With it came a relative demobilization, and a desire of institutionalization of the struggles. (Karyotis 2016)

In short, while Syriza supported all the above initiatives when in opposition, once it became the government it disregarded all the proposals that it deemed "too radical," like the self-management of the national broadcaster proposed by its workers, the treatment of the Thessaloniki Water Company as a "common," or the closing of the gold mine in Halkidiki (the Syriza stance is to make sure that the "investment" complies with environmental regulations). On the contrary, as a result of its ambivalent (and rather failed) political strategy, it has had to privatize the country's biggest port, Piraeus, selling it to a Chinese company, while the Thessaloniki and Athens water companies are again up for sale, and the Canadian mining company in Halkidiki is still operating.

Of course, after a short "honeymoon period," repression is back, Syriza-led this time, targeting especially the grassroots movement that is still demanding the cancellation of the contract with the mining company for the irreversible negative damage it has already done to the environment in their region. The occupied factory of Vio.Me, despite several visits of Alexis Tsipras and other Syriza MPs with its workers, always accompanied by regularization/legalization promises, is still facing the threat of eviction, and the country's self-identified "first government of the Left" may be the one that executes it. Tsipras himself, in a Syriza party meeting on May 5, 2016, when a disappointed member complained about the party's neoliberal policies, said, "The party is now addressing wider audiences, not just a left-wing village" (Κοκκινάκος [Kokkinakos] 2016).

The only positive outcomes of the Syriza government so far have been the granting of citizenship to second-generation immigrants (Generation 2.0) and the extension of the right to civil partnership to gay and lesbian couples. These are not minor accomplishments, of course, but neither conflicts with the neoliberal agenda of the government and foreign lenders. It could be argued that those policies have been a sign of goodwill to the Left (partial satisfaction of demands, partial carrot in Trejo's terms), which was, however, followed by a continuation of the previous neoliberal agenda, executed by a "government of the Left." In this, Syriza is proving Zibechi's argument that left-wing governments that govern rightward are the worst enemies of social movements, since they leave them without a reference point, achieving peacefully (or semi-peacefully) what the neoliberal Right was not able to achieve through repression (Zibechi 2012: 290). It is the same story that we saw in Latin America with the governments of the pink tide: a left-wing party, riding on discontent with the political system, neoliberalism, and institutional parties—discontent that was mainly created through the efforts of self-managed, horizontal, prefigurative grassroots experiences—wins the elections and then all of a sudden the *state* returns to being the main agent of social change in the political imagination (Zibechi 2009, 2012). It is interesting therefore to explore why that happens.

On Existing and Not-Yet-Existing Structures

The aim of the Movement of the Greek Squares, at least as it was expressed by the Syntagma Assembly, was twofold:

a) to overturn the austerity measures and avoid a vote on the midterm agreement by the Greek parliament;
b) to introduce direct democracy and self-organization (Syntagma Popular Assembly 2011) into the country's political life.

Once it became apparent that the short-term target was lost, with the vote on the midterm agreement of the June 29, 2011, the long-term target became the introduction of direct democracy and self-organization in all aspects of political and social life. In the words of one of the speakers at the June 30, 2011, Syntagma Assembly (just one day after the first destruction of the square by the police and the vote on the midterm agreement):

> I mean to say that it is not we who found the Square; it is the Square that found us. The characteristics were already there. Those who were obsessed with the midterm agreement. . . . I think that is over now. What is now at stake is something deeper, a bigger rupture. That of autonomy and direct-democracy. (ibid.)

The same could be said about several of the initiatives that sprang up after the Syntagma (and other Squares) experiment was over. Many of those movements were, fully or in part, putting forward all or some of the issues of autonomy, self-organization, horizontality, and direct democracy. Take for example the workers of Vio.Me, or the Workers' Assembly of Occupied ERT, or part of the Water Movement of Thessaloniki (Kinisi 136, for example, or Water Warriors), or the neighborhood assemblies and the social clinics. Adam and Teloni locate seventy such cases in Greece (Αδάμ and Τελώνη [Adam and Teloni] 2015) that were developed and are still functioning.

We are therefore talking about a third way to social change, not the traditional *reform* or *revolution* dilemma that necessarily passes from the grasp of state power in one form or another. In this case, the political demand brought forward by the movements—or at least by some of them—is that of autonomy. It is not a new demand, and the participants in these movements were aware of that and were—and are still—also making references to other such historical instances in which self-organization and autonomy played a protagonist role: the occupations and neighborhood assemblies in Argentina, the Zapatistas, the experience of the Coordinadora por la Defensa del Agua y la Vida of Cochabamba, and others (Roos and Oikonomakis 2013, 2014; Dinerstein 2014; Holloway 2002, 2010; Sitrin 2006).

The idea is for the poor and disadvantaged to be self-empowered from below in their local spaces, in an emancipatory, autonomous, self-managed way. Holloway, in his *Change the World without Taking Power* (2002), describes this "no-power"[6] road (as he calls it) as the movement of power-to (in contrast to the power-over), a movement toward emancipating human potential. It is still practiced by revolutionary movements that do make claims to territory, to the state or segments thereof (communities, villages, cities, even neighborhoods within cities), and it also has socially, culturally, and politically transformative aspects. Yet it does not aim to conquer already existing state structures, but rather to create new ones from below in a prefigurative manner. It is a road to social change that does not cling to any theoretical dogma, but rather follows the Zapatista strategy of *preguntando caminamos* (asking, we walk): "It is rather a movement outwards, a path that is made in the process of walking—walking in the dark, guided only by the light provided by the utopian star of our projection" (Holloway 2002: 221), rejecting both revolutionary vanguardism and state-oriented reformism. The nonstate power road also rejects the political party as an organizational form, on the grounds that it is a necessarily state-oriented form of organization but gives preference to autonomy and councilism—which it sees as a horizontal form of decision-making that encourages free participation with the aim of reaching consensus in its decisions (Holloway 2005). In addition, as George Katsiaficas adds, the goal of autonomous movements is "to transcend nation states, not to capture them" (Katsiaficas 1997: 196). Ana Dinerstein (2014) defines autonomy as "the art of organizing hope" in a prefigurative manner, without necessarily having a detailed future vision of the society as a whole, "seeing it," however, on the horizon. One could argue that the nonstate power road is closer to anarchism, since in its theory and practice the "means" are considered as important as—if not characteristic of—"the ends" when we are talking about emancipatory social change.

It is the kind of communitarian political approach that has been practiced in the *ayllus* of the Aymaran Altiplano in Bolivia (Zibechi 2010) or in the Argentinean neighborhood assemblies (Dinerstein 2014), the *piquetero* movements, and the recuperated factories (Sitrin 2006). Its theory and practice can be very well summarized in what the Bolivian Coordinadora Por la Defensa del Agua y la Vida, in the year 2000, described as follows: "It is not about making a small room in their house, it is about constructing a whole new house"[7] (Gutiérrez Aguilar 2008: 51).

Yet this road to social change is not one that escapes criticism either. According to James Petras and Henry Veltmeyer, this road to social change serves only one purpose: to deflect the masses from challenging the existing structures by helping them to learn how to survive within them: "Rather than directly confronting this structure in an effort to change the existing distribution of power, the aim, in effect, is to empower the poor without having to disempower the rich" (Petras and Veltmeyer 2011: 5). That's exactly the reason why, they argue, states and big international organizations (the World Bank, for example) have been very favorable to this effort and usually cooperate with like-minded NGOs. In addition, this whole process is viewed as an effort by certain governments to transfer former state responsibilities to citizens and civil society, the so-called third sector—even though, as Asef Bayat notes, "at the same time governments display apprehension about losing political space" (Bayat 1997: 12). Hakim Bey, in his *T.A.Z.: The Temporary Autonomous Zone*, adds a warning: such an autonomous nonstate power experience cannot last long. Eventually, the state will crush or co-opt it, therefore what it has to do is to sense it before that happens and "dissolve itself elsewhere/else-when before the state crushes it" (Bey 1997). Richard Stahler-Sholk (2007) warns against the pitfalls of the three different models of autonomy he identifies: a) "autonomy defined as mere decentralization," which runs the risk of simply replacing the central power structures with regional ones, b) "autonomy without resources," which involves the liberalization of the local resources, leaving the space open for transnational capital to exploit them, and c) the neoliberal "multiculturalism trap," which recognizes multiple (indigenous) identities but not their collective rights. In short, Stahler-Sholk is warning against models of autonomy that are strictly political (decentralization), strictly economical (liberalization), or strictly cultural (identity recognition), without being all-encompassing.

The main problem, however, with this kind of autonomous, self-organized, direct democratic, horizontal form of social change is that it is not there (yet). It is not a concrete institution. There is no blueprint, no revolutionary step-by-step cookbook that describes how to get there. It is based on prefiguration and it is the product of grassroots planning and execution, that very often—as one would imagine—involves trial and error. It is based, as Kropotkin argues, on the "creative power and constructing activity of the people," who aim at "developing institutions of common law in order to protect them from the power-seeking minority" (Kropotkin, Tompkins, and Capouya 1976: 57) And, of course, this constructing ability needs time to take shape and form, and necessarily passes through a great deal of trial and error: the Zapatistas, for example, have been constructing their *autonomia Zapatista* for more than two decades now, yet they keep reminding us that they still make mistakes, because they are still learning. Yet the Zapatista communities (BAEZLN—Bases de Apoyo Zapatista) decided to ignore the actual political system, national or local, of Chiapas and concentrate on building their own form of self-governance for all those years instead. Not all movements decide to do so, though, not even in revolutionary epochs when dual power—the *constituted* and the *constituent*—appears (Lenin 1917; Trotsky 1930; Rockefeller 2007).

The Leeward Port and Its Wave-Breakers
This is especially so when elections are proclaimed, as the Greek, Bolivian, Argentinean, and Spanish experiences have shown, because activists have to decide urgently whether to participate in the elections (as an expression of the constituted power) or to ignore them, and if they ignore them,

Year	2004	2007	2009	May 2012	June 2012	Jan 2015	Sept 2015
Participation	76.50%	74.15%	70.95%	65.12%	62.49%	63.94%	56.16%

Participation in the Greek Parliamentary Elections (2004–2015).
Source: Ministry of the Interior (accessed: May 4, 2016)

they must start or keep participating in self-managed prefigurative politics. The same goes for the nonactivist general public.

As is clearly visible in the table above, participation in the parliamentary elections in Greece—voters' turnout—has been steadily declining since 2004.

What is extremely interesting to note, though, is what happened between the 2009 and the 2012 elections, when the citizens' trust in the political system was at its lowest, as we have seen in the Public Issues poll (2011). In fact, that trend is not clearly depicted in voter turnout: while there was an 8 percent drop between 2009 and June 2012, and despite the overall dissatisfaction with the county's political parties, Greek citizens did turn out to vote, casting the second-largest vote (26.89 percent) for Syriza, the party they disliked *the least*, (61 percent of Greek voters expressed a negative opinion about the party). I argue that this paradox can be explained by one very simple fact: the elections as an institution were the only game in town, therefore the majority of the citizens ended up playing it. Even though representative democracy and the party as an organizational form were largely held in low regard by Greek society, once political parties started expressing popular grievances through institutional channels, the only ones available, those citizens who took to the ballot box voted for them. That fact becomes even more interesting if we take into account that while Syriza itself initially involved the movements that would mobilize under its umbrella in the internal party organizational processes, after 2012—even though the Greek society and movements were asking for a horizontal direct-democracy structure—the party starting developing a more hierarchical internal decision-making body, according to della Porta, Fernández, Kouki, and Mosca (2017). They argue:

> Although SYRIZA members changed up to 2015 due to their osmosis with social movements and anti-austerity struggles, the

pyramid-like structure impeded people from taking responsibilities and influencing the party, while at the same time no new forms
of organization or structures were created.... Notwithstanding its
great electoral victory, when SYRIZA took power in 2015 it remained
part of the old establishment in terms of organization, membership,
and decision-making structures.

It is also extremely interesting to note that in the subsequent elections,
those of September 2015, when Syriza had already broken its promise to
cancel the memorandums and get rid of the Troika, a mere 56.16 percent
showed up to vote, 35.46 percent of whom voted again for Syriza. That's an
extremely low percentage, since, according to Eurostat, the average voter
turnout in the EU in 2014 (the last available) was around 68 percent. That
can partly be explained by the fact that Greek citizens, or at least many of
those who had previously trusted Syriza, had become disillusioned and
did not turn up at the ballot boxes.

Summing up, from the evidence we have we can argue that just before
the 2012 elections participation in social mobilizations reached its apex,
only to start dropping when the 2015 elections were approaching and
Syriza was ahead in the polls, reaching its lowest point after Syriza was
elected. This observation is in line with similar experiences in other countries (Spain, Argentina, Bolivia) and was due to the monopolization of the
prospect of social change by Syriza's electoral promises and the return of
the *party* and the *state* as the main agents of change in the public imaginary.
Therefore, citizens abandoned social mobilization for party politics, at
least until Syriza became the government and broke its electoral promises.
As I have argued here, this happened because elections were the only
game in town, and once they were called and activists and voters alike had
to decide whether or not they would participate, a big share of them chose
to, with several grassroots movements splitting over the question. Once
the voters became disillusioned with Syriza as well, electoral turnout
dropped massively. What remains to be seen is whether these voters
redirected their political participation toward the typical repertoires of
protest, got involved in more autonomous projects, or chose inactivity.

Conclusion
The rise and electoral victory of a left-wing party in Greece offers us a
unique opportunity to compare its relationship with the grassroots

movements that created the wave of discontent that eventually led to the self-designated "first Greek government of the Left" with the Latin American experience of the "pink tide" of the past fifteen years. Several theorists have written about the pink tide governments and their relationship with the movements that brought them to state power (Zibechi 2009, 2010, 2012; Petras and Veltmeyer 2011, Petras 2014; Oikonomakis and Espinoza 2014; Stahler-Sholk, Vanden, and Becker 2014), either analyzing them case by case or comparing them. Yet the rise of a left-wing government under similar conditions in Greece offers a unique opportunity for a "transatlantic" comparison that searches for common patterns.

In this chapter examining the Greek experience with Syriza's "Government of Hope" and keeping in mind the lessons learned from the Latin American "pink tide" (especially in Argentina and Bolivia), I make the following observations:

a) Both in Greece and in Latin America (Argentina, Bolivia, Ecuador) we notice a cycle of protests marked by a huge disregard for the political system as a whole, representative democracy as a political regime, neoliberalism as an economic system, and the political party as an organizational form. Instead, the grassroots movements proposed self-organization, direct democracy, and autonomy. In the economic field there were two competing proposals: nationalization and socialization or collectivization of state-assets.

b) Once elections were called, they acted as "wave-breakers" for grassroots movements in terms of participation in social mobilization and in prefigurative political projects.

c) Before the elections, the main opposition party (Syriza, in this case) acted as an "institutional channel" for the grassroots movements' positions. After its election and an initial "honeymoon period" with the movements, it moderated its positions using the "(partial) carrot and (moderate) stick" strategy (Trejo 2012). The same process is apparent in the case of Argentina and Bolivia. (Zibechi 2009, 2012).

d) At least in the Greek case,[8] we also notice that once "disillusionment" took over the initial excitement with electoral politics, voter turnout dropped massively.

What remains to be seen is whether this voter turnout will be translated into renewed social mobilization, whether that mobilization will be essentially "traditional" or take on more prefigurative forms of action, and whether this low voter turnout will translate to political inactivity.[9]

Despite the social demobilization that accompanied Syriza's rise to power and the disappointment that followed it, I argue that both the rise and the fall of the Syriza hope/promise are necessary steps in a historical process toward emancipatory politics. Initially, the rise of the Left that Syriza seemed to represent relegitimized the party system, representative democracy as a governing structure, and the political party as an organizational form—during a period in which their popularity had reached its nadir. Later on, however, after Syriza's failure, all the above started to be challenged again in Greece, which may lead to the resurgence of prefigurative political processes. Finally, the "natives" may realize that they need no "sahib" to kill the monster for them. For the "rifle" is in their hands.

Notes

1 Today Myanmar (formerly Burma).
2 During the British colonial rule in India the word *sahib* was used to refer to white Europeans.—Ed.
3 For propaganda purposes Syriza chose to call its government "the first government of the Left" of Greece. Objectively speaking, even if Syriza had not made its U-turn, and even if its coalition government did not include a nationalist party, ANEL, the term would be incorrect. The first and only government of the Left Greece has ever experienced was that of PEEA (Politiki Epitropi Ethnikis Apeleutherosis/Political Commission of National Liberation), also known as "the government of the mountains." It was elected in 1944, through an electoral process in which more than two million people participated, and it governed the parts of the country (mostly rural and mountainous) that were liberated by the National Resistance (mainly by EAM-ELAS).
4 On an interesting note, seventy-two days is exactly as long as the Paris Commune lasted.
5 Beyond the critique of Gerbaudo's main argument, I would like to note here that the Syntagma Square occupiers actually rejected the name "indignants" in any language and never signed any of their decisions as *aganaktismenoi*, which was perceived as an external term imposed by the hegemonic media. They preferred to use the "Syntagma Popular Assembly" signature. In addition, the Syntagma Popular Assembly of May 31, 2011, voted in favor of placing a huge banner at the upper part of Syntagma Square, and one of the participants suggested that the movement "not be called *aganaktismenoi* (indignant), but rather *apofasismenoi* (determined)" (Syntagma Popular Assembly Minutes 2011—author's translation from Greek). A few days later, a banner reading in huge capital letters "WE ARE NOT INDIGNANT, WE ARE DETERMINED" was

placed where it would be visible during the big general strike and mobilization of the June 15.

6   This road to social change is usually described in the relevant literature as the "no-power" road (Holloway 2002; Petras and Veltmeyer 2009, 2011). In my theoretical model, though, I prefer to call it the "nonstate power" road, since it may not be leading to the conquest of *state power* (control over the state apparatus), yet it does lead to one or another form of *political power*. To put it in Holloway's terms, it may or may not lead to the *power-over*, but it certainly leads to the *power-to*.

7   Author's translation from the Spanish language.

8   I don't have the relevant data for the "pink tide," so I just add this as an additional observation that is valid for the case of Greece at least.

9   So far the refugee solidarity movement that sprang up in Greece from the second half of 2015 onward seems to be leaning toward prefigurative, autonomous, and self-organized structures. Yet we should recognize that it is too early to jump into any conclusions. That issue could very well be the topic of another chapter, in another book.

References

Αδάμ, Σοφία, and Δώρα-Δήμητρα Τελώνη [Sofia Adam and Dora-Dimitra Teloni]. "Κοινωνικά Ιατρεία Στην Ελλάδα Της Κρίσης. Η Εμπειρία Της Παροχής Υπηρεσιών Υγείας Όταν Το Εθνικό Σύστημα Υποχωρεί." [Social health centers in Greece in crisis: The experience of providing health care services when the national health system withdraws]. *INE Ινστιτούτο Εργασίας ΓΣΕΕ* [INE Work Institute of GSEE—Greek Confederation of Greek Workers], November 2015. http://ineobservatory.gr/wp-content/uploads/2016/07/MELETH-441.pdf.

Barragan, Yesenia. "Repression and Demobilization in Spain." *teleSUR*, February 12, 2015. https://www.telesurenglish.net/opinion/Repression-and-Demobilization-in-Spain-20150212-0027.html.

Bayat, Asef. *Street Politics: Poor People's Movements in Iran.* New York: Columbia University Press, 1997.

Bey, Hakim. *T.A.Z.: The Temporary Autonomous Zone, Ontological Anarchy, Poetic Terrorism.* Brooklyn: Hermetic Library, 1997. http://hermetic.com/bey/taz_cont.html.

della Porta, Donatella, Joseba Fernández, Hara Kouki, and Lorenzo Mosca. *Movement Parties against Austerity.* Cambridge: Polity Press, 2017.

Dinerstein, Ana Cecilia. *The Politics of Autonomy in Latin America: The Art of Organising Hope in the Twenty-First Century.* London: Palgrave Macmillan, 2014.

Gerbaudo, Paolo. "2011: A Year of Occupations That Changed the World." *ROAR Magazine*, April 22, 2016. https://roarmag.org/essays/2011-balance-sheet-paolo-gerbaudo/.

Gutiérrez Aguilar, Raquel. *Los Ritmos del Pachakuti. Levantamiento y Movilizacion en Bolivia (2000–2005).* Buenos Aires: Ediciones Tinta Limon, 2008.

Hardt, Michael, and Antonio Negri. *Empire.* Cambridge, MA: Harvard University Press, 2000.

———, and Antonio Negri. *Multitude*. New York: Penguin Books, 2004.

Holloway, John. *Change the World without Taking Power: The Meaning of Revolution Today*, third edition. London: Pluto Press, 2002.

———. *Crack Capitalism*. London: Pluto, 2010.

———. "Zapatismo Urbano." *Humboldt Journal of Social Relations* 29, no. 1 (2005): 168–79.

Karyotis, Theodoros. "Chronicles of a Defeat Foretold." *ROAR Magazine* no. 0 (2016). https://roarmag.org/magazine/syriza-movements-power-commons/.

Katsiaficas, George N. *The Subversion of Politics: European Autonomous Social Movements and the Decolonization of Everyday Life*. Revolutionary Studies. Atlantic Highlands, NJ: Humanities Press, 1997.

Κοκκινάκος, Γιώργος [Giorgos Kokkinakos]. "Νέα Από Το Αριστεροχώρι" [News from the leftish village] *Εφημερίδα Των Συντακτών* [*Efimerida ton Syntakton* (Editors' Newspaper)], May 5, 2016. https://www.efsyn.gr/arthro/nea-apo-aristerohori.

Κοροβέσης, Περικλής [Periklis Korovesis]. "Ν.Δ.: από την Κεντροδεξιά στην Ακροδεξιά" [New democracy: From the center right to the far right]. *Εφημερίδα των Συντακτών* [*Efimerida ton Syntakton* (Editors' Newspaper)], January 23, 2015. http://www.efsyn.gr/arthro/nd-apo-tin-kentrodexia-stin-akrodexia.

Kousis, Maria. "Η Πανελλαδική Εκστρατεία Διαμαρτυρίας Κατά Των Μνημονίων Και Των Πολιτικών Λιτότητας" [National campaign against memorandums and austerity policies]. *Κοινωνική Επιθεώρηση* [*Koinoniki Epitheorisi* (Social Review)] no. 1 (2013): 33–41.

Kropotkin, Petr Alekseevich. *The Essential Kropotkin*. Edited by Emile Capouya and Keitha Tompkins. London: Macmillan, 1976.

Lenin, V.I. "The Dual Power." *Pravda*, vol. 28, April 9, 1917. In Lenin, *Collected Works*, vol. 24. Moscow: Progress Publishers, 1964, 38–41.

Mayorga, Fernando, ed. *Estado, Ampliacion de La Democracia Y Disputa Politica. Bolivia 2000–2010*, vol. 1. Cochabamba: CESU-UMSS, 2012.

Oikonomakis, Leonidas, and Fran Espinoza. "Bolivia: MAS and the Movements That Brought It to State Power." In *Rethinking Latin American Social Movements: Radical Action from Below*, edited by Richard Stahler-Sholk, Harry E. Vanden, and Marc Becker, 285–305. Lanham, MD: Rowman & Littlefield, 2014.

———, and Jérôme E. Roos. "'Que No Nos Representan': The Crisis of Representation and the Resonance of the Real Democracy Movement from the Indignados to Occupy." University of Montreal, Canada, February 20–21, 2013.

Orwell, George. "Shooting an Elephant." London: New Writing, 1936. http://orwell.ru/library/articles/elephant/english/e_eleph.

Petras, James F. "The Most Radical Conservative Regime: Bolivia under Evo Morales." *James Petras Website*, December 30, 2013. http://petras.lahaine.org/?p=1968.

———, and Henry Veltmeyer. *Social Movements in Latin America: Neoliberalism and Popular Resistance*, first edition. *Social Movements and Transformation*. New York: Palgrave Macmillan, 2011.

———, and Henry Veltmeyer. *What's Left in Latin America? Regime Change in New Times*. Farnham, UK: Ashgate Publishing, 2009.

Portos, Martín. "Taking to the Streets in the Shadow of Austerity: A Chronology of the Cycle of Protests in Spain, 2007–2015." *Partecipazione & Conflitto* 9, no. 1 (2016): 181–210. http://siba-ese.unisalento.it/index.php/paco/article/view/15897.

Public Issue. "Πολιτικό Βαρόμετρο 97, Δεκέμβριος 2011" [Political Barometer 97, December 2011]. December 8, 2011. http://www.publicissue.gr/1944/varometro-dec-2011/.

———. "150 Έρευνες του Πολιτικού Βαρόμετρου Της Public Issue. Χρονοσειρές 2004–2015" [150 Surveys by Political Barometer of Public Issue. Time Series 2004–2015]. November 2015. http://www.publicissue.gr/12445/150-surveys/.

Rachiotis, George, David Stuckler, Martin McKee, and Christos Hadjichristodoulou. "What Has Happened to Suicides during the Greek Economic Crisis? Findings from an Ecological Study of Suicides and Their Determinants (2003–2012)." *BMJ Open* 5, no. 3 (March 25, 2015). http://bmjopen.bmj.com/content/5/3/e007295.

Rockefeller, Stuart Alexander. "Dual Power in Bolivia: Movement and Government since the Election of 2005." *Urban Anthropology* 36, no. 3 (Fall 2007). https://www.jstor.org/stable/40553603?seq=1#page_scan_tab_contents.

Roos, Jérôme E., and Leonidas Oikonomakis. "They Don't Represent Us! The Global Resonance of the Real Democracy Movement from the Indignados to Occupy." In *Spreading Protest: Social Movements in Times of Crisis*, edited by Donatella della Porta and Alice Mattoni, 117–136. ECPR—Studies in European Political Science. Colchester, UK: ECPR Press, 2014.

———, and Leonidas Oikonomakis. "We Are Everywhere: The Autonomous Roots of the Real Democracy Movement." *ECPR Conference*, Bordeaux, September 4–7, 2013. http://www.academia.edu/30352584/We_Are_Everywhere_The_Autonomous_Roots_of_the_Real_Democracy_Movement.

Sitrin, Marina. *Horizontalism: Voices of Popular Power in Argentina*. Oakland: AK Press, 2006.

Stahler-Sholk, Richard. "Resisting Neoliberal Homogenization: The Zapatista Autonomy Movement." *Latin American Perspectives* 34, no. 2 (March 2007): 48–63.

———, Harry E. Vanden, and Marc Becker. *Rethinking Latin American Social Movements: Radical Action from Below*. Lanham, MD: Rowman & Littlefield, 2014.

Syntagma Popular Assembly. "Syntagma Popular Assembly's Minutes." Syntagma Square, Athens, 2011.

Teperoglou, Eftichia, and Emmanouil Tsatsanis. "Dealignment, De-Legitimation and the Implosion of the Two-Party System in Greece: The Earthquake Election of 6 May 2012." *Journal of Elections, Public Opinion and Parties* 24, no. 2 (2014): 222–42. https://www.researchgate.net/publication/271757024_Dealignment_De-legitimation_and_the_Implosion_of_the_Two-Party_System_in_Greece_The_Earthquake_Election_of_6_May_2012.

To Vima. "Γιώργος Παπανδρέου. Ἀνάγκη εθνική και επιτακτική η προσφυγή στο μηχανισμό στήριξης'" [George Papandreou: "It's a national and urgent need to resort to the support mechanism"]. April 23, 2010. http://tovima.gr.

Trejo, Guillermo. *Popular Movements in Autocracies: Religion, Repression, and Indigenous Collective Action in Mexico*. Cambridge Studies in Comparative Politics. New York: Cambridge University Press, 2012.

Trotsky, Leon. "Dual Power." In *The History of the Russian Revolution*. vol. 1. Ann Arbor: University of Michigan Press, 1932.

Zibechi, Raúl. "Autonomy or New Forms of Domination? The Complex Relationship Between Governments and Movements." *Upside Down World*, February 23, 2009. http://upsidedownworld.org/archives/international/autonomy-or-new-forms-of-domination-the-complex-relationship-between-governments-and-movements/.

―――. *Dispersing Power: Social Movements as Anti-State Forces*. Oakland: AK Press, 2010.

―――. *Territories in Resistance: A Cartography of Latin American Social Movements*. Oakland: AK Press, 2012.

THREE

Capital Is the Catastrophe of Humanity: We Must Break It. And We Are the Catastrophe of Capital: It Must Break Us. In Other Words: Greece

John Holloway

Capital against humanity, humanity against capital. Death against life, life against death. There is no in-between. Forget the euphemisms, the in-between categories. Forget neoliberalism, colonialism, imperialism, and socialism too. Above all, forget half-hope. In the Greek crisis the antagonism stands stark.

This is not a story of Merkel against Tsipras, Schäuble against Varoufakis. It is the story of an attack by capital against the people who live in Greece and against the people of the world. Sadly, capital won, for the moment.

An interlude and a dedication: the first act of the new prime minister, Alexis Tsipras, after taking office in January 2015, was to go to Kaesariani in Athens to lay a wreath in memory of communist resistance fighters who had been shot by the Nazis on May 1, 1944. It was a symbolic act of national defiance, but it was much more than that: it was the first time that there had been such a clear recognition by the Greek state of the struggles of the communists against fascism. It was a very powerful signal that a new era had started in Greek political life, and it was a dramatic act of redemption of the struggles of all those who had lived and died fighting against oppression in Greece. A good friend of mine was so moved that she went in joy to place flowers on the grave of her father, a lifelong communist who had died just a couple of years earlier. Her bitterness at the complete reversal of the position of the Tsipras government can hardly be imagined. This article is dedicated to her father, Thanasis Koutsos, who would not (and indeed did not) agree entirely with all the ideas expressed here, but whose dignity stands in such sharp contrast to the horrible, hateful story of what happened in Greece in those months of 2015 and what is happening now. This article is my way of laying flowers on his grave—flowers of respect, flowers of refusal.

What follows is an argument in generally abstract language, but it is filled with my friend's bitterness and driven by the conviction that the only way to extract hope from the Greek disaster is to say Enough! ¡Ya basta! And not just Enough of corrupt politicians! or Enough of the political parties! or Enough of neoliberalism! but Enough of capital! There is no other future for humanity. Capitalism is our catastrophe, but we too are its catastrophe.

Capital Is the Catastrophe of Humanity: We Must Break It

Capital is a constant aggression against humanity. Developments in Greece over the last few years illustrate the force of this aggression.

The concept of capital is often forgotten in the discourse of resistance-and-rebellion or put aside as an embarrassing reminder of a past best forgotten. It is important to restore it to the center of thought.

By "capital" I understand not a thing but a way of organizing our relations with one another, a form of social relations. This way of organizing the interaction of our activities, which has not always existed and need not exist till the end of humanity, has a peculiarity at its center: we relate our diverse activities to one another through the medium of money; in other words, we exchange our products (including our own capacities to create) as commodities, things to be bought and sold.

It may be objected that we do not only relate to other people through money: this is true and very important, but there are few people in the world whose daily activity is not shaped by the need to acquire money in order to buy what is necessary for survival, either by selling products on the market or by selling their own labor power.

This arrangement of our social relations produces a dynamic. This is crucial: relating to one another through money produces not only a host of hateful phenomena in the present (exploitation, inequality, the objectification of subjects, the reification of thought, and so on, and so on), it also produces a dynamic of development that appears to be leading us toward total self-annihilation.

Exchanging our products as commodities through the medium of money means that only those things that can be so exchanged are considered (in theory and in practice) to have value. The vast richness of what we humans create is reduced to commodities, measured as money. In this society, the only activity that is considered worthy of recognition is the activity that contributes to the expansion of value (value understood in this sense, as economics understands it, as the wealth that exists as money or is convertible into money). The expansion or accumulation of this value becomes the driving force of social development. "Accumulate! Accumulate! That is Moses and the Prophets!" (Marx 1965 [1867]: 495). This is not just for the individual capitalist: it is the dynamic that dominates society as a whole and shapes human activity. Present society is based on the constant expansion of this peculiar form of wealth that is value quantifiable as money.

This peculiar form of wealth means that human growth is subjected to an external, uncontrolled faster-faster-faster. In any form of human society, there is a process of learning, as people develop new ways of doing things and more effective ways of producing. The creativeness of humans means that there is a capacity for progress. Once products are produced as commodities to be bought and sold, this advance in our crea-tive powers is measured as increasing productivity, and this becomes in turn the measure of the value of the commodity. The most effective, fastest way of producing ("socially necessary labor") becomes the criterion that defines the value of the thing produced, and the competition inherent in the process of commodity sale effects a redefinition of "progress": from being a general expression of the movement of human creativity, it is redefined as that which contributes to the cheap, efficient production of commodities. The conscious, creative process of choosing the best way to do things becomes transformed into an externally imposed, uncontrolled faster-faster-faster. The value of a commodity is measured by socially necessary labor time: what is produced today using the methods of a hundred years ago, or five years ago, or five months ago, will no longer sell—it has no value. The accumulation of value is not just a quantitative process of expansion, it is the frenetic drive of qualitative transformation. Very effective in producing cheap commodities, but this is very far from being a conscious, creative process of choosing the best way to do things, bearing in mind other people, the natural environment, and our own enjoyment, for example. Progress. The progress of destruction and death. The dynamic that we must break.

Capital is this process of value expansion. The accumulation of money (or value) is the accumulation of capital. A necessary precondition for the constitution of a society based on money is the separation of the great majority of people from the control of the means of production and subsistence. It is this separation that forces them to sell their capacity to create wealth (their labor power) as a commodity to those who control the means of production and subsistence. With the money they receive (the wage) they are able to buy what they need to survive (or not, as the case may be). This means that a society based on money is inevitably a society based on exploitation: that is to say, on the existence of a mass of people who sell their labor power as a commodity to those who own or control the means of production and who put that labor power to use in a way that either directly produces an increment of value greater than the value of the labor power (surplus value) or by indirectly contributing to the production of surplus value. This creates for the capitalist who has bought the labor power a claim on the total surplus value produced.

Inscribed in the existence of money (and capital) is a dynamic that progressively transforms all human activity into activity that expands value. What we often refer to as labor, which Marx described as abstract labor, is labor that has been abstracted from its particular creative characteristics and is recognized only for its quantitative contribution to the expansion of value. This pull of abstraction is what gives cohesion and, therefore, force to the dynamic of capital. We can think of this as a process of totalization: all activity is drawn into a totality, a single system driven by a single logic, that of the expansion of value.

This is the dynamic of capital against humanity, the dynamic of value expansion against the conscious collective determination of our needs and desires. Capital against humanity. It is more common to speak of capital against labor, but if we think of labor as that peculiar alien form into which human activity is drawn in the production and expansion of value, then it is clear that capital and labor stand on the same side of the equation. It is only if we think of labor as that which stands out against itself, that which rebels against itself, or in other words as the activity that struggles to emancipate itself from abstraction and alienation, only then would it make sense to think of the central antagonism as being that of labor against capital. But that sort of activity, the activity that struggles to emancipate itself, is rather antilabor. In other words, "humanity" as human activity that drives against labor.

Value expansion—capital accumulation—the pursuit of profit— a steamroller flattening protest, eliminating all that stands in its way.

Value expansion is reshaping the world in its image, building highways, destroying forests, wiping communities off the map to make way for mines, eliminating other forms of life, changing the climate, reshaping education to prepare children for the role they must fulfill in the expansion of capital or preparing them to accept that they have no such role to play, that they will be completely useless, expendable. Capital rules. The logic of capital prevails. Capital has become our destiny. And, more and more, it seems that this destiny is death: the massive self-annihilation of humanity. Capital is the catastrophe of humanity. We must break it. More urgent now than ever. Even if we do not know how to do it.

And We Are the Catastrophe of Capital: It Must Break Us

1. The logic of capital crushes us. And yet. This "and yet" is all-important, because without this "and yet," it would be impossible to write what I am writing. This "and yet" is all-important, because this is where "we" come in—the "we" who are more than producers of value, the "we" whose actions and thoughts do not fit without a remainder into abstract value-producing labor.

There *is* a logic of capital, but working through this logic is never an automatic process; it is always a struggle. Capital appears often to be a machine (a steamroller, as mentioned above). But it is not so. Capital is an attack upon us that may succeed or may fail. What gives this attack its peculiar force is not just the means of violent repression at its disposal, but its particular cohesion, its logic. This cohesion is a daily repeated cohering, an act of weaving social relations that is reinforced every time that we reconstitute the mediation through money of our relations with other people, every time that we integrate our activity into the process of totalizing that is abstract labor. We are all active in the daily reconstituting of a social cohesion that is destroying us. That is what makes it so difficult to resist.

Yet we do resist. We say no in all sorts of ways, sometimes individually, sometimes collectively, sometimes very consciously, sometimes without thinking. In spite of the fact that we all live in the powerful magnetic field that draws us into the active reconstitution of the system that kills us, at the same time we pull back against that magnetic force, toward something else, toward "somethings" else. When the magnetic force of capital tells us to work longer hours, we say, "No, not today, it's my daughter's birthday"; when the drive of capital pushes to destroy our village and replace it with a dam or a mine, we say, "No way," and we get together with our community to resist. When we are told that the only way in which our country can remain competitive is if we reform our ideas about education, then we say no and call a strike or occupy schools and universities. When we learn that the only jobs available (if we are lucky) are jobs that we hate or that have absolutely no meaning for us, we sit there at our desk thinking of our boyfriend. We resist, and then we resist. And our resistance will often seem quite illogical, sometimes even to ourselves. Precisely because it is illogical, it stands against the logic that we have learned at school and in the newspapers and it stands against the progress of the system that we ourselves have helped to create and help to reproduce. Yet we resist, because we can do nothing else, because resistance is the defense of what we understand as our humanity, as our dignity. And sometimes our resistance spills over into rebellion: we turn against the logic that tells us to obey and try to build a different logic, a different way of doing things. Resistance then grows into resistance-and-rebellion.

This resistance (whether or not it becomes rebellion) is an obstacle to capital and an impediment to the expansion of value. Capital is the constant movement of trying to suppress or circumvent our resistance. Capital flees from us. It may flee geographically in search of more docile or more malleable labor. It also flees into technology, replacing us with machines. This has two inconveniences, however: on the one hand, it still depends on those who design and construct the machinery; on the other, the construction of the machine costs money, so that it is necessary to exploit the remaining labor even more to counteract the effect. Capital cannot free itself from its dependence on labor, on its capacity to convert human activity into value-producing labor. The difficulties experienced in channeling human activity, directly or indirectly, into value production tend to be expressed in a falling rate of profit and therefore a slowing of accumulation, a slowing of the self-expansion of capital. This is capitalist crisis.

In crisis it becomes clear. Capital is our catastrophe: to live, we must break it. But we are also capital's catastrophe: to survive, it must break us. So simple, so stark. Capital is a way of relating to each other. To thrive it must make us conform to its logic. For humanity to survive, we must break that way of doing and that logic and establish others.

There are two ways out of the crisis. One is to restructure capital, restoring its profitability, strengthening its grip on human activity, probably taking us a step closer to annihilation. In this solution capital breaks humanity, makes it more docile, injects the unquestioned rule of money deeper into the human psyche. The other way out is for humanity to break capital, to create other ways of doing, to structure life around other values, other ideas of what gives meaning to our activity. There are millions and millions of pushes in that direction in the world, pushes against and beyond capital, traditions and experiences and experiments of living in different ways that do not have money and its expansion as their central principle. These are increasing as it becomes more and more evident that capital is a form of organization that is simply unable to secure the reproduction of a large part of the world's population, but the Greek experience makes it clear how difficult it is to turn our back on capital, to escape completely from the subordination of our life-activity to the logic of value expansion.

The third possibility is that there is no way out of the crisis, that the crisis will be a prolonged and gradually intensifying process of conflict with no clear direction. We are in a prolonged stalemate where capital is unable to tame us sufficiently and we are still unable to establish different ways of doing things on a significant scale. Crisis is a chronic illness of the system. This is akin to what Paul Mattick analyzed as "permanent crisis" in the 1930s (Mattick 1978 [1934]), but in that case the crisis was finally resolved in capital's favor: fascism, war, and then the welfare state imposed a new degree of discipline on human activity.

What has been happening in Greece is at the heart of the conflict that is shaping the world.

2. Capital against humanity, humanity against capital. So simple. But there are a couple of points that must still be explored before we come to the specific case of Greece.

First, there is the fragmented existence of capital. Although we can speak of capital as a single process of totalizing, of weaving all human activity into subservience to the expansion of value, although we can speak of a single process of exploitation in which the entire increment of value (surplus value) is accumulated by capital, and although we can speak of a single logic, a single process of cohering, this does not mean that there is a single, conscious subject that is capital. Capital exists through a multiplicity of units, individual capitals, all driven by the same logic of profit, all competing for an aliquot share of the surplus value produced. When there is a relative slowing in the expansion of capital, and consequently a fall in the general rate of profit, the competition between the individual capitals is exacerbated. The intensification of competition between capitals brings with it an intensification of the contest between individual states, as each one tries to attract capital accumulation within its borders and to lend whatever support it can to the capitals with which it is most closely associated. Since capital is essentially mobile, in constant movement in pursuit of its own expansion, capitals are not tied to particular states. Capital owned by people holding Greek passports is not predestined to be invested in Greece: the notion of a national capital is superficial and misleading. Consequently all states are in constant competition to attract capital to their territory (or retain it within their territory) by providing the most attractive conditions for accumulation: they do this in all sorts of ways, including open war, education, and monetary policy. The simple binary antagonism of capital against human activity that is the basis of the crisis thus presents itself as an antagonism between a multiplicity of actors: between capitals and, more strikingly, between states. It is through this competition between capitals and between states that the subordination of human activity to labor is imposed, and indeed opposed. The Second World War, for example, was supremely successful in imposing labor discipline in all the belligerent countries and elsewhere, but it also generated rebellion and a profound push for social reform (the welfare state), which proved to be costly for capital but was accepted in many countries as necessary for maintaining the rule of money and, therefore, labor—and, therefore, capital.

The competition between capitals supported by states facilitates the imposition of the dynamic of capital, but it is the latter, the dynamic of capitalist accumulation, that is the driving force. To mistake one for the other is disastrous: to take sides with one state against others is to participate actively in the imposition of capitalist rule. Always. The transformation of resistance against capitalism into nationalism (a theme discussed in Dimitra Kotouza's chapter) has not only led to the deaths of millions of people over the last century but has also done more than anything else to reintegrate anticapitalist sentiment into the reproduction of capital.

Imperialism and colonialism are particularly brutal forms of the competition between states to create attractive conditions for capital accumulation. Anti-imperialism and anticolonialism are often thought of as particular forms of struggle against capitalism. In fact, experience has shown these definitions of struggle to be extremely effective in channeling resistance-and-rebellion into the reproduction of capital, in many cases equally brutal. The history of the world since the Second World War attests to this: India, Africa, Nicaragua, Bolivia, and many more. To think that anti-imperialism or anticolonialism can strengthen the emancipation of human activity from labor and capital is completely misguided. Like nationalism (to which they are closely related), they involve a territorial redefinition of a conflict that is not territorial. Capital is not located in one place; it is a way of organizing our social relations. Nothing is more ridiculous and more destructive than to analyze the Greek crisis simply in terms of competition between states without situating that competition in the context of the antagonistic reproduction of the social relations of capital (for more discussion on this theme see the chapters by Panagiotis Drakos and Dimitra Kotouza).

The second point to be noted is that the expansion of debt has become a crucial part of the reproduction of capital. There is a chronic and increasing gap between the expansion of value and its monetary representation. When resistance to the ever more exigent requirements of value production expresses itself in falling rates of profit, both the reproduction of individual capitals and the employment of workers is threatened. This generates pressures on states to encourage or permit the expansion of debt, creating a situation in which claims on value expand far beyond the value that actually exists. This introduces an element of enormous instability and volatility into the reproduction of capital, since all know that the assets held by capitalists are simply claims to a part of a value-wealth that has not yet been produced. Philip Coggan comments:

> In the last forty years, the world has been more successful at creating claims on wealth than it has at creating wealth itself. The economy has grown, but asset prices have risen faster, and debts have risen faster still. Debtors, from speculative homebuyers to leading governments, have made promises that they are unlikely to meet in full. Creditors who are counting on those debts to be repaid will be disappointed. (Coggan 2011: 267)

In other words, an important part of capitalist expansion in recent years has been fictitious, dependent on the future production of surplus value for its validation.

As the disproportion between monetary assets and wealth produced grows, this leads both to increasing pressures on workers (those who produce value directly or indirectly) to produce the value that corresponds to the claims on value and to a frenzied pursuit by the capitalists to obtain relative security for the assets they hold, basically through rapid movement of their assets on the money markets.

A game of musical chairs gone mad, in which the music is increasingly wild, the disproportion between players and chairs is growing, and there is no way of knowing when the music will stop (a telling metaphor also used by Katerina Nasioka in her chapter).[1] When the music does stop, as it did for a moment in 2008, an argument breaks out among policymakers: Do we do everything possible to get the music started again, encourage the renewed expansion of debt, and carry on as before? Or do we keep the music stopped and accept all the carnage that will ensue in order to eliminate a large number of players from the game and restore the system to a healthy basis? There is of course no sovereign "we" who make this decision, but the central banks (particularly the US Federal Reserve) and other monetary authorities do have a strong influence in the way that the process develops. In this case, the dominant decision (especially by the Fed in 2009 [Geithner 2014], but followed with some differences by other central banks in the ensuing years) was to restart the music again as quickly as possible, to encourage the continued expansion of debt to avoid the collapse of the system. After a slight fall in the years between 2009 and 2012, global gross debt resumed its growth both in absolute terms and as a proportion of the world gross domestic product, so that it is now calculated in a recent report by the IMF to stand at $152 trillion, "more than two times the size of the global economy." As a senior official at the IMF put it, "global debt is at record highs and rising" (*Financial Times*, October 5, 2016). Within that total, private debt continues to be the principal part, but there has been a significant rise in the proportion of public debt. In the few years following 2008, it is calculated that more than twenty trillion dollars (McNally 2011: 2) were transferred from states to the banks in order to keep them growing, and with them the system of debt expansion that they administer. In order to achieve this, the private debt of the banks was converted into the "sovereign" debt of states. Now the banks are more stable: it is the states (and therefore their citizens or residents) that are in the center of the systemic instability. As in any game of musical chairs, it is to some extent random where the pain of elimination falls. In the case discussed in this book, the pain has fallen on Greece.

Neoliberalism is simply the political expression of a world in which capital is dominated and threatened by this enormous accumulation of debt. Neoliberalism is a world in which the range of political possibility is determined by the choice between either continuing the expansion of debt (with all that that means in terms of volatility, corruption, productive inefficiency, growing inequality, and so on), or provoking the purge of the system in order to restore efficient growth, even with all the inevitable social chaos that this will cause. Or, in terms of our musical chairs metaphor, do we continue playing the music, knowing that the game will become more frenzied and dangerous as the disproportion between chairs and players increases, and that the music will one day come to an end, or stop the music now, knowing that it will cause enormous suffering and discontent but might restore a healthy productive capitalism? This is the question that sets the bounds of political and economic debate. This is what sets the limits of "realism," the distinction between "left" and "right." Just in the last few weeks (I write this sentence in September 2016), we have seen world leaders gathered in Hangzhou, China (and clearly frightened by the growing manifestations of resentment all over the world) call for a capitalism with a more human face, on the one hand, and, on the other, an article by an economic advisor to the German government calling for a purge: "The only way out of the trap is a hefty dose of creative destruction" (Sinn 2016). Between the two options, there is a third possibility: an indefinite prolongation of the crisis, a continuation of the music combined with localized interruptions, an attempt to mitigate the crisis by focusing it on certain locations or certain groups of people.

This is the world into which the Government of Hope was born. As long as the problem was understood in terms of neoliberalism rather than capitalism, there was no possibility of a happy outcome. Neoliberalism is not a policy chosen by governments, it is simply the violence of the world in which they exist, the viciousness of the frenzied game of musical chairs in which they are forced to participate simply by virtue of being states dependent on the reproduction of capital in their territories. Any state, in order to secure its own existence, must try to promote the reproduction of capital within its boundaries: the fierce game of musical chairs between creditors and debtors that results from the enormous expansion of debt at the world level reproduces itself both within states as the competitive drive to provide the best conditions for capital accumulation and between states as each tries to make sure that the roof (which is bound to partially collapse) falls somewhere else and not on it: that it should fall in this case not in Berlin or Frankfurt but in Athens and Thessaloniki. Monetary policies are one way of playing the game of attracting investment. What distinguishes the euro from other currencies is that, having been created in the era of overwhelming debt, there is a specific aggressiveness written into its rules of functioning. The exclusion of more flexible policy options is written into its constitution: it imposes limits on the debts of its member states and permits its central bank to intervene only to combat inflation and not, as in the case of the US Fed, to combat unemployment. The euro thus embodies a particular strategy for creating favorable conditions for investment, but it is in no sense the source of the problem.

If "neoliberalism" is understood as a policy option or a political or economic theory, it begins to have the same sort of effect as "colonialism" or "imperialism." It begins as a critical concept (we are against neoliberalism, of course) and then leads us down the wrong road (we will vote for parties that are against neoliberalism) and then, once the party comes to power, it adopts neoliberal policies, not because the leaders are traitors, but because that is the world in which governments are forced to operate. No case is more dramatic than that of Syriza, but it has been the common experience of all "left" governments over the last thirty years or so. "Neoliberalism," like "colonialism" and "imperialism," has an attractive sheen that makes it part of the discourse of resistance-and-rebellion, but in effect it leads us down the wrong road, into conformity with the reproduction of capital: nowhere more dramatically than in Greece. Like colonialism and imperialism, "neoliberalism" becomes a reactionary concept. The problem is not neoliberalism: it is capital.

Socialism falls too, if by "socialism" we understand a state-led politics that would introduce radical change to reduce the ills of capitalism or even abolish them.[2] In special circumstances, where there is an abundant supply of raw materials (as in the case of Venezuela or Bolivia but not in Greece), the government may be able to respond to the force of social struggle by effecting a significant redistribution of income, but everything indicates that even in these cases, the states involved have been unable (or unwilling) to introduce changes that in any sense break the dynamic of capitalist development, with all that that implies.

Capital against humanity, humanity against capital: there is nothing in between. That is the lesson of Greece. That is where hope lies.

In Other Words: Greece

What is special about Greece? Nothing much. This is a book about Greece, but central to its argument is that there is nothing very special about Greece. Or rather, that Greece is just a particularly dramatic example of what is happening throughout the world. Everywhere in the world, the crisis of capital means an intensification of capital's attack against humanity, and everywhere there is resistance. In Greece the attack has been especially sharp, the resistance especially direct. This conflict gained an added dimension by being refracted through the state and through the election of a particularly outspoken government.

Many political parties in the world have proclaimed their radical, left-wing aspirations during elections in order to reflect or take advantage of waves of popular struggle, and many parties have then quietly abandoned those aspirations once they have become the party of government and adapted to reality (on this, see the chapter by Leonidas Oikonomakis). What distinguishes the rise of Syriza and its abandonment of the principles it proclaimed is the spectacular nature of the process.

Capital against humanity, humanity against capital: the clash in Greece has been exceptionally strong on both sides. The attack of capital has been particularly brutal, the response of humanity particularly robust.

Remember! Remember December 6, 2008! The explosion of anger and chaos after a policeman shot and killed, without provocation, the fifteen-year-old Alexis Grigoropoulos was one of the loudest screams of "no" that has been heard in this century: No to police violence. No to discrimination against the young, against migrants, against women. No to a system built on frustration. No to a system that dulls our senses, closes our nostrils, through unemployment and, sometimes worse, through employment. No to a system built on the meaninglessness of money. No too to the stale traditions of working-class struggle. As Katerina Nasioka puts it in her chapter, this was the revolt of the proletariat against the working class. There were no demands made of the state, just a roar of fury against the state and all it stood for, a roar that lasted for weeks. Here it was: humanity against capital, rage against the steamroller. No mediations, no neoliberalism, no anticolonialism, no anti-imperialism, no demands for changes in policy.

The pyres that heated the bodies of the insurgents in the long nights of December were full of products of our labour liberated, disarmed symbols of a once powerful imaginary. We simply took that which belongs to us and threw it on the fires together with all that it signifies. The great potlatch of the previous days was a rebellion of desire against the imposed canon of scarcity. This revolt was, in fact, a rebellion against property and alienation. A revolt of the gift against the sovereignty of money. An insurrection of anarchy, of use value against the democracy of exchange value. A spontaneous rising of collective freedom against the rationality of individual discipline (Flesh Machine/Ego to Provoco manifesto, Athens, 2008, quoted in Nasioka 2014: 171)

The brutality of capital's attack is intertwined with the direct force of the revolt of December 2008. The shooting of Alexis was not an isolated incident: it was part of the general constellation of capitalist aggression that was destroying any perspective for life, particularly of young people. As Panagiotis Doulos argues in his chapter, violence is integral to the reproduction of capital, and intensified violence is part of capitalist crisis.

The sharpness of social tensions in Greece was reflected in the growth of state indebtedness: it was not just the corruption of the politicians and the costs of the Olympic Games of 2004 that led to the growth of public debt but also the real gains of working-class struggle over the years in the form of pensions, working conditions, public health, and so on. This should not surprise us. The growth of debt in general is an attempt to reconcile the irreconcilable: to reconcile capitalist profitability with the fact that the material basis of this profitability is not being produced but also (and this is part of the same fiction) to resolve social tensions by granting claims to a surplus value that has not yet been produced. Where these tensions are particularly strong, the pressures increase on states to permit or encourage the expansion of debt in order to preserve some degree of "social peace" (among other things, an important element for attracting investment). And all this was in the context of the financial crisis of 2008, the worldwide conversion of private banking debt into public debt (the great bailout of the banks) and the intensification of the game of musical chairs. The ratio of gross public debt to GDP rose sharply in many countries after 2008, but this was particularly strong in Greece, where between 2008 and 2013 it rose from 107 percent to 176 percent (compared with Italy, for example, where it rose from 103 percent to 132 percent) (Wolf 2014: 81). The growing debt and the continuing social instability meant that international banks were increasingly reluctant to lend to the Greek government or would do so only at higher than usual rates of interest. This led the Greek government to turn to the European Union for support. As a condition of granting its support, the EU imposed in a series of memorandums from May 2010 extremely strict conditions to strengthen the discipline of money over Greek society.

These measures intensified in turn the resistance to the rule of money. Years of marches and protests and riots and repression followed, but they made no impact at all on government policy. Austerity, the capitalist attack, continued unabated. On February 12, 2012, when hundreds of thousands demonstrated in the streets, more than fifty buildings were burnt down in the center of Athens, police cars were set on fire, and tear gas was used far beyond the legal limits, parliament was surrounded by a police guard, and the deputies voted to approve another austerity package, another Memorandum of Agreement with the governments of the Eurozone. After that, what do you do? Where do you go?

The rise of Syriza was based both on the force of the anger expressed in the streets and the failure of the movement to achieve visible change. This is what made the rise and fall of institutionalized hope so spectacular in the case of Greece. When Syriza broke through the old party duopoly of Nea Dimokratia (New Democracy) and PASOK to win the election of January 2015, it had not yet watered down its radical rhetoric to the extent that left parties usually do in the run-up to elections. It is the force of the anger of the previous years that explains why it was able to (and needed to) maintain its radical discourse during negotiations with the governments of the Eurozone throughout the first half of 2015 and why it called the referendum of July 5 that shocked those governments, not just by the result (the great OXI—the No) but simply by its calling. It was this that made the total reversal of policy and the signing of the agreement with the Eurozone just a week later so spectacular. One expects left parties to reverse their policies after they reach government, but generally it is a smoother, gentler process. Here the radical hope voiced by Syriza simply ran into a brick wall, the wall of reality. Humanity against capital, hope against reality. Capital wins, humanity loses. Reality wins, hope loses. The old story: "Yield!" "No!" "Bow!" "No!" "Bow!" "Well, let's talk about it" "Bow!" "Yes, sir!" The onward march of Progress toward the grave. Defeat and depression.

What is this reality that so resoundingly defeated the "Government of Hope"? Is it capitalism, or was it just the particularities of the euro as a currency and a Eurozone dominated by politicians committed to neoliberal ideology? The question is important because it affects the conclusions we draw from the whole tragic experience. The issue is usually presented in the context of the negotiations around the terms of the memorandums negotiated between the Greek governments and the Eurozone leaders. Yet the basic conflict is with the money markets. The Greek state has been unable to raise loans on the money markets at normal rates of interest because the holders of money do not have confidence that it will be able to repay its loans: consequently, they demand higher rates of interest to counteract the risk of losing their money. The lack of access to loans threatens the Greek state's ability to meet its existing commitments, including the payment of debts. In the first instance, the wall of reality is constituted by money. As in the case of any debtor, the Greek state is told in effect: "If you do not structure your life according to the requirements of money, if you do not behave in a way that gives us (the banks, as representatives of money) confidence that we can expand our profits, then there is no reason why we should lend you money. The best way to give us that confidence would be to adopt measures that promote the accumulation of capital and impose social discipline, cutting back on pensions and the welfare state, putting state property on the market, introducing stricter labor laws, and so on. Otherwise, we will lend you no money. Face reality, the reality of a world organized on the basis of money. And don't complain just because 50 percent of your young people are unemployed: if their work will not contribute to the expansion of value and our profits, why should we employ them? You know the rules of the game: the only activity that counts in this world is labor that contributes to the creation of value, that is, labor that expands the profits of capital."

It is at this stage that the governments of the Eurozone and the IMF come in. But they do not create the problem. Imagine a young person (let us make him a man) who, for one reason or another (gambling perhaps, or drinking, or dedicating his days to his passion for painting, or whatever), accrues debts that he is unable to pay. The banks refuse to lend him more. The debt collectors are knocking at his door. His electricity is cut off. He is unable to find a job. He has no access to the wealth of the world and, if he cannot find some modification of the law of value, he will literally die. He learns by horrible experience what the banks announced in our previous paragraph: "You know the rules of the game: the only activity that counts in this world is labor that contributes to the creation of value, that is, labor that expands the profits of capital." He goes to his father (or his mother, or his daughter, but let us assume his father) and asks for assistance in dealing with his creditors. His father says, "All right, I will help you to deal with your creditors, but only if you give up your painting (or drinking, or gambling), break up with your lover, cut your hair, shave, train to be an accountant, and get a job." The son is furious, negotiations go on for months, and eventually the son accepts the terms imposed by the father. To his friends he complains bitterly that it is all his father's fault. He is wrong: the father's role is secondary. In his kindness or strictness, the father has simply converted himself into an agent seeking to impose the "rules of the game" on his son, trying to get his son to accept in the practice of everyday life that the only activity that counts in this world is that which contributes to the expansion of value. Similarly, the role of the governments of the Eurozone is secondary in the Greek spectacle of 2015: they are simply trying to impose the rule of money.

So simple? Yes, so simple. Clearly this is not to say that all Greeks were gambling or drinking or painting pictures, but the central issue is social discipline and the production of value (wealth that contributes to the expansion of profits). Movements on the world's money markets are the medium through which the discipline of abstract labor (that is, of labor that contributes to the expansion of capital) is imposed. After the financial crisis of 2008 and the massive conversion of banking debt into sovereign debt, the fear of sovereign default (of a state being unable to pay its debts) acquires a new importance and comes to focus on Greece (and on other countries, both inside and outside the European Union—Puerto Rico, for example, where the ratio of debt to GDP was rising particularly quickly). The Greek financial crisis is the judgment of money, transmitted through the markets, on the Greek contribution to the production of value. The financial crisis of 2008 meant a tightening of the "rules of the game" ("contribute to the production of capitalist profit or die"), and Greece was found wanting.

This is not to say that the fact that Greece is a member of the Eurozone does not play a role. It does. It excludes the possibility of devaluation of the currency as a means of imposing the sort of radical restructuring demanded by the creditors. As we have seen, the constitution of the euro is designed to exclude flexibility. The governments of the Eurozone, particularly Germany, are strongly committed to a policy of monetary strictness, partly by historical tradition but basically as a means of playing for advantage in the interstate competition to attract capital to its territory. All this means that the response of the Eurozone governments was particularly aggressive and the results particularly harsh. The fact remains, however, that the intervention of the Eurozone governments was secondary, in the same way as the intervention of the father in our previous paragraph. In both cases, they are simply seeking to impose the rule of money.

This implies that the solution of Grexit (the departure of Greece from the euro) proposed by the left of Syriza at the time would have been no solution at all. It would have simply meant the more direct subordination of Greece to the disciplinary rule of money, transmitted through the money markets. The undoubted pleasure of saying no to the European governments would have done nothing to weaken the rule of money.

And the rule of money, because of the enormous accumulation of assets that threaten to be fictitious since they far exceed the production of value, invades our lives more and more and more. Fifty years ago, the rule of money could tolerate siestas: now it is a practice that is more and more difficult to maintain. It is not just that the activities and desires and expectations and dreams of the Greek people (people who live in that part of the world) come crashing into the world of capitalist reality. It is more than that. The Greek crisis shows us that the walls of reality are closing in on us. They are a tunnel that we are forced into and that is getting narrower and narrower. The dynamic of capital is a narrowing tunnel, a progressive closing of options. In a very literal sense, there is a closure of the world, a closure of what is possible, a closure of dreams, of hope, of thought. Depression: a recurrent theme in the accounts of Greece after the summer of 2015. From hope to depression.

How Do We Break It?

We must turn that depression around. We must extract hope from what happened. We must learn from the disastrous experience of the Syriza government. How do we avoid going round and round in circles, from one party or leader that promises hope and change to another and then another? If we are going to learn from the tragedy of Greece, then theoretical reflection is important.

Halfway hope is a disaster. That is perhaps the most important lesson of the Syriza government.

Hope is a powerful emotion. The projection of a better future, the often desperate searching for a way out, a way forward, against-and-beyond present conditions. It is constantly manipulated by politicians, is perhaps the basis of their existence. In the case of Syriza and its rapid rise to the point of winning the Greek election of January 2015, it was their central slogan: hope is coming. Many of their supporters believed the slogan, thinking that this time the government would be different. Within six months, hope was transformed into disillusion, into depression. Whenever a left party wins an election, one expects that it will soon abandon its promises, but in this case it was different, more spectacular. More depressing. Left-wing party politics was pushed to its very limits, and it failed.

Or perhaps, in killing hope, it succeeded? There has to be a certain cynicism in the leaders of left-wing parties, a certain awareness at least that they are leading hope up the garden path and into conformity with that which is hoped-against. If it were not so, then why did Tsipras not resign when the agreement with the Eurozone leaders reversed everything he had proclaimed up to then? Of such people we can agree with Eduardo Galeano when he says, referring to politicians and their promises: "The only sin that cannot be forgiven is the sin against hope" (Galeano 2017: 224).

Yet left-wing parties cannot be reduced to their leaders: it is their supporters that matter, the huge number who really hope that the party might bring significant change (whatever their doubts). For them, the "good people" who vote for the Left because they want justice, because they oppose oppression, there can be no doubt that the reversal of the referendum result was the failure of hope.

Halfway hope: hope genuinely felt but not learned, not thought through. Not a *docta spes*, as Ernst Bloch (1986 [1959]) would put it. Hope that has been poured into a container that holds: the party. Hope that has been defined so that it can become realistic: nonsensical because hope, by definition, cannot be defined, cannot be contained. Hope put in a bottle: very attractive, but it is bound to fail. And it did fail in July 2015. Hope contained, bottled, lost. But it could be something else: it could be that the bottle breaks, that hope escapes, emancipated, emancipating.

Syriza bottled the hope-anger that surged in December 2008 and fizzed through the years that followed, gave it direction, defined it, put on a shiny label, gave it a vigorous shake in the referendum of July 5, then simply let it fall on the ground with the agreement of July 13. Hope spills on the ground, depression follows, but there is more. Try it for yourself, dear reader. Take a glass bottle of (dare I say it?) Coca-Cola, shake it vigorously for several minutes, drop it on the ground and watch it explode. Cry a little, if you like, as you see the liquid disperse, because you are thirsty. But there is much more than that. You see the bubbles, the explosion, feel the power of the shattering, the thousand fragments, the vigor of the gas escaping. We are that shattering. We are the hiss and the fizz. We are the breaking of the logic of containment.[3]

Two possible outcomes, then. The first, the obvious: the Government of Hope failed, there is no hope, we can only conform, depression, embitterment. Containment wins, capital wins, ever-present anger takes other routes, increasingly familiar routes—nationalism, violence, drugs, crime, migration. The second possible outcome of the Greek crisis is the shattering of containment, the hiss and the fizz, an emancipating hope, a different logic, a different politics.

A struggle against the first outcome: this book is part of that struggle. No answers (asking we walk), but some thoughts:

1. The dramatic crash of the Syriza government as a Government of Hope is the death of state-centered politics, the death of left social democracy. There is no point in going in that direction anymore. Syriza pushed left-wing state government as far as it could go, and it crashed. Podemos, Corbyn, Sanders, even the Pirates of Iceland are a ridiculous anachronism: it is as if the news of what happened to Tsipras and Syriza had not reached them yet. Or perhaps they think that the Greek experience has nothing to do with them, that it was just special circumstances, nothing to do with the dynamic of capital.

Greece is the death of halfway hope, the death of euphemisms, the death of antineoliberalism, anticolonialism, and anti-imperialism. Institutionalized hope is no hope.

But why then do people in other parts of the world and in Greece itself go on as if nothing had happened, as if Syriza could just be explained in terms of betrayal or mistakes, as if it is just a question of being a little bit more to the left? Perhaps it is because, as Leonidas Oikonomakis puts it in his chapter, it is the only game in town.

2. The title of this article. Capital is the catastrophe of humanity—obvious. We are the catastrophe of capital, and it must break us. We are the crisis of capital, and to resolve its crisis it must break us, break our resistance, break our humanity. What has happened and is still happening in Greece

is a major achievement by capital in this direction, a major victory. Yet we are still there. Refusal is deeply ingrained in our lives. Capital is still in trouble, still has major problems that stand in the way of the advance of Progress. Our resistance to having our communities destroyed by roads or mines or dams, to having to work longer hours and faster, to being refused access to socially produced wealth, to the destruction of the environment, or quite simply to the meaninglessness of life under capital: all these resistances arise and arise again. Perhaps there is a fatal flaw in our character as humans. Perhaps there is an ineradicable push toward wanting to determine our own lives that never ceases to spoil capital's plans.

We are the crisis of capital, but as Panagiotis Doulos points out, this is not enough. We are the crisis of capital and proud of it, but to be the crisis of capital is not yet to be its destruction. The subject of crisis is not the same as the subject of revolution. The strength of our resistance is the stalemate of capital, but we need a checkmate. We need somehow to go forward from being the crisis of capital to being its downfall and replacement.

Does this mean a new formulation of the old distinction between reform and revolution? No, because that distinction is posed from a standpoint of knowing, and we do not know. We can criticize reformism, the pointless attempt to bring about radical change through the state, we can point to the disaster of Syriza, but when we are asked what is the right path, we have to say that we do not know. The distinction between reform and revolution becomes a distinction between those paths that clearly lead back into the accumulation of capital (and this includes all state-centered approaches) and those paths that look as if they are worth exploring, that look as if they could at least puncture the logic of capital. There is no correct line, no right path, but there are paths that are clearly wrong and there are could-be paths.

Or perhaps better: there are paths that are clearly wrong, and there are no other paths. Perhaps the very fact of being an established path means that it is the wrong path. The only paths that can take us against-and-beyond capital are the paths that we make by walking them. That is why, necessarily, we walk asking, not by following a map. The instrumentalism inherent in the reform/revolution dilemma (the best means to arrive at this end) falls. Perhaps, then: there are wrong paths and no right paths. Perhaps all paths are wrong except for those that we make walking. We, and then those who come after, for communizing is simply that, to make paths walking. To make the path by walking on it (*el camino se hace al andar*) is not just a form of struggle, it is already the creating of a communizing world.

3. It has become common in recent years to think of looking for an anti-capitalist way forward in terms of a "Plan C." There is an excellent discussion of this in Theodoros Karyotis's chapter. The very notion of a "Plan C" takes us back into an instrumentalist framework, as Panagiotis Doulos points out, yet it confronts us with an important issue. We must eat. Even to walk a new path, we must eat.

For most of us, eating is related to a monetary income derived directly or indirectly from capitalist employment. There is a simple, logical chain: if you want to eat, get a job; if you want a job, you must attract capital; if you want to attract capital, you must make conditions attractive for capital. It does not make sense to say, on the one hand, "We want more jobs," and, on the other, "But we are not prepared to accept the conditions imposed by capital." If we do not want to accept the conditions imposed by capital, we must find a way of breaking our dependence on capitalist employment. How do we do that? One of the lessons of the Greek crisis is surely that that is our weakness. We can scream "no" to the cuts in pensions and education imposed by capital (by the creditors through the mechanisms of the Eurozone), but if capital does not come to Greece, then our sons and daughters face a life of poverty and/or emigration. And even if the politicians were to listen to our protests (which they do not), then it would make little difference: capital would run away even faster. The "no" to capital cannot take us very far unless it is accompanied by the construction of other ways of living, the creation of what might be called another mode of production. This is sometimes referred to as the construction of the common, a helpful concept if we bear in mind that the common is always a movement against-and-beyond the rule of capital, a communizing. The apparent sobriety of the idea of a "Plan C" perhaps helps us to confront the disturbing reality of capitalist power, yet neither sobriety nor a single plan can be the key to rupture, to a multiplicity of ruptures.

4. A multiplicity of ruptures. The thousand fragments of glass that shoot out in all directions as the bottle that contained hope explodes, unified not by any institution but by the invisible force that propels them. So many fragments of emancipating, unbottled hope. If capital is a totalizing

process, an abstracting of human activity into value-producing labor, then we move in the opposite direction: detotalizing, de-abstracting recuperation of the force of self-determining activity. The repudiation by and of capital (we repudiate capital, and capital repudiates us) does not just drive us into physical and moral misery, it can also release a new creativity. The creation of a million cracks in the texture of capitalist domination, a million spaces or moments in which we build, by choice and by necessity, other ways of living, of relating to one another, of producing what we need to live, a million cracks unified by the mutual repudiation of humanity and capital: that is probably the only way out of the nightmare. Cracks that will always be contradictory, because we are still caught in the catastrophe of capital, but cracks that nevertheless help us to create alternatives, that help us to be ready for the fire next time.

5. Fire next time. There will be a next time. The social situation in Greece continues to get worse: there is no recovery of economic growth, no recovery of incomes, no recovery of employment, and it is unlikely that there will be in the foreseeable future. It will almost certainly be impossible for the Greek government to meet the commitments made in the agreements with the Eurozone. Anger grows.

"Fire next time," taken from James Baldwin's book in the early sixties on the situation of the blacks in the United States, is the title of the last chapter of a book by the economics commentator Martin Wolf on the financial crisis (Wolf 2014). The financial collapse of 2008 and the drastic measures taken by the governments of the world did not solve the problems of capital. Capitalism today is still characterized by a "savings glut," as the economists put it (Wolf 2014), a massive overaccumulation of capital (as Marx put it), a mass of capital that is unable to find the conditions for its self-expansion. The game of musical chairs continues, more and more intensely. It is unlikely that the concerted efforts of capitalists and their politicians (and their armies) will be able to postpone the next financial collapse for very long. Fire next time: what the Zapatistas call "*la tormenta*," the storm. A gathering social storm blowing through the world: a storm that is already there but is likely to become much worse.

Capital is humanity's catastrophe: we are capital's catastrophe. An intensifying antagonism in which the two sides clash head-on, one side wins, the two sides regroup, there is a new clash, perhaps in the same place, perhaps somewhere else. And so on, clash by clash, down the hill to annihilation. Or perhaps, clash by clash, up the hill to emancipation. The Greek crisis of 2015 was such a clash, and there is no doubt that it ended in capital's favor, that it imposed discipline and conformity in Greece and elsewhere, that it pushed humanity down the hill, closer to destruction. But the clashes will continue, are continuing, sometimes quietly, sometimes explosively.

There must be an element of preparation if we are to ask the question: How do we get out of here? How do we break capital? The present is intense, the present is struggle, but there must also be preparation for a possible future crash. If we think of the present capitalist attack as austerity (at least where it is not outright war), then how do we respond to a superausterity? For Greece, you may think the present situation is awful, and you must ask: but what will you do the next time round?

What the Greek experience tells us, loud and clear, is that there is no solution within capitalism. There is no possibility of a kind capitalism. The massive global overhang of debt makes that impossible. To talk of building toward a "progressive solution" within capital (Varoufakis and many others) is just so much nonsense. Greece has simplified the world dramatically: that is the great lesson. Capital against humanity, humanity against capital. Capital goes or else both humanity and capital go. There is no other way out.

How do we get rid of capital? The basis has to be "No, we'll do something else." The fragmented, detotalizing creation of different worlds, a multiplicity of cracks in capitalism, in which we build other ways of living. If we do not have that, then no amount of anticapitalist fervor can take us anywhere, because at the end of the day we have to eat. Tear down capitalism on Saturday, but if we do not have access to noncommodified wealth on Monday, then we are forced to rebuild what we destroyed two days earlier.

The creation of cracks is the basis, but these cracks have to flow into, or be accompanied by, a massive, tumultuous "no" to capital. Not to neoliberalism, colonialism, imperialism, fascism, just a simple "no" to capital, to the absurd, horrendous form of social organization that is human catastrophe.

Notes

1   The metaphor has been used frequently in relation to the financial crash of 2008. See, for example, the book *After the Music Stopped* by Alan Blinder, in which he begins by quoting the "immortal words on July 8, 2007, of Chuck

Prince, then the CEO of Citigroup": "When the music stops . . . things will be complicated. But as long as he music is playing, you've got to get up and dance. We're still dancing" (2013: xv).

2   Some might prefer to use the term "social democracy" here, but I think we must go further. What falls is the idea of "socialism" as some sort of halfway house between capitalism and communizing.

3   This metaphor should be used with caution: it will not work if you use a plastic bottle.

References

Blinder, Alan. *After the Music Stopped: The Financial Crisis, the Response and the Work Ahead*. New York: Penguin, 2013.

Bloch, Ernst. *The Principle of Hope*, vol. 1–3. Oxford: Basil Blackwell, 1986 [1959].

Coggan, Philip. *Paper Promises: Money, Debt and the New World Order*. London: Penguin, 2011.

Galeano, Eduardo. *Hunter of Stories*. New York: Nation Books, 2017.

Geithner, Timothy. *Stress Test*. London: Random House, 2014.

Marx, Karl. *Capital*, vol. 1. Moscow: Progress Publishers, 1965 [1867].

Mattick, Paul. "Zur marxschen Akkumulations- und Zusammenbruchstheorie." *Rätekorrespondenz*, 4 (1934); reprinted in Spanish in Karl Korsch, Paul Mattick, and Antonie Pannekoek. *Derrume del Capitalismo o Sujeto Revolucionario, Cuadernos del Paso y Presente*, 78. Mexico City: Siglo XXI, 1978.

McNally, David. *Global Slump: The Economics and Politics of Crisis and Resistance*. Oakland: PM Press, 2011.

Nasioka, Katerina. "Ciudades en Insurrección: Oaxaca (2006) y Atenas (2008)." PhD diss., Instituto de Ciencias Sociales y Humanidades "Alfonso Vélez Pliego," Benemérita Universidad Autónoma de Puebla, 2014.

Sinn, Hans-Werner. "The Global Economy Is Caught in a Trap: The Only Way Out Is Creative Destruction." *Guardian*, September 27, 2016. https://www.theguardian.com/business/2016/sep/27/the-global-economy-is-in-throes-of-self-inflicted-malaise-since-2008.

Wolf, Martin. *Shifts and Shocks*. New York: Penguin, 2014.

FOUR

On Antimemorandum Struggles and Democracy That Is (Not) on the Way

Giorgos Sotiropoulos

Beware of words without definition, they are the preferred instrument of schemers. . . . It is they who invented the beautiful aphorism: neither proletarian nor bourgeois, but democrat! . . . What opinion couldn't manage to find a home under that roof? Everyone claims to be a democrat, even aristocrats.
—Auguste Blanqui, letter to Maillard, June 6, 1852

Syntagma Square, May 2011, beginning of the *indignados* movement in Greece. A massive assembly taking place in the "lower square" of Syntagma Square announces that "for too long, decisions have been made for us without us" (Resolution of the Popular Assembly of Syntagma Square, May 28, 2011). The communiqué named the lack of access to power centers as the source of evil and concluded leaving few doubts as to how that could be solved: "Direct Democracy Now!" At the same time, in the "upper square" in front of the parliament, the crowd waves national flags—mostly Greek but also Spanish, Egyptian, Tunisian, and Argentinean, all states that had recently witnessed popular uprisings—making insulting gestures, chanting slogans, and hosting discussions in thousands of small impromptu groups. This famous division between the "upper" and "lower" Syntagma Square, while visible and therefore existing, should not be reified. If "upper" and "lower" define two *places* but also two *forms* of struggle, the limits between them were blurred, as proven by the continuous movement of people from one to the other. So, rather than two different fronts, there were two massive flows that permeated each other, producing a heterogeneous but unified entity, the *aganaktismenoi* (the Greek word for "indignant," or *indignados*, following the example of the Spanish

15-M movement) (Giovanopoulos and Mitropoulos 2011; Rocamadur 2011; Sotirakopoulos and Sotiropoulos 2013).

The aganaktismenoi were a moment within a movement of massive resistance against the austerity measures and the internal devaluation sanctioned by the memorandum that accompanied the loan agreement between the Greek state and the Troika (EU, ECB, IMF).[1] Therefore, it is a fact that the heterogeneous crowd that took to the streets met on the basis of a negative denominator: they were all against the memorandum. But it was not only a desire of denial that brought the aganaktismenoi together and mobilized the masses during the time of antimemorandum struggles.[2] There was, at the same time, a positive investment in democracy.[3] Perhaps the upper-square protests were not about direct democracy (although, importantly, some of those who found the lower square popular assembly to be too "leftist" created their own popular assembly in the upper square). But what clearly ran through the entire movement was the conviction that—either because of corrupt politicians or due to more structural factors—democracy in Greece was not working as it should, and the shift toward a better democracy would be attained through the immediate activation of popular sovereignty.

All this outlines the emergence of differentiations and confrontations during the antimemorandum struggles—which peaked during the movement of the aganaktismenoi—between democracy as a militant activity and democracy as a system of governance. This distinction is no historical novelty. On the contrary, it would be no exaggeration to claim that it has been following democracy throughout its entire modern history. In fact, there is no such thing as a unified and linear "history of democracy," but rather a historical production of two separate forms, whose interaction throughout history has been full of contradictions and tensions.[4] On the one hand, democracy defines a state form: namely, a set of procedures and rules that organize power and codify the relations, roles, obligations, and rights of the political structure within a specific territory. In this case, the ultimate locus of democracy consists in the elected bodies of representation. Its function par excellence is to legitimize the state form and government decisions, implemented under the auspices of popular mandate. On the other hand, democracy appears as a militant practice from below—as democracy-as-movement—that demands direct participation in the exercise of power, meaning the production of authority and law. In this case, the ultimate locus of democracy is constituted by the streets and the massive assemblies. While the former legalizes the prevailing situation, the latter stands critically against it, questioning in practice the dominant distribution of roles through the production of flows of deterritorialization. While the former pertains to the state, democracy-as-movement is *against* the state, that is, against the formal differentiation between rulers and ruled and against the consolidation of hierarchic structures of (political) power (Abensour 2011).

From an emblematic perspective, the distinction is between representative and direct democracy. While quite telling, this distinction tends to simplify the matter by reducing it to a formal, model-related difference; it downplays their similarities—for both forms revolve around notions of popular power, equality, and freedom—and, importantly, their historical dialectic. We will be returning to this point further on. For the time being, underlining the conceptual and historical distinction between the two forms of democracy will suffice. What I have tried to point out is that this distinction between "democracy-as-state" and "democracy-as-movement" allows us to approach the recent cycle of struggles in Greece (and around the world) in a way that enriches a mere economic and class analysis.

While embodying the resistance of the subaltern classes in the face of the austerity policies and the devaluation imposed by international and domestic elites, the struggles also reflected and reproduced the long-standing tension between the two forms of democracy. This chapter will take a closer look at the stakes of this proposal in order to show, on the one hand, that the tension and the dialectic between the two forms of democracy constituted a driving force as well as a limit for the movement in Greece. According to this perspective, the recent cycle of struggles in Greece ended with the signing of the third memorandum by the Syriza-ANEL coalition government, marking the defeat of the antimemorandum movement. On the other hand, I will try to avoid a rigid and regulatory distinction between a "good" democracy-as-movement and a "bad" democracy-as-state, quite common in the radical-activist spheres. In fact, I consider it more fertile to use the defeat of the recent antimemorandum movement as a starting point for a critical reflection on democracy as a signifier of flows of emancipation. Through this reflection, which acquires the form of a journey through history, we will finally arrive at a point of friction with the historical conjuncture, exploring the dynamic and potential of democracy-as-movement within the context of an ongoing crisis of democracy-as-state.

From Postdemocratic Consent...

Drawing from research conducted by Michael Oakeshot on this topic, Margaret Canovan (Arditi 2007: 42–49) makes a distinction between two dimensions in modern democracy: one is "pragmatic" and is linked to the production of legitimizing procedures of governance and the administration of social tension through consent and noncivil confrontation; the other is "redemptive" and has to do with the promise of a better world through the massive mobilization of the political body and the establishment of true popular sovereignty. It is quite tempting to draw this distinction in full correspondence with the distinction between democracy-as-state and democracy-as-movement and to argue that the first form turns democracy into a clearly formalist procedure, while the second—in the face of this soulless formalism—activates the suppressed messianic force of popular will. In fact, this activation, while conflictual by definition, can be formulated in therapeutic terms. For example, during the recent cycle of struggles, democracy-as-movement did not aim as much at overturning the democratic state as at saving it from itself. But although a certain parallelism undoubtedly exists between the two formalizations, we cannot speak in terms of absolute symmetry but rather of inscription and convergence. From this viewpoint, the conceptual distinction proposed by Canovan (ibid.) helps to explain the historical relation between democracy-as-state and democracy-as-movement. More specifically, for democracy-as-movement to emerge, the democratic state must fail in its effort to coalesce and conceal the void between the pragmatic and the redemptive dimensions of democracy.

It is common knowledge in critical theory that democracy has become the absolute fetish since the fall of the Eastern Bloc. It has been portrayed as something beyond the optimal form of governance: it has essentially been promoted as a hyper-historical "necessity" invested with a messianic power of ecumenical dimensions. As *existing ecumenism*—for it could be empirically proven—the liberal, democratic state became the only path of salvation for all nations. Of course, problems and imperfections had been detected in existing democratic regimes but to question democracy was to risk regressing to some type of totalitarianism. The only correct path was that of gradual improvement, following a course of evolution through which the dominant discourse not only projected its own image into the future but at the same time also renounced the revolutionary "exaggerations" of the past. This led to a delegitimization of any practice that did not fit into the institutional network of liberal democracies and, therefore, legitimized military and police interventions in cases where the—now global—democratic order was being threatened. In fact, what rendered the redemptive dimension of democracy even more *totalizing* is that the existing model of liberal democracy was defined as the best form of democracy in its own right. Thus, the pillars of liberal democracy—representation, rule of law, civil society, and the free market—became the necessary ingredients for the fulfillment of the world's democratic destiny.

This posture seemed to find its historical validation in the expansion of liberal democracy the world over and in the geometric growth of the number of states adopting this form. But no matter the effort to identify true formalism with redemptive teleology in the form of the liberal state, this was continually confronted with reality. For, the more democracy donned a messianic guise, the deeper the processes of *de-democratization* of the sociopolitical structure became; processes defined by Colin Crouch (2000) as the (now popular) notion of "postdemocracy."[5] This term is surely quite indicative, but no matter how we conceptualize them as a whole, we are talking of specific historical processes: the domination of the technocratic-economic rationality promoted by neoliberalism; the destructuring of the logic of collective rights embodied by the welfare state; the globalization of capital flows and the simultaneous accumulation of power in international centers and institutions of power that are not accessible to forms of popular control; the production of a sui generis one-party system, characterized by the alternation in power of two parties with no essential ideological or programmatic differences; the transformation of the electoral process into a consumerist spectacle defined by polls and image-makers (Brown 2013: 83–198).

In this context—which became even grimmer through the fierce exploitation of the labor force in the periphery and in capitalist centers, migration flows, growing inequalities, and "humanitarian" wars—the rejoicing of liberals rightly seemed, in traditional Marxist terms, to be pure ideology: a camera obscura that concealed the fact that the liberal democratic state did not constitute a point of convergence of pragmatic administration and the promise of redemption but actually broadened the gap between them, turning the two dimensions into conditions for the reproduction of the existing relations of domination and exploitation. It is in this ever-growing gap that Canovan detects the emergence of populism (Arditi 2007: 46–48). Yet, as she recognizes, it is precisely in this interstice that the massive democratic movements of the last decades emerged, questioning the establishment of the democratic promise. Democracy became directly related to flows and anti-institutionalizations produced by the movement as it advanced. So, if Wendy Brown (2013) is right in pointing out that everyone, from Bush and Berlusconi, Derrida and Balibar, to the Italian communists and Hamas, was a democrat, below this surface of consent lurks a profound confrontation (which, we must not forget, had casualties such as Carlo Giuliani)[6] between the liberal democratic state and the collective movements that promoted democracy as a future promise rather than an already existing ideal.

Therefore, it would be unfair—at the very least—to say that democracy-as-movement had no influence on the prevailing situation. But existing movements failed to cause profound flows of reform or seriously threaten the stability of democracy-as-state, with the exception of the antiglobalization movement at its height (between Seattle and Genoa), and this, obviously, in the cases where there was a stable democratic state to threaten. Socially founded on the expanded middle classes (which now included the working class) and financially grounded on the reproduction of global flows of credit, debit, and loans, an extensive "postdemocratic consent" was achieved, which was reflected in the relatively unhindered hegemony of the mentioned "bipartisan one-party system." In Greece, this postdemocratic consent was linked to the vision of "modernization" and "European completion" that reached its highest point in 2004, the year of the Athens Olympic Games, when the domestic industry for the production of international successes produced its brightest results (Sakellaropoulos 2014).

... to "Real Democracy" ...

The crisis that broke out in 2008 put this expanded consent on trial, a consent that reduced democracy-as-movement to the sphere of activism—sometimes significant but by definition a minority. It also led to a crisis of representation, particularly in states that were greatly affected by the economic crisis, such as Greece. This provided the negative context for the emergence of democracy-as-movement against democracy-as-state in terms of a massive uprising. Even during the days "of the squares," the differences between the separate mobilizations were numerous and important. Yet they all shared a common denominator that became the consciousness of the international movement itself: the crowds that took to the streets were a de facto negation of the government claim that having won the elections gave them the right to implement measures of austerity and impoverishment (Hardt and Negri 2012; Endnotes 2014). This brings us back to the starting point of this chapter: "the squares" were the culmination of the anti-austerity struggles, as well as of an escalation of the conflict between democracy-as-state and democracy-as-movement. In other words, the occupied squares, beyond their specific demands—in the case of the aganaktismenoi, it was to stop the medium-term austerity program from being voted—constituted events where democracy-as-movement reached a *high point of tension*, for they passed from denouncing the lack of democracy to producing "real democracy"—a democracy that, at the discourse level, stood critically against the existing (not very) representative democracies.

It is important, at this point, to underline that the emergence of democracy-as-movement was not only the result of acts of protest. Unlike Egypt, for example, where the very act of uniting in public was an act of rupture, in Greece, a peaceful protest in front of the parliament building is a practice provided for by democracy-as-state and a constitutional right. Therefore, if the occupation of Syntagma Square or equivalent occupations in Madrid and New York were simple gatherings that validated the prevailing role distribution, we could not speak of democracy-against-the-state, but rather of a symbolic validation of democracy-as-state. However, democracy-as-movement appears to the extent that the mobilized bodies produce flows of deterritorialization and lines of escape from the prevalent situation.[7] These flows of deterritorialization abrogate the distribution of roles that the democratic state validates and, at the same time, territorialize democracy as a *becoming*, as a militant practice from below. That is why we stress that Syntagma Square was not only the place where scarcity was denounced; it was also a construction site for "real" (or, as it was named in this case, "direct") democracy. Negri and Hardt (2012: 56) grasp this dimension of the international Occupy movement when they point out, "The encampments are a great factory for the production of social and democratic affects."

The choice of the word "affect" may seem peculiar at first sight, but it is quite enlightening. The democracy-as-movement that was produced in the occupied squares obviously had to do with organizational forms (the first and foremost being the "popular assembly" form) imbued by a pragmatic rationalism that tried to render them operative and, at the same time, materialized their protocols of appearance: circularity, non-consolidation of roles, horizontality, equality in decision-making and in the production of discourse. Nevertheless, no matter how crucial the issue of organization might be—as it also highlights the pragmatic dimension that democracy-as-movement ascribes to it—the "democracy of the squares" did not limit itself to the construction of an organizational form but spread to the production of an affective field that included new forms of experience, correlation, and socialization. These new forms practically renegotiated the fundamental categories of the existing political imaginary such as "citizen," "popular sovereignty," and, ultimately, the very notion of "democracy." This emotional activation of the political imaginary was obviously territorialized in certain "positive" practices that speak of the "degree of democracy" within the movement and also grant it a prefigurative dimension that certifies an alternative, better democracy. But we must not fall into the trap of separating the practices of the movement into distinct forms of struggle to be hierarchized and chosen or rejected by the piece. On the contrary, we must understand democracy-as-movement in the recent cycle of struggles in Greece in all its multiplicity: from the different activities that took place during the occupation of Syntagma Square—the popular assembly, the thematic assemblies, and the working groups, as well as the political discussions that emerged spontaneously in small groups of people—to the local popular assemblies that constantly grew, and from the massive demonstrations to the extended clashes with the state forces of repression. Insofar as they are moments of one and the same movement of protest that interacts dialectically with democracy-as-state, all these practices represent both a positive and a negative dimension. In this sense, democracy-as-movement has a dialectic structure.

This dialectic structure is not constituted in reference to a state power that is simply "above" but to the state as a legal order that validates and legitimizes a certain configuration of what exists, that is, a set of social relations. This means that during their mobilization the participants of democracy-as-movement come up against the social roles on the basis of which they initially mobilized, regardless of whether, in the process, they move on to a de facto denial of these roles or confirm them as the foundation of a new political configuration.[8] In this sense, in more abstract terms, the dialectic between democracy-as-state and democracy-as-movement also has to do with the relation of democracy-as-movement with itself. This is an element that eludes the "interclass" critique that is so popular in radical debates. In its more simplified form, this critique looks down upon the antimemorandum movement, and more specifically the aganaktismenoi, as "interclass mush"; at the same time, it regrets the lack of class consciousness among the laboring classes that participated in the mobilizations. Of course, the interclass nature of the protests was nothing new; in fact, it was fully expected, not to say *typical*. The memorandum is the necessary legal expression of a process that is completely real, as real as the 25 percent decrease in living standards it put its stamp on. Considering that this decrease did not only affect one class but many different social groups—especially the so-called popular strata: wage workers, the unemployed, freelancers, pensioners, small property owners—the flows of denial of the austerity measures would inevitably assume a heterogeneous, interclass form. But the issue is not only that the accusation of interclassness lacks critical edge as an *empirical* conclusion, as all massive movements usually transcend clear class divisions. The issue is that, as an empirical fact, the coexistence of different social classes (as well as sexes) in terms of political equality reveals the democratic character of a movement. For democracy has to do precisely with the noncorrespondence of social function and political capacity and the subsequent assertion that, regardless of whether one is a public servant, a student, a scientist, an unemployed or employed worker, or a pensioner, he or she can participate in the production of authority and law. More specifically, democracy-as-movement produces in the form of an immediate presence with constitutional force what the democratic state ratifies under the form of a constitutional class of representation. It is in the context of this separation that the subjective figure of the citizen, a typical category ratified by the state, turns into an active quality against-the-state; not necessarily against the state form as such, of course—as an abstract dominant class that is ruled by law—but rather against the prevalent, institutionally established and consolidated class of representation and the distribution of political roles and attributes.

One could argue that this text fails to mention the patriotic character of the mobilizations, particularly those of the aganaktismenoi. Indeed, national identity was not only an element that created a common ground in the massive mobilizations. It was constantly in the forefront, giving an air of "national resistance" to the struggles and linking absolution from the memorandum through the validation of popular sovereignty to the imaginary of a restored national independence. As will be discussed further on, the intensity and extent of democracy-as-movement were limited by the boundaries of the uprising of a nation in search of its lost sovereignty. More specifically, the absence of immigrants at a time when the Greek proletariat is more multinational than ever is an issue in its own right, even more so considering the movement constitutes a noninclusive identity. Yet the existence of a "national-popular" element in no case obliterates the massive character or democratic dimension of the antimemorandum movement. The "national" as a form of intervention is always problematic in its extensions, but it is not reactionary or fascist by definition. To deny this is to render the revolutionary experience of the twentieth century incomprehensible, especially in the colonial world (Losurdo 2016).

Therefore, even with its patriotic coating, democracy-as-movement in memorandum Greece appeared as a massive, multidimensional flow of desire that opened up a horizon of absolution, while at the same time producing a rudimentary version of the organizational structures required for its realization. But precisely because we are referring to a movement that is materialized as a negation of what exists and is, therefore, a confrontation of collective forces, the issue of intensity is crucial in the proposed analysis. The core of this problematic is whether the resulting structures materialize their protocols: was the principle of equal capacity embodied in Syntagma Square or was a new bureaucracy established that allowed the members of certain political formations to pull the strings (Rocamadur 2011: 81–83)? But it also has to do with the depth and intensity of the rupture with democracy-as-state and, therefore, with the social relations it validates. In this sense, we must be clear that no revolution has taken place in Greece in recent years. The revolutionary overturning (or transformation) of the existing state has not even appeared on the agenda as a tangible possibility. Even the "simplest" violent overthrow of the government that seemed to be within the reach of the movement during the riots of February 12, 2012 (Woland 2012) was finally proven unattainable, precisely during the same events. But while the conclusion that the movement was reformist and not courageous enough to take the next step might be true as an empirical ascertainment, it is not in the least helpful. If we are to have a clear image of how we went from the squares of indignation and the nights of fire to the electoral victory of Syriza and, finally, to the third memorandum, we must go deeper into the dynamic, the contradictions, and the limitations of the movement that emerged in Greece in 2010–2015.

... Back to the Democratic State

So, let us return to the interclass issue. In their dimension of democracy-as-movement, the antimemorandum struggles opened up a field of concrete negotiation of the existing social roles and identities. This does not mean that all those participating ignored their social position or its corresponding interests. There was a (largely genuine) effort to practically negate all class divisions through the declaration of an equal capacity and the de facto production of a community of struggle. This was particularly so in the occupied squares, where assemblies reinforced the common ground between the participants. Unfortunately, however, there is no bypassing the material dimension of belonging to a certain class, which inevitably defines, to a great extent, the interests and desires of the subjects.

Regardless of the importance of the notion within the tradition of critical theory that ideology obscures consciousness (Dillet 2016) post-democratic consensus was not based on an ideological "veil of deceit," even if it was woven with fantasies and illusions systematically reproduced from above. On the contrary, it was founded on the fact that a significant part of the population—be they left-wing or right-wing, conservative or progressive—were materially and psychologically attached to their living standards. Therefore, within such a regime of desire, it was more than likely that they would attempt to defend those standards against the attack or reclaim them when they began to fall apart.[9] This defensive stance assumed by the antimemorandum movement did not deplete its dynamic. As the political mediators that ratified these terms were collapsing through the memorandum—the clearest example being PASOK, whose rate of electoral support dropped from over 40 percent to under 10 percent—the desired defense/restoration also demanded a reform of the political system, thus opening up a horizon of *change.* It is in this gap between the tackling of the social crisis and the hope of the good life that democracy brings that democracy-as-movement emerged. The dynamic of change that was developed within this field allowed for the emergence of minority groups of participants that gave a particularly radical and confrontational content to the desire for negation and change; as a result, the mass of protesters went far beyond their starting point. It is highly unlikely that all those who took to the streets expected to participate in massive popular assemblies or extended clashes with the police, but they did, carried away by the flows that articulated democracy as a movement against the (existing) state.

But although there were flows of struggle with particularly radical and conflictive characteristics at moments that must not be looked down upon as mere *reminders of a possibility*, the antimemorandum movement as a vessel of democratization and change remained trapped within certain boundaries. In fact, the very common desire that constituted the antimemorandum movement as a force of assertion and not a simple force of denial—that is, the investment in democracy as a positive outcome of the struggles—produced further internal deviations. Simply put, the democracy desired by a young left-wing protester whose point of reference is the Paris Commune and the workers' councils is not the same democracy as the one pursued by a middle-class right-wing Greek citizen whose landmarks are the 1821 War of Independence and "Goudi."[10] Although they both fight for the restoration of lost popular sovereignty, the former invests in the movement as the bearer of "true" democracy, while the latter believes in a democratic nation-state. In this sense, the movement incorporated and internally reproduced the divisions that existed between itself and the Greek state as the democratic legal order.

Even though it constituted a minority, the radical tendency very often set the tone for the movement. But the critical mass of the antimemorandum movement maintained its conservative character (in the sense of a movement that wants to preserve an already existing situation). This is where the interclass critique acquires a truly political resonance, for, indeed, the massive movement did not challenge the existing class divisions beyond the field of political immediacy and a critique of the inequalities in the distribution of wealth and privileges. Therefore, not only did the project of "real" or "direct" democracy not expand into the field of economic and productive flows; more importantly, it did not criticize the social roles themselves (something easier said than done) but rather asserted them as such. Public servants wanted to conserve their position and their vested social rights; young students wanted to see their diplomas acquire true value; the unemployed wanted to be employed; small business owners wanted to continue as such. This is how the path was paved for the prevalence of a political discourse (both left- and right-wing) that used the populist figure of the virtuous and innocent people under attack by a treacherous elite and a corrupt political class to legitimize, in the context of Greek society, the interests and privileges of social groups that had long-standing relations of nepotism with the democratic state, while at the same time impeding the development of internal deviations in favor of the subaltern classes.

This failure of the massive movement to escalate into an explicit class struggle that would rupture the national community is closely linked to the fact that democracy-as-movement could not go beyond the pursuit of the democratization of the existing state. The confrontation with democracy-as-state—a confrontation present in all democracies-as-movement, for they challenge in practice the existing political roles and structures of representation—did not escalate to a point of rupture and certainly not to a point of revolutionary dynamic. This is precisely when the possibility of a Syriza emerged.

For their critics to their left, Syriza and other equivalent parties that arose during the recent cycle of struggles, such as Podemos, express the defeat of the movement or even contributed to it. For their supporters, these parties constitute—one way or the other—the institutional expression of the movement in the central political scene. While they are not wrong, both approaches tend to simplify the situation and remain attached to resolved political statements. Regardless of whether they participated in the movement, as Syriza did, or emerged directly from it, as occurred with Podemos, these parties are not simple institutional expressions of the power or the powerlessness of movements (anyhow, this characterization makes sense only when linked to a specific target, horizon, or desire). They constitute *material mediators between the two forms of democracy* and are driven and legitimized by the claim that they can articulate democracy-as-state with democracy-as-movement in terms others than those of antagonism, following the example of Latin America (Linera 2015). Acknowledging the existing democratic deficit, or perhaps the *postdemocratic contract*, they propose democratizing the state through the force and energy of movements from below. In the most sophisticated analyses, the relation between the party and the movement is conceived in dialectic terms, thus recognizing an inescapable contradiction and tension in the articulation of the two forms as one unitary form of governance that is capable of challenging the neoliberal model of governability (Kioupkiolis 2014).

This theoretical foundation is obviously crucial for the reproduction of said model of articulation, and it is no coincidence that the inability to refer to it at present—that is, after having signed the third memorandum— has caused a significant identity crisis for the governing party, Syriza.

But what I wish to point out is that, before it was theoretically convincing (or, inversely, before it was criticized), Syriza's aspiration to become the institutional mediator between democracy-as-state and democracy-as-movement expressed a tense desire that was responded to by—and therefore encountered in—the flows of escape and change produced by the movement. These flows did not achieve radical reform but rather pursued the democratization of the state and the restoration of vested social rights. This does not mean no possibilities opened up; however, the further radicalization of the movement required certain preconditions that were not met. These included the intensification of desire to a point that could not be expressed politically by forces of the "constitutional front," such as Syriza.

I do not claim that Syriza's electoral victory is solely the result of its connection to the movement and the will to use it as a means to democratize the state. If anything, Syriza's (admittedly moderate) populism was equally important, a populism that managed to bring together, through the image of the "tormented" people, the heterogeneous hope for restoration and change that fueled the antimemorandum struggles. What I want to stress, contrary to the thesis that if there was no party like Syriza the movement would have escalated to the point of the desired revolution, is that the antimemorandum struggles and Syriza were a reflection of each other. As a collective investment within a field of forces, desire is not a static measure, but rather power in movement, and is, therefore, open to flows of radicalization. But this means that just as desire can acquire a revolutionary dynamic under certain conditions, it can also, once again under certain conditions, acquire a moderate dynamic. In fact, usually both occur and aim at a relative dynamic and correlation. From this viewpoint, Syriza—and reformism as a general phenomenon—is not a plot created by "those in power" to deliberately cultivate illusions that prevent the subaltern classes from seeing the revolutionary Truth, but rather the political expression of a desire from below for change in non-revolutionary terms. So, if Syriza was able to participate in the movement, it was because it constituted a specific crystallization of it, a part(y) of it. In its party form, Syriza obviously acquired its own cohesion, creating an external relation with social flows, especially the flows of struggle. This, in turn, opened up the possibility that a party could constitute an obstacle to a struggle or even sell it out. But to understand this external character in exclusively negative terms of obstacle and misdirection is to ignore, on the basis of the imaginary of nonmediation, the dialectic—and therefore permeable—relation between the party and the movement. Therefore, while it allegedly gives the subaltern classes a force of immediate emancipation, it essentially ends up victimizing and underestimating the movements from below and treats its participants as actors who fail to see their true interest.

What we suggest is quite different. If Syriza's mediation contributed to the decision of the movements to take the parliamentary road, at the same time its proposal to deploy the movement as a force of democratization of the existing state resonated with the desire of the critical mass of the movement. This ultimately allowed Syriza to express in the central political stage and amid a crisis of representation the promise of a better future, one without austerity, one with justice and true democracy: true popular sovereignty. Therefore, a consistent critique of Syriza cannot but turn against the antimemorandum struggles. And, if this criticism does not wish to reduce the matter to a weakness of spirit or a lack of consciousness, it must also critically analyze late capitalist social formations and, more specifically, the Greek social configuration.

Arguably, it is too soon to judge the venture that Syriza represents in Greece, for it is just emerging in Europe. I do not question the fact that this peculiar coming together of democracy-as-movement and left-wing populism that appeared in Greece is still in its infancy, at least in Europe, and that there are no guarantees of further development (on the contrary, what seems to be on the rise is mainly right-wing populism). Yet we can assess certain incidents that point toward the existence of specific dynamics and tendencies, especially in what refers to Syriza and Greece.

If something can be said with absolute certainty, it is that the Syriza-led government has failed dramatically to live up to the idea that it is a vessel of democratization through initiatives from below and through the articulation of democracy-as-state and democracy-as-movement. But the issue is not only that an allegedly antimemorandum government signed a new memorandum and is implementing measures that go directly against its former program. And this is not to underestimate the extent to which Syriza, far from constituting an obstacle to austerity, has become a vessel of neoliberal rearticulation that promotes austerity and internal devaluation as a way to tackle the crisis and internalize competitiveness as a crucial element of social existence. Nevertheless, what is equally worrying is that the government is taking the postdemocratic high road: fast-track omnibus bills with no real consultation, adoption of a technocratic approach to politics as a process that concerns a few experts, not opening spaces of production and articulation of political discourse from below. Even the notorious July 5 referendum turned out to be a political maneuver and was, therefore, interpreted on a discretionary basis. To sum up, the prevailing situation was not challenged in the least: continuing along the lines of all parties previously in power, Syriza advances on the basis of a popular command that is conceived as a quantitative fact, rather than an active and ever-renewed activity that unravels the distribution of roles between the rulers and the ruled.

This critique does not downplay the pressures, extortions, and obstacles the present government encountered in its negotiations with the country's creditors. Neither does it bypass the structural coercions that make a party moderate its agenda. But one cannot simply overlook political choices and decisions made in the name of a "structuralism" that tricks itself into believing that one can talk of politics without talking of accountability. There is a certain inconsistency, to say the least, when someone promises the creation spaces of real democracy and that the memorandums will be torn up, and then castigates these promises as populism, as Prime Minister Alexis Tsipras has done. Furthermore, no matter the influence of external factors, there is no changing the fact that Syriza currently constitutes a de facto vessel of neoliberal articulation and of the state of emergency that implements it and, therefore, stands against the movement it once tried to express. But the issue remains much more complex. Regardless of Syriza's responsibilities, the solution is not as simple as putting the blame on the specific party or even on wretched social democracy or shameful reformism. Neither do we solve anything by asserting that the two forms of democracy cannot be articulated, thus implying that the only true solution is for democracy-as-movement to resist its state-ification so as to remain true to its institutional definition as "direct." For, even if this goal is considered feasible or fair, it does not put an end to the discussion; it opens up many issues and causes for reflection. This is precisely the context in which, I suggest, the recent cycle of struggle in Greece opens up a field of critical reflection on democracy as the conveyor of the promise of emancipation and justice.

Irresistibly Powerless

How is it that an ancient Greek term that reflects the particular conditions of the polis has been used in such different historical and social circumstances? There is something *attractive* to the word, to say the least. Etymologically speaking, it does not amount to the promotion of a timeless conception of democracy. As Kondylis (2014: 104) would have it, definitions such as "democracy is" can turn into "bad metaphysics." Therefore, a theoretical exploration of democracy does not constitute an analysis of essence but rather an anatomy of the form. On the other hand, the very existence of historical forms of democracy welcomes a field of theoretical generalization that—without rendering it ahistorical—does not dissolve democracy in its historical and social conditions, but acknowledges it has the cohesion of a theoretical subject matter. In other words, because democracy appears in time as an ideal inscribed in struggles from below, it must be examined theoretically as such.

Etymologically speaking, democracy gives "the power" to a collective entity it defines as "demos." Yet although "demos" is defined as the totality of the political body and, therefore, as an interclass collective entity, Aristotle (2009: xxii) insists on defining democracy as "the rule of the poor." In this formulation, Aristotle systematically expresses the opinion that prevailed in ancient Greece. "Demos" also refers to the totality of citizens—a people, in this case the people of Athens—but, first and foremost, it refers to the poor. There is a lot of talk on poverty and on the need to fight it. But the poor must not be conceived as a sociological category defined through economic measurements—those who are not wealthy enough—but rather as a word that defines a life based on shortage and on a radical inequality. Being poor means you are "below." Therefore, the profound contempt the ancient scholars of the aristocracy had for democracy was related to the fact that those who were below by definition were now acquiring "a state." As the rule of the *plebeians*, democracy was a scandal; and if we are to judge by the reactions of present-day "patricians" in the face of the emergence of democracy-as-movement, it still is (Rancière 2014).

This power of the poor must not be conceived as the occupation of an already existing position of power, but rather as the invention and production of qualitatively different forms of power that challenge the prevailing hierarchies, roles, and relevant relations of command and submission. Precisely because the poor are defined by the fact of radical inequality, precisely because they *are* this inequality, to have the power is to invalidate the structures that define them existentially and materially as inferior. Thus, democracy articulates an experience of freedom not as privilege but as an equating activity (Rancière 2007; Abensour 2011). Furthermore, to the extent that the production of binding decisions takes place among equals, there is a promotion not of imposition—founded on the possibility of violence—but of dialogue and persuasion; that is, of nonrepressive forms of producing and making binding decisions. Democracy, of course, is imposed upon its (wealthy) opponents, and this is a crucial issue that we will return to.[11] But the essence is that the production of flows of power through the coming together of equal parts—which are equal precisely because they are not *identical*, that is, because there exists between them a dimension of difference—has a specific protocol of realization. One that includes institutional forms where power does not distance itself from the political body by tracing a vertical relation of submission, an "above" that must necessarily activate a mechanism of repression for its own reinforcement but is part of it, an immanent quality articulated through forms of discourse and knowledge based on dialogue and consultation.

As a result, democracy became historically identified not only with the perspective of popular rule but also with the pretension of handling differences in terms of nonimposition, acceptance, and compromise. The rule of the poor is (inevitably) the rule of *nobody* or a nonrule of "all": a principle of equal capacity (Rancière 2007; Abensour 2011). This expresses an ambiguity that becomes materialized in the notion of demos itself, which can mean the poor, the majority, or the entire political body: a *people*.

It must be stressed that the intention of this article is not to establish ancient Greek democracy as a normative model on whose basis subsequent historical crystallizations of the democratic form are to be judged. But it would be misguided—to say the least—to leave the reappearance of the term to the philhellenism of certain bourgeois polymaths. In fact, historically, this would come up against the deeply ambiguous stance of even the most liberal sectors of the bourgeoisie toward the notion of democracy (Chimber 2013: 54–76). To the extent that the struggles of those below are not reflective reactions, but rather flows that are activated and permeated by productive investments of desire, one can reasonably presume there exists something in the essence of the term "democracy", a certain connotation that allows it to stand historically as a symbolic projection—an *Idea*—of struggles that are so far apart in space and time: from the emancipatory struggles of slaves and women to the struggles of the labor movement, both revolutionary and reformative. The most typical connotations of the term, which have accompanied it since antiquity, are freedom and equality, which come together as a "proposal of equal liberty" (Balibar 2002). To be on the safe side, just as "it is by no means obvious that the hunger which was satisfied [by] Neolithic humans . . . is the same kind of thing as the hunger that is satisfied by dining in a five-star restaurant" (Geuss 2008: 4), so the differences in the material parameters of the life of a fifth-century peasant or housewife and a nineteenth-century worker or suffragette (and so on) also modify the content of any motivating ideas of freedom and equality. Yet one cannot ignore the drastic presence—in the form of anticipation and activity—of a notion of equality and freedom in the face of repression and exclusion. Democracy appears, precisely, as the definition of this collective expectation and activity and, therefore, as the *vessel* of the desire for freedom and equality that mobilizes them. In fact, when democracy is the central stake in a struggle, equal liberties are raised to the level of a state category, namely, of institutionalized legal relations.

In the revolutionary tradition, it is common to criticize democracy in one way or another for not truly materializing freedom and equality and for laying the foundations for class domination.[12] But although there is a clearly empirical basis to this criticism, it tends to miss the point. As an investment of desire that is closely linked to the expectation of a better life, democracy refers to productive flows that practically validate the possibility of equality and freedom and without which the latter would be simple abstractions. Therefore, the very productive materiality of democracy as a movement from below—democracy-as-movement—also allows for this critique. Importantly, as the expression of a desire that goes beyond the prevailing situation, democracy constitutes the historical expression of the imaginary of vindication of those who are below; a vindication that can span from having direct access to the creation of laws, the self-organization of production, and the common administration of community resources to the right of a young person to drink beer and smoke pot whenever and wherever they might wish to do so. And this imaginary, this plebeian utopia of true democracy as a fair and good life, might experience defeats, might be limited to small minorities, but it is unbeatable at its core, for each time it is defeated it is confirmed. Democracy is invincible because *each incident that might seem to nullify it can be credibly presented as the result of its absence.* This does not mean that a democratic regime cannot be overturned; quite the opposite. Even less so does it mean that all democratic decisions are "correct" (to make such a judgment, one needs specific criteria of correctness). It is rather that domination, repression, authoritarianism, and so on—that is, political forms that are necessary for the existence of systems of exploitation and exclusion—could not stand as proof of democracy's dubious nature, for democracy is a historical condensation of all that these political forms of power deny: freedom, equality, pluralism, popular sovereignty. Therefore, the violation of these principles will always appear as a *democratic deficit*, subsequently activating the vision of "true democracy" in terms of a movement against the prevailing situation.

This lands us at the center of one of the numerous paradoxes of democracy. For if the latter is invincible and, therefore, *irresistibly captivating*, it is at the same time extremely unlikely that it will be materialized through its protocols of appearance. Did this not become obvious during the present cycle of struggles? Either as a militant activity or as a popular mandate expressed in the election results, "democracy" was unable to successfully resist austerity policies. Such a blocking of predominant policies would mean that the movement that linked the end of austerity to the perspective of real democracy is capable of imposing its collective will upon the (allegedly democratic) institutions of power and the international political and economic elite that controls them, to whom, naturally, the demand for social justice through profound democratization sounds quite menacing. The issue here is that, in speaking of a correlation of powers, we speak of a capacity to impose what democracy presumably rejects. What Marx and Engels clearly understood is that democracy, *and especially democracy-as-movement*, exists in a dialectic relation with dictatorial regimes in that it has the capacity to impose extreme measures upon those who go against collective will.[13] Obviously, the dialectic between democracy and dictatorship raises huge questions, as a sound analysis of the revolutionary experience of the twentieth century reveals. But this does not legitimize a comparative delimitation of these notions that ultimately denies the problem itself (e.g., Petkas 2014). As a militant decision-making activity, democracy imposes its decisions upon all those who are beyond the field of representation—the famous "1%," for example, which does not fit into the community of the "99%"—in terms of an inviolable popular mandate. To the extent that popular will fails to impose itself, popular mandate is a dead letter: democracy is defeated. Yet if it is imposed, its victory—meaning the materialization of democracy—passes through procedures that are, strictly speaking, not democratic.

The dialectic of democracy and dictatorship goes beyond the revolutionary experience of the twentieth century. It spreads historically from the Paris Commune and the abolition of slavery in the United States of America to the rebellion of the Athenian *demos* against Isocrates—who *imposed* the return of Kleisthenes—and brings us face-to-face with what democracy carries within and tries to exorcise: civil war. In the context of contemporary political science and theory, these two terms are usually conceived as opposites, a distinction historically founded on the fact that during the twentieth century (parliamentary) democracy and civil war were posed as practical alternative strategies.[14] Yet this historical relationship cannot be conceived in purely external terms. From as early as ancient Greece, democracy has been haunted from within by civil war as the fragmentation of the political body, a potential expression of the noncohesiveness of the "sovereign people." This issue is obviously related to a society's class composition, for civil war is (potentially) also class war. But what is of concern here is the inscription of civil war in the very definition of democracy; it is, at the same time, the power of one side, those who are below, the people, as well as a way of politically administrating difference.

Because a people are socially divided, they cannot be identical to their political representation as a unitary, dominant subject.[15] Therefore, as I noted previously, democracy as a signifier of popular domination is innately ambiguous, for the power of the people is never the same as the power of the plebeians. On the one hand, a democratic regime cannot be such if it does not grant equal power, rights, and obligations to the political body in its entirety. On the other, the dimension of plebeian power as a vindication of those who are below accompanies democracy precisely to the extent that it defines forms of power through which the subaltern classes— those who are "below"—can become "equal" by participating, directly or through forms of representation, in the production of authority and law. Thus, democracy as plebeian sovereignty encompasses the perspective of the fragmentation of democracy-as-state. Historically, this immanence of civil fragmentation appears when the evolution of democracy-as-movement against democracy-as-state reaches a certain degree of intensity and, more specifically, when opposition to the state becomes so intense that it poses an issue of constitution and openly clashes with the organized interests and privileges that are validated and protected by the existing state; the private ownership of the means of production is an example of this. Then the people are inevitably fragmented, and democracy is posed from below as a battle cry against the social status quo and from above as a reason to conserve it. The example of 1917 Russia is more than telling in this case (Kolonitskii 2004: 75–90). This does not mean the development of democracy-as-movement unavoidably leads to civil war: there can be— and there have been—flows of true democratization without the struggles that produced them assuming the form of an armed conflict. In fact, the forms of democracy that have existed in the state form—as democratic states—have, in a sense, been the result of historical compromises (we will not, at present, examine the reasons that led to said compromises). Yet as democracy brings forward the spectrum and the promise of the power of those who are below, or else an equality that challenges in practice the given state of affairs, it also entails the possibility of rupture of the political body and the short-circuiting of the democratic administration's internal tensions and antagonisms. If, indeed, the outcome will be civil war is a question of historical circumstance, among others. All those who aspire to the outbreak of such a civil conflict should better think well about what it would really mean and what the consequences would be. But civil war is not the contrary to democracy but rather a symptom of its internal tensions. For that reason, just like dictatorship, civil war is also a notion that constitutes a *boundary* from the viewpoint of democracy.

This discussion obviously revolves around power as a constitutional category of the political. Yet during the entire analysis the issue of power is inscribed within a broader framework, for the popular sovereignty that democracy entails is a precondition for the plebeian utopia, vindication, and justice for those who are below. On this level of justice, which constitutes a vindication, democracy never appears only as an abstract political relation but as one that is materially interwoven with the expectation of change and the improvement of social living conditions. More specifically, democracy promises that what really matters—however one might perceive it—"will eventually reach everyone" (Papageorgiou 2015: 477). In this sense, democracy-as-movement is not simply a movement for democracy but a dimension of movements for social (and therefore state-related) change. From ancient to modern-day Athens, democracy-as-movement is inscribed within flows of social reform to whose materialization it contributes. To what extent the resulting transforming flows have a dynamic of reform or revolution is important but secondary. The essence is that if democracy is the condition and the content of the plebeian aspiration for a better and fairer life, the latter goes beyond democracy. But from this viewpoint, democracy's promise of redemption takes us from the limits of democracy to *democracy as a limit*.

In the struggles against austerity, in the struggles against the destruction of local communities and the natural environment, the movements always come face-to-face with capital, which is more than an abstraction; it is embodied in very real interests that are organized at the level of (local, national, transnational) political power. It is no surprise that the struggles for democratization involve the issue of social justice, but they tend to reduce it to issues of wealth redistribution. I do not underestimate this demand or the way in which it is linked to the establishment of democracy: historically speaking, the accumulation of wealth has been directly linked to the accumulation of power. The dominant are always the wealthy, and it is no coincidence that democracy emerges as a historical questioning of this identification of power and wealth. But while democracy as a movement constitutes a hands-on critique of the power of wealth, as a critical notion it does not touch all the forms of capital's domination.

A clear example of this is money. More than a general equivalent, it is a basic form of mediation in social relations. As such, the money form has always occupied a constitutional position in the processes of capital reproduction and accumulation. But at present, in the days of financial capitalism, the meaning of money has been qualitatively upgraded. This becomes apparent in the rule of financial capital and of institutions such as banks, whose too-big-to-fail power is now openly discussed as a problem in public dialogue. But the "power of money" goes much deeper, in the sense that the power of the banks constitutes the material expression of the penetration of the money form in everyday life. "What is money?" asks *Pieta*, the exceptional film by Kim Ki-duk, and the answer is simple and clear: "the beginning and the end." The issue here is that, in order to question the authority of the banks, one must question the power that money has on human lives. This does not necessarily amount to the immediate abolition of money, as a sometimes naive ultraleftism proposes, but to the need of being able to question its rule in practice; that is, its role in the reproduction of social existence. And while democracy-as-movement brings this issue to the fore by attacking privileges, the inequality of wealth, and corruption, the production of flows that challenge the money form is not only an issue of democracy; it spreads across questions such as what we produce and why, what is it that defines the value of things, and what does and does not matter in life. Regardless of how abstract these questions might sound, they are practically linked to the stakes of true resistance against neoliberalism and to the prevailing tactics of tackling the crisis. The forms of realization of capital such as money (or commodity and value) are not only the cornerstones of the power of the institutions that impose austerity and the devaluation of labor power; they are also the material precondition for the existence of the latter as such. Therefore, to posit these questions as practical issues with an intensity that would render them crucial would mean to shift the desire for social justice from criticizing the injustices of capitalism to criticizing the capitalist form of production itself. Inversely, the fact that these issues were no more than minor stakes in the recent Greek cycle of struggles—as in similar movements in other countries—shows that the question of an alternative mode of production did not appear on the agenda with great intensity. That is why democracy is defined here as the power as well as the *boundary* of the struggles: in setting democracy as its goal, the movement showed its incapacity to imagine a noncapitalist world.

Epilogue

> *For you these from me, O Democracy, to serve you ma femme!*
> *For you, for you I am trilling these songs.*
> —Walt Whitman, "For You O Democracy"

It is not hard to corroborate that the processes of de-democratization mentioned at the beginning of the chapter continue with increasing intensity since the outbreak of the crisis. Of course, tendencies must not be confused with completed situations. The citizens of the Greek (or another Western) state do not live in a totalitarian biopolitical camp. Yet there is a global tendency of transition to a postdemocratic security state, despite partial differences in intensity and scope. Particularly through the escalation of the war on terrorism but also through policies for the control of migrant-refugee flows, the security state not only deepens its structures to the detriment of any existing democratic rights or procedures, but also manages to do so with the approval of the citizens themselves, as the recent massive army and police operations in the US, France, and Belgium prove. And while there are clearly structured and structural rationalities that drive the entire process, there is no reason to regard the latter only as a targeted and carefully planned production of a "new totalitarianism" from above. If, indeed, authoritarianism is turning into a more and more endemic operation of liberal democracies, it is probably the result of a true crisis of the democratic state. Neither is it simple (without wanting to exclude this possibility) to resolve the crisis from above through a typical dismantling of democracy, as occurred in certain countries during the interwar period. Quite the opposite. It is—will be—a particularly complex and risk-laden procedure, for democracy remains the cornerstone of the legitimization of the existing capitalist social formations, at least in the West. A legitimization that had until recently been accomplished through the (always relative) democratic administration of social antagonism—particularly the relation between capital and labor—on the one hand, and the incorporation of the aspirations that modern societies continually produce, on the other.

According to the perspective outlined in this chapter, the recent electoral results in various European countries—from Greece to Portugal and Spain and, of course, the election of Donald Trump in the United States—can be seen as expressions of the ongoing crisis of democracy-as-state. The collapse of the traditional two-party system and of the "political families" of the postwar era that created it (Barontini 2015) expresses the failure to politically represent a big part of the social body; this was a precondition for the stability of democracy-as-state in recent years. Despite their particularities, all mentioned cases show that the heightened tension between democracy and capitalism (the impossibility to administrate the economic crisis in democratic terms) and between democracy and state (the impossibility to democratically govern and administrate the social flows) are a sign of the times. Although this possibility cannot be discarded, for the time being there are few indications that there will be a fast solution to the crisis of the democratic state through a new (post-) democratic consensus.

The emergence of democracy-as-movement in Greece has been analyzed in this chapter as a result of the crisis of democracy-as-state and the gap between pragmatic administration and the hope of deliverance that accompanies it. In fact, the Greek case is quite relevant for a number of reasons. First, it corroborates Lazzarato's (2015: 13) claim that the movement cannot yet constitute itself as a revolutionary force but rather "tests its force (still too meager) and that of Empire (still too great), then retreats." Second, and directly linked to this, democracy-as-movement appears for now in therapeutic terms, without however being able to succeed in that goal. The case of Syriza reveals how difficult it is to succeed in this endeavor that is slowly spreading from South to North and to the core of the capitalist world (Jeremy Corbyn in England, or even Bernie Sanders in the United States).[16] In this sense, the moments when democracy-as-movement displays its power, placing friendly powers that try to represent it in government, are the very moments in which its incapacity to radically challenge the powers of this world becomes apparent.

If we are to assume, as we have reason to, that the global crisis will continue in its complex expressions—from the strictly economic to the issue of the migrant-refugee flows—the dialectic of democracy-as-state and democracy-as-movement will continue to manifest itself. What this chapter essentially argues is that in Greece as elsewhere a potential upsurge and victory of the struggles against the prevailing policies for the administration of the crisis will pass through the expansion of flows of profound democratization, that is, through the consolidation of democracy-as-movement. At the same time, however, this consolidation—any historical victory of democracy-as-movement—will reveal the limits of democracy but also democracy as a limit. And while there is no point in discoursing the future and prefiguring a happy or sad end to the dialectic procedure we are discussing, we can reflect on the processes of reform that go "beyond" democracy and incorporate it in ways that define it and are defined by it, that differentiate it and are differentiated by it. This "beyond democracy" has been historically represented by communism or even socialism, notions that inscribe democracy within a historical horizon of the social emancipation of the subaltern classes and, more specifically, of the working class. It is well known that these notions are now obsolete. But just as their unexpected mention in the television series *American Crime* might suggest, this obsolete character can also be an indication of their power, of their nature as an ultimate solution to the intolerance of modern capitalist societies. In such a case, the goal would be to once again expand the connection of a certain notion of communism (or even socialism) with both the experience and the imagination of the subaltern classes. This is what occurred in Latin America, despite all the existing limitations. Such a possibility could turn democracy-as-movement into one dimension of a process of creating a different world.

Notes

1   The loan agreement and the measures that accompanied it were an answer to the Greek economic crisis that assumed the form of a "sovereign debt crisis."

In theory, the debt and the measures that accompanied it aimed at helping Greece avoid bankruptcy and, in the long run, set its economy on track for development. The outcome was a long-standing recession. This does not mean the creditor discourse on their intentions was a complete lie, although the solidarity rhetoric is so hypocritical it is obscene. The international institutions did, indeed, want to avoid a disorderly default of the Greek state, for that would have unexpected repercussions for the EU and possibly the world economy. They also believed the measures would boost development in the long run. Of course, the real issue is *what* one means by this term. In general terms, the measures promoted a very deep and intense restructuring, affecting mostly the economy in ways that would allow for a new cycle of accumulation and assist toward the assimilation of the supremacy of capital and, therefore, of the power institutions that embody it. This is sufficiently proven by the three main directions of the measures: readjustment of the capital-labor relationship in the interest of the former, concentration of capital through the attack on small properties, and the creation of fields of investment and private accumulation through extensive privatization (Sakellaropoulos 2014; Children of the Galley 2011, 2012). But the content of the readjustment, the rationality that guides it and structures it, seeps into a broader readjustment of the Greek society through the assimilation of the system of norms that constitute neoliberalism (Dardot and Laval 2009; Athanasiou 2012).

2   This time period extends roughly from May 5, 2010, the day the first memorandum was voted on, until the referendum of July 5, 2015.

3   Obviously, this does not deny that there are antidemocratic tendencies within the aganaktismenoi, be they related to a traditional Bonapartism or to a more contemporary technocracy. Yet the dynamic of these tendencies in the Syntagma protests should not be overemphasized. For the most part, the aganaktismenoi were the peak of a movement whose opposition to the memorandums was expressed through the invocation of a better democracy and not its authoritarian abolition.

4   The two forms of democracy mentioned here have been studied from many different perspectives, but they are usually not discussed together. Alain Badiou's article "A Speculative Disquisition of the Concept of Democracy" (2005: 78–95) is a significant exception.

5   The acknowledgment of a historical transition toward a postdemocratic condition does not insinuate the idealization of liberal democracies or an unquestioning acceptance of the dipole democracy/totalitarianism through which the liberal capitalist regimes projected their own self-image. Free elections and the incorporation of the labor movement have always been conditional and filled with gray zones, especially in countries with a heightened "communist danger," such as Greece or Italy. Also, it should not be ignored that in all contemporary massive democratic states there exists a zone of lawlessness which exceeds the democratic lawful order and legitimizes the authoritarian and arbitrary power of the state, even on the supposedly "sovereign people." On the last point, see Buck-Morss, 2002: 2–35.

6   On Friday 20, 2001, Carlo Giuliani became yet another casualty of democracy when he was shot dead by a police officer (Mario Placanica) while participating in the antiglobalization demonstrations against the G8 in Gaetano Alimonda square, in Genoa.

7   The present analysis, just as the text in general, owes much to the conceptual arsenal provided by the work of Gilles Deleuze and Félix Guattari from *Anti-Oedipus* (2013) onward.

8   Yet even such a confirmation is never a simple reproduction. A worker that truly "has the power," a true power of participation/influence in the production of authority and law, is no longer simply a "worker."

9   This is not a novelty either, just as it does not negate the production of radical characteristics and tendencies within such a movement of defense/restoration. See, for example, the study on the popular movements of the early industrial period by Craig Calhoun (1982).

10 The latter refers to a military movement that launched an armed revolt from the Athenian neighborhood of Goudi. Although it expressed a complex socio-political situation, the Goudi movement has been inscribed in the collective imaginary, especially of the conservative and right-wing social sectors, as an act of patriotism against the "treacherous politicians," hence the recurring declarations that today's politicians shall be taken "to Goudi."

11 In traditional historiography, the development of democracy is identified with the reforms of certain legislators that belonged to the aristocratic class, such as Solon and Kleisthenes. Yet this is only half the story, as the production of democratic forms is related to a long history of popular revolt that the various regime changes answer to and try to regulate. The most characteristic example was when the aristocrats of Athens, with the help of Sparta, tried to institute an oligarchic regime. The masses rebelled against this coup, sent Isocrates away and imposed Kleisthenes so that he would make the necessary institutional reforms to establish Isonomia (equality of rights for all), that is, the first form of democracy (Ober 1996: 32–52).

12 For a critique that goes beyond the overused revolutionary renunciations of democracy, see Troploin 2008. For a more historically orientated, but equally insightful critique, see Canfora 2006.

13 This dialectic is formulated, though not analyzed, by Badiou (2005). It also runs through the historical narrations of Luciano Canfora (2006) and Domenico Losurdo (2015).

14 A very interesting analysis of the phenomenon of civil war was recently formulated by Giorgio Agamben (2015). For a more historical perspective, see Traverso 2016.

15 This, of course, poses the question of the extent to which there can ever be absolute symmetry between reality and representation. To the degree that the social is defined in terms of multiplicity, as a being-together, it follows that each individual representation, each identity group—even that of the working class—is noncohesive. In this sense, in a classless society the dissolution of the political body would remain imaginary. Anyhow, the tension and ambiguity that we can diagnose in the definition of democracy historically acquires its

content from the reality of class antagonism. An interesting discussion on this issue, albeit in a different conceptual context, can be found in Abensour 2011: 73–88.

16 Jeremy Corbyn has been elected head of the British Labour Party. Bernie Sanders was a candidate for the Democratic presidential nomination and Hillary Clinton's main opponent within the Democratic Party in the 2016 US elections.

References

Abensour, Miguel. *Democracy against the State: Marx and the Machiavellian Moment.* Cambridge: Polity Press, 2011.

Agamben, Giorgio. *Stasis: Civil War as a Political Paradigm.* Edinburgh: Edinburgh University Press, 2015.

Arditi, Benjamin. *Politics on the Edge of Liberalism: Difference, Populism, Revolution, Agitation.* Edinburgh: Edinburgh University Press, 2007.

Aristotle. *Politics.* Oxford: Oxford University Press, 2009.

Athanasiou, Athina. *Η κρίση ως "κατάσταση έκτακτης ανάγκης"* [Crisis as a "state of emergency": critiques and resistances]. Athens: Savvalas, 2012.

Badiou, Alain. *Metapolitics.* Translated by Jason Barker. London: Verso, 2005

Balibar, Étienne. "Three Notions of Politics." In *Politics and the Other Scene.* New York: Verso, 2002.

Barontini, Danielle. "Το τέλος των 'πολιτικών οικογενειών' της Ευρώπης" [The end of Europe's "political families"], December 2015. https://aenaikinisi.wordpress.com/2015/12/.

Brown, Wendy. "We Are All Democrats Now." In Giorgio Agamben et al. *Democracy in What State?* 83–198. New York: Columbia University Press, 2013.

Buck-Mors, Susan. *Dream World and Catastrophe: The Passing of Mass Utopia in East and West.* Cambridge, MA: MIT Press, 2002.

Calhoun, Craig. *The Question of Class Struggle: Social Foundations of Popular Radicalism during the Industrial Revolution.* Chicago: University of Chicago Press, 1982.

Canfora, Luciano. *Democracy in Europe: A History.* Oxford: Blackwell Publishing, 2006.

The Children of the Galley (TPTG). "Burdened with Debt: 'Debt Crisis' and Class-Struggles in Greece." In *Revolt and Crisis in Greece: Between a Present Yet to Pass and a Future Still to Come,* edited by Antonis Vradis and Simitris Dalakoglou, 245–78. Oakland: AK Press/Occupied London, 2011.

———. "Burdened with Debt Reloaded: The Politics of Devaluation." *libcom. org,* April 12, 2012. http://libcom.org/library/burdenned-debt-reloaded-politics-devaluation.

Chimber, Vivek. *Post-colonial Theory and the Specter of Capital.* New Delhi: Navayana, 2013.

"A Contribution to the Critique of Political Autonomy." *troploin,* 2008. http://www.troploin.fr/node/17.

Crouch, Colin. *Post-Democracy.* Cambridge: Polity Press, 2000.

Dardot, Pierre, and Christian Laval. *The New Way of the World: On Neoliberal Society*. Translated by Gregory Elliot. London: Verso, 2009.

Deleuze, Gilles, and Felix Guattari. *Anti-Oedipus: Capitalism and Schizophrenia*. London: Bloomsbury, 2013.

Dillet, Benoit. "Deleuze's Transformation of the Ideology Critique Project: Noology Critique." In *Deleuze and the Passions*, edited by Ceciel Meiborg and Tuinen van Sjord. New York: Punctum Books, 2016.

Endnotes. "The Holding Pattern." *Endnotes* no. 3, September 2013. https://endnotes.org.uk/issues/3.

Geuss, Raymond. *Philosophy and True Politics*. Princeton, NJ: Princeton University Press, 2008.

Giovanopoulos, Christos, and Dimitris Mitropoulos, ed. *Δημοκρατία under Construction: Από τους Δρόμους στις Πλατείες* [Democracy under construction: From the streets to the squares]. Athens: Ekdoseis A/synecheia, 2011.

Hardt, Michael, and Antonio Negri. *Declaration*. New York: Argo Navis Author Services, 2012.

Kolonitskii, Boris I. "'Democracy' in the Political Consciousness of the February Revolution." In *Revolutionary Russia: New Approaches to the Russian Revolution of 1917*, edited by Rex A. Wade, 75–90. London: Routledge, 2004.

Kioupkiolis, Alexandros. *Για τα Κοινά της Ελευθερίας* [For the commons of freedom]. Athens: Ekdoseis Exarcheia, 2014.

Kondylis, Panagiotis. *Planetary Politics after the Cold War*, 2014. http://www.panagiotiskondylis.com/resources/Planetary%20Politics%20after%20the%20Cold%20War%20by%20Panagiotis%20Kondylis.pdf.

Lazzarato, Maurizio. *Governing by Debt*. Cambridge, MA: Semiotext(e), 2015.

Linera, Alvaro G. *Κράτος, Δημοκρατία και Σοσιαλισμός* [State, democracy, and socialism]. Athens: A/synecheia, 2015.

Losurdo, Domenico. *Class Struggle: A Political and Philosophical History*. New York: Palgrave Macmillan, 2016.

———. *War and Revolution: Rethinking the 20th Century*. London: Verso, 2015.

Ober, Josiah. "The Athenian Revolution of 508/507 BC: Violence, Authority and the Origins of Democracy." In *The Athenian Revolution: Essays on Ancient Greek Democratic and Political Theory*. Princeton, NJ: Princeton University Press, 1996.

Papageorgiou, Kostas. "Ισότητα και Δημοκρατία" [Equality and democracy]. In *Δικαιοσύνη και Δίκαιο* [Justice and law], edited by Stavros Zouboulakis, 477–92. Athens: Artos Zois, 2015.

Petkas, Petros. *Δικτατορία του Προλεταριάτου και Εργατικά Συμβούλια: Δυο Ασύμβατες Έννοιες* [Dictatorship of the proletariat and workers' councils: Two incompatible concepts]. Thessaloniki: Ekdoseis Panoptiko, 2014.

Rancière, Jacques. *Hatred of Democracy*. London: Verso, 2014.

———. *On the Shores of Politics*. London: Verso, 2007.

Resolution of the Popular Assembly of Syntagma Square, May 28, 2011.

Rocamadur. "The 'Indignados' Movement in Greece." *SIC: International Journal for Communization* no. 1 (2011): 75–193.

Sakellaropoulos, Spiros. *Κρίση και Κοινωνική Διαστρωμάτωση στην Ελλάδα του 21ου Αιώνα* [Crisis and social stratification in twenty-first-century Greece]. Athens: Ekdoseis Topos, 2014.

Sotirakopoulos, Nikos, and George Sotiropoulos. "Direct Democracy Now! The Greek Indignados and the Present Cycle of Struggles." *Current Sociology* 61, no. 4 (July 2013): 443–56.

Traverso, Enzo. *Fire and Blood: The European Civil War, 1914–1945.* London: Verso, 2016.

Woland (Blaumachen and friends). "The Rise of the (Non-)Subject." *libcom.org*, February 28, 2012. https://libcom.org/library/rise-non-subject.

FIVE

Crisis, State, and Violence:
The Example of Greece

Panagiotis Doulos

1

"A sinking ship."[1] With this expression, Greek prime minister Giorgos Papandreou announced, in April 2010, the beginning of the "guardianship" of the Greek state by the so-called Troika, the mechanism composed of the International Monetary Fund, the European Commission, and the European Central Bank. At that moment, the Greek state was unable to obtain a loan from the markets in order to cover its financial needs and found itself at risk of defaulting. Dominant discourses presented the Greek crisis as unrelated to the 2008 world financial crisis, a problem affecting only the Greek people, a result of state corruption and incompetence, as well as a "cultural" issue.[2] Thus, an image of the Greeks was constructed that depicted them as untrustworthy, irresponsible individuals who did not work enough and lived beyond their means. The debt became an inescapable condition with a moral foundation, like a mistake that acquires the form of individualized guilt. As Katerina Nasioka points out:

> The Greeks are portrayed as the weak link in the European chain, a lazy, backward, and unlawful nation that has, for years, been borrowing money without putting in the necessary amount of work. Now, they are being called to pay for their mistakes or for the mistakes of their corrupt politicians.... According to neoliberal theory, the crisis can be "solved" through onerous economic measures and sacrifices made by the citizens for the salvation of the country, the

banks, and the prevailing financial system, with the acceptance of memorandums that dictate the privatization of everything that belongs to the common sphere and, of course, the continuance of the loans, the debts, and the dependence. However, the result of this measure is mainly to enlarge the "dangerous classes" and destabilize the system even more, for capital must not only secure the preconditions for its perpetual reproduction but also establish the legitimization of capitalist relations. (Nasioka 2012: 116)

The medicine prescribed during the debt crisis as the only solution for this "malady" was austerity.[3] With the signing of the first Memorandum of Understanding—the agreement on the package of austerity measures—the Greek state obtained an eighty-billion-euro loan in order to fulfill its obligations; the agreement included measures that had to be enforced as a precondition for the country's salvation, such as the reduction of the social state and the restructuring of social relations. The result was a massive attack on social and labor rights. The reforms imposed by the memorandums went hand in hand with the "law and order" doctrine. As Werner Bonefeld (2006: 252) points out, "Obedience to law, order and constitution is not sufficient—one is now also required to love them." In this context, the appearance of the strong state was a necessary condition for the implementation of neoliberal policies or, even better, for the intensification of capital's aggressiveness. The divisions that existed within the working class at that moment were crucial in constructing social consent and the acceptance of "necessary reforms." Strategies such as moral panic or the massive channeling of guilt and fear were deployed to create social division and demoralize the working-class struggles. That is why labor reforms were not implemented at once, but occurred gradually and were increasingly focused on specific groups. Thus, the rights of the workers were suddenly perceived as "privileges," as in the case of public servants, who were considered more "protected" and linked to party corruption. At the same time, social and anticapitalist movements were often characterized as terrorist. The zero-tolerance doctrine was imposed, accompanied by discourses on "lawlessness." The implementation of austerity policies went hand in hand with the rise of state repression.

Local resistance—such as the struggle in Skouries, in the northern Greek region of Halkidiki, against a gold mining corporation operating in the area—was met with harsh direct and indirect repression and was often portrayed by the Greek state as an act of terrorism or crime. The criminalization of the antiauthoritarian sphere was also a common practice of that period. A characteristic example is that of anarchist Tasos Theofilou, accused of robbing a bank on the island of Paros in August 2012 and of participating in armed organization Conspiracy of Fire Cells (Συνομωσία Πυρήνων της Φωτιάς).[4] The fact that he was an anarchist was enough for the judicial authorities—on demand of the district attorney—to consider him guilty, even if the evidence proved he had not been present at the crime scene. Furthermore, self-managed and antiauthoritarian endeavors, such as the Villa Amalia squat,[5] were described as centers of lawlessness and were violently evicted. Anti-austerity struggles were also dealt with similarly and faced state repression. The concept of debt crisis was a pathogenic symptom of Greek society, and the reforms introduced were the remedy. Any social resistance was portrayed as the face of this malady so that state violence could be justified.

It is no coincidence that protests were met with increasing aggressiveness by the police special forces and the power apparatus: this rise was directly related to the aggressiveness of the violent reforms the state was trying to impose upon society.[6] If, in times of crisis, the state exists in a *state of emergency*,[7] then "the law of necessity is the law of violence—it imposes order with the force of law, so that the rule of law can be applied again, once the emergency is over" (Bonefeld 2006: 249). State violence itself is the violence that legitimizes its mode of existence and, as Walter Benjamin points out, "The tradition of the oppressed teaches us that the 'state of emergency' in which we live, is not the exception but the rule. We must attain to a conception of history that is in keeping with this insight" (Bonefeld 2006: 247).

But how do we perceive crisis? In Goethe's *Faust*, Mephistopheles (cited in Bartra 2016: 51) says, "Who hath the power, has still the right; The What is asked for, not the How. Else know I not the seaman's art: War, commerce, piracy, I trow, a trinity we may not part." How do we understand this testimony by Mephistopheles and its relation to capitalism and crisis?

First, thinking of crisis as anomaly means we find normality in capitalism. In other words, crisis as anomaly acquires the form of an exception, a temporary disease that must be overcome so that we can return to normality or, more specifically, to a healthy condition. But if crisis lies at the center of capitalist relations as a "chronic disease," what we perceive as "crisis" is no more than the intensification of capital's aggressiveness. That is a constant crisis with intensities and multiple manifestations that express the core of the unreality of capitalist society: in this contradictory and antagonistic society, what is considered normal is no more than the expression of an *abstract violence*,[8] which is present at all levels of every-day life in a society characterized by general injustice and exploitation. Crisis is not an anomaly in capitalism's operation, but rather the form of exception as the norm. Piracy, war, and commerce express the logic and the brutality of the capitalist world.

Second, as an extension of the 2008 crisis, the debt crisis was a field for the reconfiguration and reterritorialization of social relations. Its appear-ance as pathogenic and as a matter of individualized responsibility went hand in hand with the idea that sacrifice was necessary and conducted in the name of the common good. Austerity was the price individuals had to pay for their sins. Six years on, the results of these policies can be seen in the incessant increase in unemployment rates and the drastic decrease in the minimum wage. Therefore, the employers were the only ones favored by the labor reforms. The debt crisis allowed for the implementation of a new area of disciplines on the social body. It was not only about the reduc-tion of "labor costs" in order to impose the "increase in competitiveness," but also about the reconfiguration of the disciplined body of the workers. Although control, as Gilles Deleuze mentions in his *Societies of Control* (1992), is the new form that will characterize today's societies, what we see is that present-day capitalism operates on the basis of the violent and dialectic circuit between discipline and control, where "man is no longer man enclosed, but man in debt" (ibid.: 6).

The memorandum programs demanded the reduction of the social state. Sectors such as public health care and other social services had to reduce their operational costs, leading to a decrease in the living stand-ards of the poorest social strata. The words of Neil Whitehead (2011) take on a real existence: "We will all become part of Marx's 'disposable indus-trial reserve army,' with eroding economic resources, dwindling legal status, no enforceable human rights, [and] become merely 'killable bodies' as Giorgio Agamben terms it." In fact, the dominant discourse during the first years of crisis, according to which we all had to make sacrifices for the good of the nation, translated into the poor and the workers having to sacrifice themselves. A state of emergency was activated in the name of debt, leading to a reduction of labor, human, and social rights. In this context, the existence of human beings serves to satisfy the needs and desires of the capitalist economy. The money form is more important than the value of human life. In the capitalist world, the freedom of the markets turns into the *absolute spirit* and expression of individual freedom. The individual must be the abstract representative of the impersonal laws of the market. The *solitary subject* is always the only one responsible for the insult (hubris) committed for not having been able to adequately follow the routes that the market gods had defined as normality: everyone is equal in the face of property and general inequality. This precept constructs a locus of discourse in which the subject's compliance to the "realism" of the logic of capital is compulsory. When *lines of escape* from this captivity emerge, the power of the state is there to remind the subjects of their obligations.

Furthermore, the media adopted and reproduced the discourse on the necessity of the reforms, justifying the aggressiveness and violence of the state. In their narrative, austerity equaled the salvation of the country, which was always linked to the salvation of the banking system, the increase in competitiveness and discipline, and the reduction of "labor costs" and the social state. If, as Karl Marx said (1994: vi), "in every epoch the stability of the state power signified Moses and the prophets to the entire money market and to the priests of this money market," why should it be any different today? If one followed (and still follows) the media during the period of the Greek crisis, one would observe that the markets are presented as abstract forces with a will of their own. As other gods, when they are destabilized, they demand restoration. According to this logic, anti-austerity protests gave the country a bad name and constituted a violation of human rights; that is, they defended personal interests against the good of the country.

An important element that completed the puzzle was the growth and consolidation of neo-Nazi party Golden Dawn during the first years of crisis. As a consequence, the police displayed tolerance toward increasing attacks against immigrants, homosexuals, social activists, and so on. It is no coincidence that half the police force voted for the neo-Nazi party (Lambropoulos 2012). The Golden Dawn groups were also directly or indirectly supported by the media. The violence of state power and the violence of said groups are, in fact, indistinguishable. For example, in the pogrom against immigrants that took place in the center of Athens in May

2011[9] (TVXS, 2011) the violence of the logic of "collective responsibility" and "social cleansing" is justified on the pretext of avenging the assassination of a Greek man by immigrants. In October 2012, while the police were torturing protesters who had participated in an antifascist demonstration, the police spokesperson declared, "There is no doubt that the Greek police always respect human rights and don't use violence" (Margaronis 2012). Yet torture within police stations with the blessing of democracy is nothing new or exceptional. On the contrary, it is the expression of the strong state whenever the establishment of "law and order" in favor of capitalist normality is deemed necessary.

As we can see, the state crystallizes capital's aggressiveness and transforms its interests into universal interests. According to Deleuze and Guattari (2004: 512), "In principle, all States are isomorphic; in other words, they are domains of realization of capital as a function of a sole external world market." The Greek example does not escape this condition. The intensification of capital's aggressiveness could not take place without the mediation of the state apparatus. If the reformations and reterritorializations of social relations are processes of their renormalization, these processes are violent and have multiple expressions. Thus, the objective of austerity was the intensification of the exploitation of the labor force and the constitution of an order through the establishment of a social discipline that does not doubt capitalist brutality. According to Bonefeld, "Every liberal constitution entails the real possibility that the class antagonism between capital and labour is reproduced within the state, that is, the very institution charged with codifying and regulating bourgeois interests as universal human interests" (2006, 239). At any given moment, the solitary subject must satisfy the voracious appetite of the markets, which appear as abstract and invisible entities. Furthermore, the appearance of capital as universal consciousness is not only the expression of an idiocy in which the poor are the only ones to blame for their catastrophes; it is the language of a world that mystifies its existence in order to legitimize its violence. The words tweeted in 2012 by Adonis Georgiadis, then minister of the right-wing government, reveals this honest idiocy: "Those who do not adapt, die" (Hatzinikolaou 2012).

It is no coincidence that the debt crisis acquired the characteristics of national and individual guilt. And it is no coincidence that neoliberal and nationalist discourses coexisted harmoniously either. The construction of the image of an internal or external enemy determines the Other who must be "exterminated," metaphorically or not, in order to preserve oneself. Thus, the contradictions and antagonisms of oneself acquire the appearance of a neutralized and false homogeneity. The idea of the nation is the first example of this false appearance that allows for the unification of opposites in a way that the latter remain separated within the former. This paves the way for collective guilt aimed at the individual. The intensification of the capitalist crisis requires a false collective identity, an imaginary subject that must pay the price for its sins and be sacrificed for salvation. The subjects who do not accept this condition are classified as the Others who must disappear from the social map. In the years preceding the Syriza–Independent Greeks coalition government, we observed the construction of this type of narrative that linked nationalism to neoliberalism through the idea of national salvation and imposed the reforms and austerity policies of the memorandums: austerity is, at the same time, the guilt and the salvation of the country. This connection between divine punishment and salvation legitimizes the strong state.

During the first two austerity programs, the presence of the police in the streets of Athens became the norm. The "law and order" doctrine was linked to the freedom of the market. The first governments to support austerity collapsed. It became clear that the debt crisis resulted in the decline of the parties traditionally in power and in the rise of left-wing party Syriza. Before coming to power, Syriza adopted an anti-austerity and antineoliberal discourse. But what happened afterward? What changed after the Syriza government? What is the importance of its discourse on the state, democracy, and the markets? What is the importance of the referendum? And what does it mean to turn *Oxi* into *Nai*, No into Yes?

2

In the discourse of the Left, the state conserved its autonomy with regard to capital and the markets. Thus, neoliberalism appeared as the bad expression of capitalism, an expression that had to change so that there could be capitalism with a more human face. Importantly, there was also faith that representative democracy could beat the markets and austerity. Through this bizarre matrimony of Poulantzas and Keynes, Syriza declared the memorandum went against the country and its democratic institutions, while at the same time insisting it sought a solution within the Eurozone. Syriza believed democracy could change the neoliberal structure of the EU, at the heart of which Germany constituted a dominant voice and appeared as the source of all evil. Syriza's campaign promises had been to free the country from the memorandums, begin "real negotiations" on the debt, and implement policies that would allow for a fair development. In this sense, bourgeois democracy acquired the mystified form of the "voice of the people" that goes beyond the oligarchy of the markets. That is, "real democracy"—as the expression of the will of the people—and Reason were able to overcome the power of the markets, expressed in the institutions of the Troika and the memorandums.

In January 2015, Syriza won the elections with the catchphrase "hope is on the way" and formed a coalition government with right-wing party Independent Greeks (ANEL). But this hope never escaped the administrative logic of realpolitik. It is no coincidence that Syriza representatives stated that the proposals of the Greek government were realistic and reasonable and, for that reason, the government could attain a good agreement and commitment with the "Institutions," the name that simply replaced the "Troika." The agreement reached between the government and the Institutions in February 2015 was the first act to mark the distance between Syriza's campaign promises and its decisions, which did not break with the logic of austerity. At that moment, the government insisted the agreement was temporary—unlike the memorandums—and useful for attaining a final agreement that would put the country back on the track of development and provide a solution to the debt crisis.

The negotiations for a final agreement continued until June 28, 2015, the moment at which Prime Minister Alexis Tsipras called for a referendum on July 5 on the demands made by the Institutions, that is, the proposal made by Jean-Claude Juncker (2015). During the week preceding the referendum, the Greek state was on the verge of defaulting on its payments and was under a regime of capital controls: economic transactions were restricted, the banks were closed, and constraints were imposed on cash withdrawals. The discussions taking place in the streets of Greek cities had a taste of "strange happiness" but were also permeated by fear and anguish regarding the future. Long queues in front of ATMs,[10] the city frozen in a state of shock, intense debate: these are all parts of the pendulum that oscillated from hope to despair and back, and built up through the expectation of the great event of the referendum. This is the context in which the subject was convoked to decide on whether or not to accept the bailout package, the proposal of the Institutions. Meanwhile, in a delirious narrative, the media played on apocalyptic images of an impending catastrophe in case of a victory of Oxi (No). The result of Oxi was presented as a vote in favor of Grexit. But what could that mean? In the words of John Holloway (2015: 30):

> Grexit, the exit of Greece from the Eurozone, would probably make little difference. . . . Its merit would be to prolong and magnify the cry of No to the capitalist attack but, as a policy, its implications would be not so very different from those imposed through the negotiations. If Greece is to remain a capitalist society, and whether or not there is a default on the debt or part of it, it has to provide conditions that are attractive to capital, and that, almost certainly, includes introducing labor reforms, cutting back on the welfare state, reducing pensions, privatizing state-owned assets, and so on.

But in the narrations of Remain—those in favor of Nai, of Yes—exiting the euro equaled descending into hell. Namely, when one is left outside the magic world of money and its fetishized forms, the only promise left is that of a catastrophe of mythical proportions. Nai seemed to be the only path. The euro became linked to European identity and to Greece's permanence in the European Union.[11] If, according to Walter Benjamin (2005: 2), "capitalism is a purely cultic religion . . . and has no specific body of dogma," in this case the allegory between theology and economy at the level of the flow of discourses no longer seems so symbolic. Just as the great prophets once announced the world to come and the terror of an imminent catastrophe, so the different empiricists and representatives of the *voice of reason* in newspapers and television channels, priests of the economy defending the principle of reality, based their predictions on figures that always tasted like a promise. It is no coincidence that, when a strategy of power is presented as a one-way street, it is always followed by a narration that warns of a future biblical catastrophe. To hold on to power, the order of modern reason deploys the biblical ghosts whenever it considers it necessary, so that the forms of discipline and control acquire true existence. Consequently, although a change of currency would not mean exiting capitalism, this did not stop the emergence of a rhetoric that played against the backdrop of the metaphor of leaving Eden, warning of complete destruction if the Oxi were to win. The Greek example plainly shows that when the representatives of the bourgeois class tell us we must be realists, it is no more than a precept for our compulsory adjustment to the principle of reality in theological terms (IEK 2015).

On July 5, against this campaign of terror, the Oxi obtained 61.3 percent of the Greek vote. The majority of the "Greek people" rejected austerity. In theory, this result was a victory of democracy against all the threats of the media and the prophecies of an impending catastrophe. The prime minister, who based on his discourse on the power of democracy, had the right to reject a new memorandum of austerity. A week later, Oxi turned into Nai. The government accepted an austerity program that was worse than the one rejected the previous week. This decision was denounced as the outcome of EU blackmail, and many representatives of the foreign media spoke of a "coup d'état" against the Greek left-wing government (#ThisIsACoup).

The Greek government accepted the third austerity program and has, until now, enforced its demands. Once again, austerity is the only alternative. It makes no sense to debate whether this was an act of treason or the government was blackmailed and had no other option. In winning the second elections in September 2015, the "second government of the Left,"[12] with the slogan of "getting rid of the old, winning tomorrow," legitimized austerity as a decision of Greek society, in the sense that the latter *knew what it was voting for*. Once again, the reforms needed for the country to return to development justify state violence and are accompanied by references to the "Greek humanitarian crisis." This discourse allowed for the restoration of the order of representative democracy. Capitalist barbarity wears many masks. When Leviathan wears the mask of humanism, it is because he wants to satisfy capital's voracious appetite.

The failure of the "progressive" government reveals to us that the myth of a more humane capitalism passes through the ideology of the autonomy of the bourgeois state and the strength of representative democracy. In fact, the "New Left," such as Syriza and Podemos, is no more than a neo-Keynesian logic with a Marxist cliché. Marx would never have imagined a minister of finance quoting the third volume of *Capital* to justify austerity policies. If "austerity is being used as a cover-story for class war against the poor," according to self-proclaimed erratic Marxist and former minister of finance Yanis Varoufakis, the Syriza government applies every letter of the memorandums as another form of "class war" (Stone 2015).[13]

The referendum was a "false" dilemma that marked the end of democratic illusions. In this sense, all dilemmas posed by the state are "false" dilemmas, for each result and proposal must legitimize the logic of capital and not the opposite. The referendum was a vote for the sake of voting, a formal dilemma aimed at helping the government in its negotiations with the Institutions, in which the subjects had to vote on accepting or rejecting a proposal that, at that point, was no longer on the table.[14] Regardless the outcome, the referendum could not change material conditions for the lower classes. "If elections could change the world, they would be illegal," reads a spray-painted slogan on a wall of the neighborhood of Exarchia,[15] famous for the activity of antiauthoritarian and anticapitalist groups. There can be no bourgeois state outside the logic of capital; more specifically, the administrative logic of representative democracy is the other side of the logic of capital. But even if the value of the referendum was a symbolic one, what are the real consequences and importance of this symbolic dimension?

The importance of Oxi lies in the denial of terror and in the nonlegitimization of austerity. Certainly, Oxi was not a homogeneous scream.[16] On the contrary, it was a heterogeneous scream that did not necessarily reject the core of capitalist relations. This heterogeneity is revealed by its scope, from its nationalist dimensions to the perspectives of resistance against the world of markets and capitalism. But in the cynical world of capitalist realism, the Nai would confirm the total acceptance of the order of compulsory adaptation. Also, the Oxi revealed democracy cannot be a vessel of radical change. On the contrary, democracy exists to preserve things as they are. When the phantom of popular will and the majority acquire a voice, state power translates it in favor of capitalist interests; the transformation of Oxi into Nai expressed this aspect of capitalist society. Yet the Oxi constructed a memory that does not only reject the legitimization of austerity, but also that of bourgeois democracy. It is a memory that speaks of dignity. Certainly, the Oxi was not an expression of hope in radical change, but it was a moment of dignity and of not saying yes to everything.

3

The failure of progressive governments is the failure of an ideology that distinguishes between a good and a bad capitalism, and the failure of the logic of the power of the "people" as an abstract phantom of representative democracies. The absurd thought that there can be a good state or a good capitalism ignores the fact that in capitalism the state is a bourgeois state. That is, it presumes the existence of "good" states that would be democratic in the context of a humane capitalism. But what could follow the end of illusions? Or, better, is this the end of illusions? After the experience of the referendum, Greece seems to have sunk into a massive depression. Realism in its total form is the discourse that there is no alternative, that capitalism is the only possible horizon. Discourses on changing the world, or even aspects of it, are presented as childish, irresponsible dreams. But the other side of despair is the birth of a new illusion, such as DiEM25,[17] or the rebirth of an old nightmare, such as the rise of nationalism in Europe. In the first case, realism returns under the guise of a systemic Left.

In his article "The Courage of Hopelessness," Slavoj Žižek (2015) shows us that "true courage is not to imagine an alternative, but to accept the consequences of the fact that there is no clearly discernible alternative: the dream of an alternative is a sign of theoretical cowardice." According to this logic of alternative realism, "grassroots self-organization cannot replace the state, and the question is how to reorganize the state apparatus to make it function differently. . . . We are thus brought to demand more than just political democracy: the democratization of social and economic life too" (ibid.). It is not surprising that Žižek invites us to remain *trapped in a new dream*, the democratization of the institutions and the demand for more transparency. In the DiEM25 manifesto (2016), the key phrase is a "surge of democracy"; the ultimate demand, to "democratize Europe." But in this type of "movement"—quite in vogue right now—the dominant identity of the modern world is not challenged. "Democracy is the identity between the rulers and the ruled, regardless of the means through which this identity is obtained" (Comité Invisible 2014: 70) and, by extension, the identitarian classifications of the mode of capitalist production.

If one of the forms of the fetishization of social relations that constructs the myth of the modern world is the separation between the spheres of the political and the economic, dreams of a fair capitalism through its democratization are more than an illusion. In fact, they imply a different form of realism and of disciplining the social body, insofar as they do not deny the core elements of capitalist brutality, but instead assert them. These narratives renaturalize exploitation and oppression and shift the weight of the problem from capitalism to a specific form of its aggressiveness. The separation between good and bad capitalism, along with a longing for the "good old" welfare state, propose a new reterritorialization of the subject within capitalist normality. Thus, capitalist violence is relegitimized through embracing an alternative and progressive realism. In other words, these logics confirm that everything will be fine if we give a human makeover to the "capitalist hydra," to use the term of the Zapatistas (EZLN 2015).

On the other hand, the rebirth of the nationalist ghosts of the past has reactivated "old" nightmares. The growth of nationalist parties in Europe's parliaments reveals this tendency. Under the pretext of the refugee crisis and the "war on terrorism," the fabrication of new external enemies and the generalized control of the populations that this entails are justified through the state of exception. Immigrants and refugees must be detained and kept invisible in "reception centers" for their own "safety," thus turning into *naked lives*. On the Greek islands, the tombs of refugees and migrants with the epitaph of "anonymous" express the form and value of human life within capitalism: disposable bodies without the stamp of the individual, without a name or a "true existence." Those who manage to survive the dumping site of the Aegean Sea face imprisonment in "reception centers," being treated as human garbage or turned into a new form of a naked labor force on European soil. These bodies are the norm of this world, not the exception: the statistics of the "humanitarian crisis," an administrative problem that reveals the inhumanity of the capitalist machine.

Xenophobic discourses construct the image of the Other as an external threat to the identity of the "European"; to this end, they reassert the need to preserve the order in times of economic crisis. The operation of the capitalist economy is accompanied by racism, with the dystopias of the present always echoing those of the past. In the name of safety, law and order, and the preservation of European values, the discourses of the high priests of the economy meet the nationalist voices that defend the state in a state of emergency. In the administrative logic of the strong state, subjects have the obligation to participate in capitalist normality. In this case, the ideological facade of the state serves only to paint the same brutality with different colors. The real negation of capitalist brutality is a crime, given that people are "reduced to walk-on parts in a monster documentary film which has no spectators, since the least of them has his bit to do on the screen" (Adorno 2005: 55). In times of crisis, the aggressiveness of capital and state violence are intensified. The television screens flood us with images of new threats, enemies, and diseases in order to confirm the permanent state of exception as a divine fact, one that the subject must accept and never challenge.

The movements that reject this type of logic turn into the enemy within. The eviction, in August 2016, of three squats operating in solidarity with refugees in Thessaloniki is a clear example of this (Karyotis 2016). The promise of terror can always have many faces. The capitalist hydra is there to remind us that brutality can appear in multiple forms. If we do not want to be part of this "monstrous documentary," the question is how to open paths with our negations, paths that do not reproduce the nightmare of the angel of history and allow us to look at the future instead of the storms of the past.

Conclusion

Crisis is inherent in capitalism, not a glitch in its operation. What appears to be a crisis of capitalism is no more than the intensification of state violence and capital's onslaught. In this context, the "storm" (EZLN 2015) is not a specific manifestation of capitalism, such as neoliberalism; rather, capitalism itself is a permanent storm with multiple intensities. When the capitalist machine is in crisis, social relations are violently reformed and reterritorialized so that there can be a return to capitalist normality.

The grammar of capitalist brutality turns this world upside down, and its words demand we gladly accept our catastrophe. In capitalism, freedom is another word for death. In this sense, there is an antagonistic relation between the freedom of the markets and the freedom of humans. For most people, capital's prosperity amounts to poverty. The debt crisis appears as the responsibility of the subjects themselves, a responsibility to be assumed with sacrifice so as to attain salvation. Debt acquires a moral form, according to which the subjects are the only ones to blame for their catastrophe, while the memorandums appear as an inescapable destiny. The individualization of guilt is needed in Greece so that austerity policies can be presented as the only salvation. Neoliberalism and nationalism walk hand in hand, particularly during the first years of the Greek debt crisis. Guilt as divine retribution played an important role in the confirmation and legitimization of state power and its violence. The doctrines of "law and order" and "war on lawlessness" became materialized through the repression of anti-austerity struggles and anticapitalist movements, while social and labor reforms were presented as the only alternative, as *salvation*.

Syriza's promise of being the "hope [that] is on the way," as well as its pledge to avoid memorandums, never escaped the logic of realpolitik. The failure of the "first government of the Left" is the failure of a logic that does not reject capital but rather asserts it. In other words, it is the failure of the promise of a more humane capitalism and of the promise that representative democracy can defeat the impersonal forces of the market. But should we speak of failure or treason? As Edith González Cruz (2016: 6) points out: "The examples of Greece and of the so-called end of the cycle of progressive governments in Latin America show that the democratic state itself does not break with the logic of capital accumulation but rather maintains and guarantees it and, in some cases—when the Left wins—even manages to pass reforms the Right was not able to pass. Capitalism is annihilating us."

Indeed, in the administrative logic of representative democracy, the other side of the logic of capital, the state's ideological guise is of no importance; what matters is its efficiency in guaranteeing and reproducing capitalist normality. If the Greek experience is but a moment in the constant crisis of capitalism, one question that comes to mind has to do with the subject of the crisis. John Holloway's proposal (2016) that "we are the crisis of capital" is right,[18] in the sense that capital depends on our doing and on our discipline. However, at the same time, we must think of how to become the force that will destroy the production of the capitalist continuum and terror. If the example of Greece teaches us that the state is not part of the solution, we must invent a new hope beyond the state and capital. That means, paraphrasing Friedrich Nietzsche, that critical thought must encounter our *doing*, in Holloway's terms, in an act of chaos and entropy that will give birth to a star that dances against capitalist brutality. Our chaos and entropy constitute the movement against the capitalist order and its borders, the negation and destruction of the images and effigies of what is not real in this world, our capacity to construct a different type of social organization, one without exploitation and inequality.

In this context, the idea of a "Plan C" deployed by Theodoros Karyotis in his contribution to this book seems to me a different way of talking about a program. I find it difficult to imagine practices such as self-organization as a program. Self-organization, rather, reveals our capacity to think of a different social organization. The idea of a "Plan" can also reduce social resistances to an issue of strategy and, thus, trap them within an instrumental logic where social movements become something programmed. In a recent article, Raúl Zibechi (2017) quotes and applauds the Leninist aphorism that "revolution does not happen, it is organized" and goes on to add emphatically: "regardless of one's opinion of the Russian leader, this decision is the core of any revolutionary struggle." Can we really distinguish between these two moments, that is, between the revolutionary act itself and its planning? Can we identify the Zapatistas or antiauthoritarian movements with a "Plan"? No. I believe the logic of the "Plan" reduces them to something they are not and does not reveal their potential of existing against and beyond capitalism. The concept of a "Plan" seems like a different instrumental form of alternative realism and functionalism. The danger of the "Plan C" narrative is that it can be considered the only realistic proposal in the face of the ineffectiveness of "Plans A," "B," or "X," and so on. But autonomous movements go beyond a simple temporary proposal to the capitalist crisis. This is what distinguishes them from "Plan A" or "Plan B," which are mere strategies for the return to a fairer capitalism. According to this kind of logic, crisis is something temporary that can be resolved. We cannot place demands for the restoration of a capitalist order with a human face in the same cadre as the movements that reject capitalism and want to destroy it in its totality. For the latter, capitalism is not in crisis; capitalism *is* crisis. Grassroots movements are a constant and contradictory creation of spaces and times against and beyond the logic of capital and the state, but they do not have a ready recipe for revolution.

In conclusion, the question is not how to embellish the capitalist hydra so that it appears more fair and humane; it is how to open, through our negations and entropies, paths toward the annihilation of the nightmares of the angel of history. In terms of Benjamin (1973), this means that we cannot wait for any Messiah to save us from the impending storm; we can become the true state of exception against the permanent state of exception. The storm is here, now. This is the challenge.

Notes

1   On the announcement of Giorgos Papandreou and its symbolism, see the chapter in this book by Leonidas Oikonomakis.
2   On the 2008 crisis and its shifts, see the chapters in this book by Katerina Nasioka and John Holloway.
3   For the relation between crisis and pathogenesis, see Lynteris, 2011.
4   As Tasos Theofilou himself points out (*athensindymedia*, January 24, 2016), the trial was a parody. Although the evidence of the robbery and his participation in the Conspiracy of Fire Cells were constructed and contradictory, Theofilou was sentenced to twenty-five years in prison for robbery and acquitted on charges of participation in the Conspiracy of Fire Cells. This last decision was appealed, however, and criminal proceedings are ongoing.

5   Villa Amalia was an antiauthoritarian squat with self-organizational traits in the center of Athens, in existence since the 1990s. On the squats in the center of Athens, see Katerina Nasioka (2017).

6   In fact, there is no separating the aggressiveness of the police from the aggressiveness of the violent reforms. The dramatic decrease in minimum wages and all social and labor rights reforms were part of the violent and "necessary reforms" made in the name of emergency. If the bourgeois state must be efficient in order to guarantee the reproduction of capitalist relations, the intensification of capital's aggressiveness implies the intensification of the aggressiveness of state violence. That is, the state must impose social discipline against social struggles in order to guarantee capital accumulation. In this sense, we must not only look at the forms of aggressiveness of capital and the state but also at the struggles against said forms.

7   In *Homo Sacer* (1998) and *State of Exception* (2005), Giorgio Agamben tries to trace Walter Benjamin's thought on *exception as the rule* and its relation to sovereignty, law, and violence; that is, how domination has the divine right to decide who lives and who does not. Agamben analyzes Benjamin's work through Foucauldian categories such as biopolitics and biopower to resolve the theme subjects: the relation between law, exception, and life. Indeed, in this analysis, the sovereign is in a permanent state of exception and lawlessness, in a relation within and outside the law.

8   On abstract violence, see Žižek (2008: chapter 1).

9   On the pogrom against immigrants in the center of Athens, see the chapter in this book by Dimitra Kotouza.

10 The "storm" of images of enormous queues in front of cash machines presented by the media were, undoubtedly, more dramatic than what was really going on in the streets of Athens.

11 We must not forget that the Eurozone and the European Union are not the same. A country can be a member of the European Union without belonging to the Eurozone. Being a member of the Eurozone means adopting the euro as the country's official currency. The United Kingdom, for example, was able to be an EU member state without being part of the Eurozone.

12 When Syriza won the elections in January 2015, it adopted the phrase "first government of the Left." In this context, "second government of the Left" is ironical, following Syriza's triumph in the second national elections and the enforcement of the third memorandum. On this phrase, see the chapter by Leonidas Oikonomakis in this book.

13 The notion of "class war" that is found in Greek anarchist and autonomist pamphlets expresses the conflicted character of class struggle, which in orthodox Marxist terms appears as a determinist and mechanical movement. Following his resignation as minister of finance, Yanis Varoufakis used this same term to criticize austerity policies. For Varoufakis, however, the dynamic of this notion is not the same. As Vasilis Grollios (2016) points out, Varoufakis, as an erratic Marxist, perceives Marx's work as an economic theory and not a critique of political economy, resulting in a positivization of Marx's critique.

In consequence, it reduces Marx's critique to an instrumental logic trapped in capitalist normality.

14 On June 29, 2015, the European Commission withdrew its proposal. Therefore, the Greeks had to vote on a proposal that was no longer valid. Meanwhile, the Commission backed the Nai, using the phrase "Greece is Europe, Europe is Greece" (*I Eláda íne Evrópi, i Evrópi íne Eláda*) and, at the same time, different scenarios were created in relation to the Oxi and the exit of Greece from the Eurozone.

15 On the neighborhood of Exarchia, see Katerina Nasioka 2017.

16 On the concept of the scream, see Holloway 2002.

17 DiEM25, the Democracy in Europe Movement 2025 is a European political movement (party) founded on the initiative of Yanis Varoufakis that launched officially on February 9, 2016. On this, see https://diem25.org.—Translator's note.

18 In words of the author (2016): "We are the crisis of capital, we who say *No*, we who say *Enough of capitalism!*, we who say that it is time to stop creating capital, time to create another way of living. Capital depends on us, because if we do not create profit (surplus value) directly or indirectly, then capital cannot exist. We create capital and if capital is in crisis, it is because we are not creating the profit necessary for capital's existence: that is why they are attacking us with such violence."

References

Adorno, Theodor W. *Minima Moralia: Reflections on a Damaged Life*. London: Verso, 2005.

Agamben, Giorgio. *Homo Sacer: Sovereign Power and Bare Life*. Stanford: Stanford University Press, 1998.

———. *State of Exception*. Chicago: University of Chicago Press, 2005.

Bartra, Armando. *Goethe y despojo. Los costos del progreso, el sur, la incertidumbre, los demonios*. Mexico City: UAM-X, CSH, 2016.

Benjamin, Walter. "Capitalism as Religion [Fragment 74]." In *Religion as Critique: The Frankfurt School's Critique of Religion*, edited by Eduardo Mendieta, 259–62. New York: Routledge, 2005.

———. "Theses on the Philosophy of History." In *Illuminations*. New York: Schocken Books, 1969.

Bonefeld, Werner. "Democracy and Dictatorship: Means and Ends of the State." *Critique* 34, no. 3 (December 2006): 237–52.

Comité Invisible. *A nuestros amigos*, 2014. http://lhblog.nuevaradio.org/b2-img/A.nuestros.amigos2014.pdf.

Deleuze, Gilles, and Félix Guattari. *A Thousand Plateaus: Capitalism and Schizophrenia*. London: Continuum, 2004.

———. "Postscript on the Societies of Control." *October* 59 (Winter 1992): 3–7. https://cidadeinseguranca.files.wordpress.com/2012/02/deleuze_control.pdf.

DiEM25. "A Manifesto for Democratising Europe," 2016. https://diem25.org/manifesto-short-version/.

EZLN. *Critical Thought versus the Capitalist Hydra I: Contributions by the Sixth Commission of the EZLN*, 2016.

González Cruz, Edith. "¿El fin de las ilusiones electorales?" Presentation at *Segundo Congreso de Estudios Mesoamericanos*, June 27–30, 2016, Quetzaltenango, Guatemala.

Grollios, Vasilis. "Syriza's Delusions and the Nihilism of Bourgeois Culture." *Constellations* 23, no. 3 (September 2016): 404–12.

Hatzinikolaou, Nikos, "Άδωνις: Όποιος δεν προσαρμόζεται πεθαίνει" [Adonis: Those who do not adapt, die]. *Enikos*, November 30, 2012. http://www.enikos. gr/politics/101186,AdwnisOpoios-den-prosarmozetai-pe8ainei.html.

Holloway, John. *Change the World without Taking Power*. London: Pluto Press, 2002.

———. "Critical Thought versus the Capitalist Hydra." In EZLN. *Critical Thought versus the Capitalist Hydra I: Contributions by the Sixth Commission of the EZLN*. Durham, NC: PaperBoat Press, 2016.

———. "NO, NO, NO." *ROAR Magazine* no. 0 (2015). https://roarmag.org/wp-content/ uploads/2015/12/ROAR-Issue-0.pdf.

Institute of Research and Destruction (Ινστιτούτο Έρευνας και Καταστροφής, IEK), "Σκέψεις και σημειώσεις πάνω στην αρχή της πραγματικότητας και τις νέες μορφές μαγείας" [Thoughts and notes on the principle of reality and the new forms of magic]. *IEK*, June 26, 2015. http://iek.espivblogs.net/2015/06/26/ σκέψεις-και-σημειώσεις-πάνω-στην-αρχή/.

Juncker, Jean-Claude. Transcript of President Jean-Claude Juncker's press conference on Greece, July 29, 2015. http://europa.eu/rapid/press-release_SPEECH-15-5274_en.htm.

Karyotis, Theodoros. "Criminalizando la solidaridad: La guerra del Estado griego contra los movimientos de base." *Diagonal*, August 4, 2016. https://www. diagonalperiodico.net/global/31129-criminalizando-la-solidaridad-la-guerra-del-estado-griego-contra-movimientos-base.html.

Lambropoulos, Vassilis G. "Ένας στους δύο αστυνομικούς ψήφισαν 'Χρυσή Αυγή'" [One in two policemen voted for "Golden Dawn"]. *To Vima*, May 11, 2012. http:// www.tovima.gr/afieromata/elections2012/article/?aid=457088.

Lynteris, Christos. "The Greek Economic Crisis as Eventual Substitution." In *Revolt and Crisis in Greece*, edited by Dimitris Dalakoglou and Antonis Vradis, 207–13. Oakland: AK Press, 2011.

Margaronis, Maria. "Greek Anti-fascist Protesters 'Tortured by Police' after Golden Dawn Clash." *Guardian*, October 9, 2012. https://www.theguardian. com/world/2012/oct/09/greek-antifascist-protesters-torture-police?CMP=twt.

Marx, Karl. *The Eighteenth Brumaire of Louis Bonaparte*. New York: International Publishers, 1994.

Nasioka, Katerina. *Ciudades en Insurrección. Oaxaca 2006/Atenas 2008*. Guadalajara: Cátedra Interinstitucional-Universidad de Guadalajara-CIESAS-Jorge Alonso, 2017.

Nietzsche, Friedrich. *Thus Spoke Zarathustra*. New York: Cambridge University Press, 2006.

Stone, Jon. "Austerity Is Being Used as a Cover-Story for Class War against the Poor, Yanis Varoufakis Says." *Independent*, September 25, 2015. http://www.

independent.co.uk/news/uk/politics/austerity-is-being-used-as-a-cover-story-for-class-war-against-the-poor-yanis-varoufakis-says-10516247.html.

Theofilou, Tasos, "Για το εφετείο μου στις 24 Φλεβάρη» [On my court of appeal on January 24, 2016]. *Athens Indymedia*. https://athens.indymedia.org/post/1554547/.

TVXS. "Πογκρόμ κατά μεταναστών στο κέντρο της Αθήνας" [Pogrom against immigrants in the center of Athens]. *TVXS*, May 12, 2011.

Whitehead, Neil L. "The Divine Hunger: The Cannibal War Machine." *Counterpunch*, July 1, 2011. http://www.counterpunch.org/2011/07/01/the-cannibal-war-machine/.

Zibechi, Raúl. "El poder de abajo." *La Jornada*, January 6, 2017. http://www.jornada.unam.mx/2017/01/06/opinion/018a1pol.

Žižek, Slavoj. "The Courage of Hopelessness." *New Statesman*, July 20, 2015. http://www.newstatesman.com/world-affairs/2015/07/slavoj-i-ek-greece-courage-hopelessness.

———. *Violence: Six Sideways Reflections*. New York: Picador, 2008.

SIX

Whose Lives Matter? Nationalism, Antifascism, and the Relationship with Immigrants

Dimitra Kotouza

The contemporary sociopolitical context in Europe and North America of economic crisis, a refugee crisis, and the rise of popular "anti-establishment" nationalist, xenophobic, racist, and antidemocratic politics has intensified the urgency for analyzing the question of nationalism. The question of how and why such politics gain popularity has not yet led to enough self-critical discussion on the left. Nationalist and ethnocentric discourses in popular politics have often remained naturalized and invisible, through a desire to not alienate powerful popular feeling, and through a separation of a left nationalism of "class interests" from a "bad" far-right nationalism. The tradition of this nationalist form of thought and practice on the Left is very long, but in this crisis it has appropriated anti-imperialist, antiglobalization, antifinance, and antineoliberal discourses to oppose austerity as ostensibly originating from agents outside the nation-state. Antifascism has also often taken on a nationalist guise in recent years, mobilizing, most notably, on behalf of Russian nationalism in the Ukraine conflict, but also in references to the Second World War national resistance in Greece. A critique of these tendencies is not merely an argument for internationalism as an abstract principle, but also has an immediate material impact both upon the forms and outcomes of collective action and upon those excluded by it. This is what I aim to demonstrate here, using examples from the recent social movements in Greece.

The ethnocentric production of the dominant political subject in movements as a Greek national citizen against "foreign" political and economic influence was particularly evident in the period between 2010 and 2014, when movements against the restructuring and antifascist movements were at their strongest. I will begin by discussing the mobilizations of this period: the succession of the Movement of the Squares, the empowerment of Golden Dawn, antifascism, and these movements' relationship to immigrants' collective action. In doing so, I will highlight the theoretical and practical limits of the nation-centered response to imposed immiseration, in both its right- and left-wing manifestations. These are limits that have only been substantially challenged by immigrants' own battles for freedom of movement and against the racialized barriers to the means of subsistence. I conclude by discussing the relevance of these considerations for the present situation in Greece and elsewhere.

The Unity of the "People"

Despite the fact that the restructuring imposed in Greece since 2010 has been, above all, an attack on the direct and indirect wage, the dominant subject invoked in the high points of this period's movements (the Movement of the Squares, large demonstrations, antidevelopment movements, such as those of Keratea and Skouries, and most of the new neighborhood assemblies) tended to be a national one, which befitted the interclass composition of these movements. By early 2011, there was an escalation of violence in social confrontations, from the antipolice riots of Keratea against the opening of a landfill, to disruptions at national anniversary celebrations and personal assaults on politicians, to the increasingly confrontational (and heavily policed) demonstrations at Syntagma Square, until the climax of the February 12, 2012 riots. These antipolitical mobilizations reflected a crisis of representation, as well as a crisis of parliamentary politics. They were framed as a confrontation between the "people" or "citizens" and the representatives of the state who betrayed them by favoring national and international elites and giving up control to "foreign" agencies, such as the International Monetary Fund.[1]

The Movement of the Squares was one of the most significant episodes of this tendency. It began on May 25, 2011, only a few days after a four-day anti-immigrant pogrom orchestrated by Golden Dawn in the center of Athens to avenge the mugging and murder of a Greek man by, according to the police, three Afghan men.[2] The pogrom resulted in twenty-five hospitalizations and the murder of a young Bangladeshi man, Alim Abdul

Manan (TVXS 2011; Sunderland et al. 2012; Eleutherotypía 2014). The event was only mentioned by small minorities in the assemblies that took place at Syntagma Square, which was filled with Greek flags. The movement, like those before it, mobilized the subject of the Greek citizen or people toward the rejection of Greece's political system and the austerity contained in the midterm program of reforms. "Burn the parliament" was one of the most popular slogans in opposition to established politicians and foreign political and economic control over the country.

This antipolitical popular national unity was not straightforward, however. The takeover of the square was divided from the very beginning into an upper section, facing the parliament, and a lower section, which was the main part of the occupation. The division was already evident from the Facebook calls to join the protest. Some event pages, filled with Greek flags, were calling on all "indignant Greek citizens" to rise up,[3] while others, following the Spanish example, called on everyone to unite under the demand for "real democracy." The upper section was where nationalist organizations, such as the "300 Greeks," had set up stalls.[4] It tended to attract crowds with Greek flags, ultramasculine groups of young nationalists, and conspiracy theorists holding eccentric homemade banners. The lower section was where assemblies were held. This section was dominated by activists from the left and anarchist political scenes, who had hope that a "political fermentation" through discussion would generate new political subjectivities and unite the movement. Political affiliations were not openly revealed, because one of the founding rules was for the protest to be "partyless," "colorless" (in the sense of party color, not skin color), and "flagless" (with the exception of the Greek flag). Indeed, on the first day, even a union demonstration was driven out of the square as representing a certain kind of political "color." For the Right, this was in the name of national unity, while for anarchists and radical democrats this was an opportunity for building self-organization and direct democracy.

The "direct democratic" imaginary promoted a system of inclusive, bottom-up decision-making, self-organized resistance, and mutual support in neighborhoods and workplaces. It was captivated by the notion that a more "decent" life would be possible, if only the citizens had the political power. Indeed, the movement's practice of organizing, working, sharing, thinking, and even living together, for those who had set up tents in Syntagma Square, provided to many participants a sense of solidarity and hope that a lot could be achieved by finding others who were hit by the crisis. But the boundaries of the movement's self-organized practice against the social relations it opposed were perforated in many respects. Most importantly, it was able neither to recognize its internal divisions of class nor to challenge the racialized national boundaries presumed by its imaginary. Despite the left and anarchist class-based discourse in the assemblies, the calls for expanding self-organization into workplaces, and the eventual coordination with the general strikes called by the GSEE (Genikī Synomospondīa Ergatōn Elládos—General Confederation of Greek Workers), most of the movement's activity and composition was interclass. The dominant citizen-based, democratic discourse was intrinsic to this interclass character, explainable by the austerity measures' devastating effect on small businesses. Debates around the question "What is to be done?" were thus unable to refer to a common class experience, and the discourse of class conflict came up against the principle of national popular unity.

The imagined unity of national citizens organizing democratically against a failed system of government also meant that immigrants were excluded not just exceptionally by racist individuals but *by definition*, by the very concept of citizenship, except in the token action of inviting immigrants' organizations to speak and organize events for a day. It was then normal that Golden Dawn's pogrom was not discussed. The unspoken—but unambiguous—boundaries of the space were national and racial. Despite the active expulsion of violent racist groups from the occupation, the movement's definitional citizenship and common-sense nationalism was rarely challenged. The call for "direct democracy" and self-institution itself also appealed to national pride, with evocations of ancient Athens.[5] Again, the democracy, while direct, was also exclusive: it was the Greek citizens who were naturally presumed to be the participants.

The distinction between the lower and upper parts of the square was then blurred, particularly in the large demonstrations, where the national framing legitimized the expansion of antipolice violence beyond the usual young anarchist rioters: many people were rioting with Greek flags as weapons. The notion of a national popular unity that went "beyond politics" was the driving discursive undercurrent of the movement when it reached mass proportions, both in its upper and lower parts. This was, after all, not only a protest against the entire political system, but also against imperialism, harking back to the nationalism of the seventies movements but no longer under the hegemony of the labor movement. Under such conditions, anti-imperialist ethnocentrism was at risk of lapsing into something more worrying. Mikis Theodorakis, the eighty-something-year-old antidictatorship activist and composer of songs for that struggle, staged a rally at Propylea near Syntagma while it was occupied, and his supporters joined the square demonstration. The rally was massive, and his speech was indicative of broad tendencies already present: "Our national wealth," he warned, "will be taken over by 'Turks' and 'negroes from Tanganyika.'"

These tendencies provided a favorable environment for groups of "autonomous nationalists" to attempt to take part in the movement. Their temporary presence, demanding "jobs for Greek workers," and some violent attacks on immigrants by small groups of young men, took place in the context of a "popular" national unity, in which immigrant workers did not belong and could thus be considered a threat. This nationalist, racist tendency, while representing a minority in the square, would grow through this period up to 2014, as was most evident with the rising strength of Golden Dawn (Chrysī Augī) in the 2012 elections. Although the squares movement did not directly *instigate* this rise, it did reveal the strong appeal of nationalist discourse and patriotic direct action as forms of opposition to the restructuring.

Nationalism "from Below" Meets Neo-Nazi State-Backed Terror

These tendencies soon greatly exceeded what initially appeared as a productive polyphony or was dismissed as mere "common-sense patriotism." Concurrently, ultranationalist politics were gaining strength in the rest of Europe (the victories of UKIP and Front National in the 2014 EU elections, as well as the questioning of "multiculturalism" in light of the May 2013 riots in Sweden and the later empowerment of the Swedish Democrats). This fact placed the Greek situation in the context—if not at the edge, given its geographical location—of anti-immigration discourse in the EU more broadly. After the elections of May and June 2012, the radical wing of this nationalist tendency, which up to that point had been mainly visible through the presence of flags and patriotic slogans in demonstrations, was taken over, at least at the level of the spectacle, by a thuggish national socialist party, Golden Dawn, which entered the parliament for the first time with eighteen seats (6.92 percent). The formation of a three-party coalition government led by New Democracy (Nea Dimokratia) in one of its most far-right cabinet configurations, alongside the empowerment of Golden Dawn and the impressive advance of Syriza, which came second with 27 percent, brought an end to the succession of mass demonstrations that had culminated in the riots of February 12 (in which the antipolitical nationalist element was also present).[6]

The low election result of Golden Dawn in comparison to Syriza should not be interpreted as reflecting the marginality of racism in this period. In fact, in 2012 and 2013, Golden Dawn built massively upon extremely favorable media coverage and support from New Democracy leaders, opening party branches across Greece, recruiting plenty of new members, and establishing itself in third place in polls. The majority of its support came from young unemployed men (Georgiadou 2014), against the common assumption that this was a "petit bourgeois" phenomenon. This was phenomenal for a party whose main activities have been racist vigilantism, demanding the expulsion of all immigrants, venomous condemnation of "treasonous politicians," and delusional narratives about the superiority of the Greek "race." In this environment, it became commonplace for outrage against established politicians to come with racist anti-immigration discourse.

Even during the preelection period, however, it was clear that there was potential for such a development. The main political parties had decided to take advantage of the opportunities provided by the strengthening of popular nationalism by shifting their discourse toward openly racist anti-immigration statements and policies, in the name of the health and safety of citizens. Their attempt was partially successful, insofar as a government was formed on this basis, the succession of massive demonstrations was halted, and the dominant debate shifted to an old-style altercation between Left and Right reminiscent of the civil war over the question of fascism. The New Democracy–led government zealously pursued the line of citizens' health and security, with heavier policing and spectacular forms of social control against immigrants and those pushed to the gendered social margins of citizenship, such as sex workers and gay and noncisgender people, as well as those who were homeless or addicted to drugs. This was added to the heavy police repression of demonstrations, strikes, local grassroots campaigns, antifascists, anarchists, and the broader Left, whose patriotism was questioned. Police action was often accompanied and sometimes spearheaded by vigilante Golden Dawn attacks on immigrants and political opponents. With electoral empowerment and sympathizers within the government and mainstream media, Golden Dawn soon got away with another murder, that of Shehzad Luqman (Xynou 2013), an immigrant from Pakistan. The openly racist government only became concerned about Golden Dawn's lethal violence and began to prosecute the party's leaders when one of its members murdered a Greek man, the antifascist Pavlos Fyssas.[7] This, of course, did not put an end to racist state practices, and support for Golden Dawn has not fallen below 7 per cent since.

Antifascism, Anti-imperialism, and the Nation-State as a Limit

Antifascism was the broader Left's response to this far-right hijacking of popular nationalism, and it represented its change of attitude toward racism in comparison to the Movement of the Squares. Despite appearing as a diversion of aims, antifascism was also a fight against the restructuring, because of the way in which racism was blatantly cultivated by this period's governments as part of their strategy to control social discontent against austerity. While Golden Dawn presented itself as antirestructuring, in practice its gangs were systematically used by employers and landlords to terrorize Greek and immigrant workers who dared to protest and immigrant tenants who failed to pay rent. Golden Dawn's discourse diverted all discussion of the restructuring to forays against immigrants. Its long-running feud with the Left, as well as its history of strong connections with army and police leaderships and important sections of Greek capital (shipowners and shipbuilders), left no doubt as to the strategic importance of Golden Dawn for the continuation of the restructuring.

But although this turn to antifascism seemed finally to prioritize questions of racism and abuse against immigrants, the separation between antifascist and immigrants' own actions remained. Antifascism was, true to its name, a political fight against Golden Dawn, as opposed to a fight that was directly concerned with the immediate material interests and needs of immigrants. Antifascist actions were carried out almost exclusively by Greek activists, with the primary aim to obstruct Golden Dawn actions, to "invade" spaces dominated by the party, and to promote antifascist politics. Local antifascist actions encompassed demonstrations through areas where large immigrant populations were intimidated by Golden Dawn; festivals and open discussions; propaganda material; pressuring landlords not to rent to Golden Dawn; and "antifascist defense groups." The latter attempted to drive Golden Dawn gangs out of certain areas, by fighting them on the street and vandalizing their offices, shops, and the cafés they frequented.

It is clear that the antifascist movement did not prioritize the cultivation of direct links with immigrant communities. While the fight against Golden Dawn may have contributed to the creation of spaces where immigrants felt a little safer, this was done without much collaboration or discussion with immigrants themselves. Immigrants did not gain more say or more control over conditions in their neighborhoods, where they continued to be treated as visitors, as an alien body in a neighborhood controlled by its "real" (Greek) residents. The antifascist struggle was then mostly a fight among citizens over how to treat "foreign" noncitizens, who themselves remained voiceless and nameless.

Antifascism also often took a contradictory nationalist guise—but one not without historical precedent. The antifascist camp was diverse, consisting of the entire spectrum of the Greek Left, from social democratic and socialist parties (even including DIMAR, which was part of the government coalition until June 2013) to insurrectionist anarchists. Yet, in frequently deploying the history and historical political discourse of the classic division between Left and Right in Greece, it tended to produce a left unity around this tradition. Despite long-running divisions within this left spectrum over the issues of nationalism, statism, and democratism, the dominant antifascist discourse across this spectrum tended to draw analogies between the German occupation during the Second World War and German hegemony in the EU, and to reawaken a nostalgic mythical image of communist antifascist national resistance.

While initially this anti-imperialism was most characteristic of the parties left of Syriza (and the left wing within it), in the crisis it tended to expand to extra-parliamentary factions, and even to anarchist and antiauthoritarian groups.[8] Slogans reminiscent of the civil war became more common in antifascist demonstrations led by anarchists,[9] despite their traditional enmity toward the Communist Party. The antinationalist left opposition has been small, mostly composed of preexisting antifascist groups.[10] For Syriza, which had grown into a serious election contestant, this reunification of the Left around traditional lines of political opposition between competing left and right patriotisms provided ideal conditions.

Anti-imperialism has been one of the corollaries of strengthening international hierarchies in the crisis. Its growth as an ideological trend can be understood in the context of the worsening position of Greek labor in the international labor market, as the restructuring, imposed by European institutions, the IMF, and Germany as Greece's major creditor, compressed the value of local labor power. This undervaluing of labor power in Greece as opposed to other EU countries, and particularly Germany, was frequently interpreted as a transfer of value from "Greece" to "Germany." (The quotation marks have been used here to indicate the absurdity of discussing national economies and their diverse populations as unitary entities between whom acts of exchange take place.) The lack of distinction between different classes and business interest groups, state property and finances, common and private land, national economies and nationalist narratives, produces the image of the suffering looted motherland that is much more than the sum total of its people.

Left-wing anti-imperialism, to be sure, can be much more sophisticated than this.[11] Many Greek Marxist economists have developed theories of this kind of value transfer via trade imbalances in the Eurozone (Mavroudeas and Paitaridis 2014; Lapavitsas 2012). These theories acknowledge that domestic capital is always the first to benefit when the local price of labor power goes down. They do not equate a country's working class with its capitalist class and its ("collaborating") government. Yet analyses that lay blame on core-periphery relations within the Eurozone also tend to support national economic autarky (EU exit) and place special importance on industrial capital and its nationally integrated development for overcoming the crisis (Mavroudeas 2011; Mavroudeas and Paitaridis, 2014).[12] This positive emphasis on national production and growth misapprehends Marx's work as economic science instead of as a critique of the political economy. Its focus on the "real" value of productive labor versus the "fictitious" value of finance does not move beyond the fetishism of capital (Rancière 1976; Milios and Dimoulis 2004) produced by the distance and apparent disconnection of finance capital from labor and the process of valorization. The problem here is not only that the production of value and the continuation of exploitation is untouched by this critique. This approach is not sufficiently distanced from fetishistic forms of anticapitalism, not recognizing that finance is not merely a superfluous epiphenomenon in the world economy, an abstract level that can be dispensed with by choice, so that concrete nationalized capitalist development can continue undisturbed. It is a necessary, integral part of capitalist structures and circuits of valorization. A nationalized

capitalism, at least in the present configuration of international capitalist production and accumulation, can hardly exist without finance and
cannot grow without competition. The formation of the Economic and
Monetary Union (EMU), and Greece's entry in it, was not an act of defeat
for Greek capitalism but an act that aimed at strengthening Greek capital
by facilitating competition, achieving market freedom, and centralizing
monetary policy so as to make structurally impossible the satisfaction of
wage and welfare demands (Bonefeld 2002, 2013). Exposure to this competition was seen as favorable for Greek capital in the period of growth,
both because it allowed more stable access to markets in Western Europe,
unhampered by inflation, and because competition produces pressures
toward the restructuring of domestic capital and labor markets toward
higher productivity.[13]

Analyses that focus on economic dependency also fall prey to the
classic anti-imperialist productivist and moralistic accusation of lack
of patriotism against the upper classes and power-holders of a country
whose labor power is cheapened and its industrial productive forces
are left "underdeveloped." The living tradition of left civil war discourse
concerning bourgeois collaborationism matches this narrative perfectly,
while the repeat appearance of Germany as the enemy is uncannily
fitting.[14] In this narrative, the working class is the genuine representative of "the Greek people"; it represents the nation itself. From this point
on, the discourse on "treason" can easily cross the boundaries of "left"
and "right" political discourse: leading politicians can be "traitors" both
because they "collaborated" with the Troika and because they allowed the
"invasion of illegal immigrants" (Linardīs 2015), both of which are taken to
affect negatively the relative price of the domestic labor power.

Drakos's chapter, in this book, is worth discussing, for it goes further
than the authors discussed above in theorizing Greece as "peripheral"
and in understanding the form of power in contemporary capitalism not
as a form of abstract domination but as domination by an international
cosmopolitan *elite*. As such, this approach moves away from a critique
of capital and toward a version of elite theory, but it also attempts to
avoid the above implications of the theory of dependency, by claiming
that it is compatible with proletarian internationalism and antistatism.
Yet Drakos's historical analysis repeatedly returns to the contradiction
between a conception and practice of revolution as the takeover of a state
and a territory and the practical problems, such a *national* state faces

once established in attempting to stand against its "capitalist" outside by establishing, necessarily, some form of autarky and military presence. Internationalism under such conditions can only exist as military alliances among insurgent states. The contradiction Drakos identifies is correct, but he stops short of drawing theoretical or practical conclusions from it that would question a conception of revolution as necessarily evolving into the defense of a nation-state. His conclusion is that internationalism is an abstraction if its priority is not to fight against hierarchies among national states. The paradox here is that one can only fight against these hierarchies from the position of a weaker nation-state, and thus the affirmation of that nation turns out to be presented as the first step toward internationalism. Having downplayed the relative international position of Greece as a white European nation benefitting from the history of colonial racialization, this analysis risks valorizing Greek nationalism as compatible with internationalism.

At play in such analyses are two forms of fetishism that enhance their contemporary appeal, but also severely limit their critical capacity. First, as already mentioned, and most relevant for the present crisis, debt, finance, and globalization have been fetishized. With debt at the core of the Greek crisis, international finance has appeared as the parasitical element that sucks the life out of the "real" local capitalist production and economy. And indeed, the restructuring was imposed through a matrix of international political and economic structures interrelated with the constraints of financial governance, the contemporary distributed and decentered power of finance to control the actions of states, businesses, and workers through risk assessment (Sotiropoulos et al. 2013). In turn this abstract, distributed power has been personified as a national and international elite of powerful politicians and financiers dominating the nation-state and its "people." It appears to be this elite that has used international institutions to erode national sovereignty and invalidate democratic processes. The predominance of the demands for democracy, the retrenchment into anti-imperialist nationalism, the spread of (often classic antisemitic) conspiracy theories, and xenophobia reflected the way in which the restructuring was imposed politically.[15]

Second, there is the form of fetishism that relates to the historical experience of the national state, economy, and labor. The ideology of nationalism, of a people with a common origin, destiny, and belonging, and the associated rage against external control and intervention, the fear of immigrants and their labor, cannot be understood as based on mere ideological falsities. They are founded, at the most banal level, on the historical production of nation-states as organized political and economic communities, involving past and present power relations among nation-states and capitals and racialized hierarchies of labor, which have real validity in daily experience. Thus the existence of national and racial separations is not the mere *appearance* of capitalist social relations, the instantiation of a capitalist essence, but its historical reality. Workers have historically organized in national terms, and international solidarity has rarely ever entailed a demand for the complete dissolution of borders and boundaries of ethnicity. If today's movements become entrenched in defending the interests of a *national* citizen, and, for the Left, a national working class, it is because, when labor interests and demands are defined as dependent upon economic growth (in this case, the idea of pushing forward Greece's thwarted industrial development), as is the case in most socialist perspectives, these interests cannot but be local and national. Labor power only exists today as internationally differentiated and hierarchical, and the labor struggles of each country, insofar as they fight for "jobs," can only fight for their own respective position in the international labor market.

This de facto nationalism of labor demands was less evident in the labor mobilizations of this period than in Golden Dawn interventions against them. Still, these mobilizations did not *question* their national and ethnic limits by forming effective ties of solidarity with immigrant workers. Left antifascism then remained, to a great extent, circumscribed by its focus on a political conflict, which, despite its questioning of Golden Dawn's racism and proclaiming proletarian internationalism, did not go far enough in challenging the tradition of left antifascist patriotism and practically confronting the social divisions between Greek and immigrant proletarians. This is intimately related to the fact that struggles in the crisis in Greece did not produce a radical questioning of proletarian conditions of existence, and did not move far enough beyond the demand for the reinstatement of jobs (whether dependent upon employers or cooperatively "created"), which might perhaps also have permitted a deeper questioning of the nation and its economic survival. Instead, the empowerment of anti-imperialist nationalist discourse showed that the labor demand in the crisis has been premised upon the indirect affirmation of capital, that is, the affirmation of a (successful) restructuring, even if it were to be an "alternative" restructuring led by the Left, which purports to reinstate growth and employment.

The inability of resistance to austerity, as well as antifascism, to move decisively beyond nationalist discourse limited its ability to question the imperatives of government: economic management, labor productivity, the management of populations. This is the point where, at a moment of crisis, the preservation of the national community against external or internal "threats" can weaken the critique of racist violence. The persistence of nationalist anti-imperialist discourse within the Left and the antifascist movement betrayed the extent of this inability, which is not only ideological but also practical, to separate national capitalist accumulation from the struggle for subsistence, even when the wage relation no longer guarantees subsistence for an ever-broader section of workers. While conservative-authoritarian nationalism identified with the state and its function of law enforcement in a desperate attempt to maintain its relative social position, left nationalism attempted to represent a class automatically defined as national, with declarations of solidarity to immigrants presupposing and failing to effectively question their separation. The left imaginary of international and interethnic solidarity is then faced as a contradiction, and the nation-state is faced as an internal as well as external limit (the repressive apparatus).

Immigrants' Action, Solidarity, and the Hunger Strike
It is worth looking at some examples from 2010–2014, which I believe demonstrate the typical distance between immigrants' collective action and forms of solidarity toward them, as well as showcasing some positive examples of solidarity. Above all, these accounts aim to demonstrate the importance of immigrants' mobilization against the invisibility imposed by ethnocentric viewpoints and to point out the enormous strength required against the heavy force of the state and a society that racializes them as abject, passive, and insignificant. These actions were the other side of this period's dominant, nationally unifying opposition to the restructuring. Immigrants demanded the most basic of things, most of which Greek citizens take for granted: freedom from detention; to walk in the street without the fear of police harassment or a deadly assault; freedom of movement; or, even less audaciously, an end to abuse by guards and access to health care when in detention. Here, I pay attention particularly to the hunger strike and occupations of public space as means of struggle,

which, in my view, pose a significant threat to racism and ethnocentrism despite their limitations. I will discuss the more recent developments of the refugee crisis and the implications for the present in the next section.

The first important immigrant mobilization of the crisis period was the hunger strike by 300 North African immigrants from January to March 2011 demanding legal permits to stay in the country.[16] With help from a broad section of the Left, including anarchists and antiauthoritarians, they occupied a space at the Athens Law School and were immediately attacked and racialized attack by right-wing students, government politicians, and the mainstream media, who presented the strikers as indigents bringing dirt and disease (Mastoras and Vradelīs 2011; To Éthnos 2011). Within four days, the government threatened a police invasion of the university unless the hunger strikers were rehoused (Papadiochos 2011) but nonetheless failed to push the occupation out of sight, away from the center of Athens (Autonome Antifa 2011). Fifty more immigrants began a hunger strike in Thessaloniki on February 14, and, after forty-four days and the hospitalization of more than one hundred strikers, they won renewable legal permits to remain and the reduction of contributions necessary for health care access for all workers. However, this did not last. Over the following years, the strikers were involved in continual protests to have this agreement implemented. In 2014, the six-month renewable permits granted to some of the hunger strikers stopped being renewed. They were subsequently charged with illegally staying in the country and were fined and imprisoned (Fóroum Metanastōn Krītīs 2014).

Despite this eventual defeat, the strike was a significant step forward for immigrants in Greece, who for the first time initiated and carried through a major mobilization, placing their issues center-stage in a racist political scene. Yet, the separation between the immigrants and their politically motivated supporters became clear even in this relatively successful collaboration between them. The political mediation of the action by left parties alienated anarchist and antiauthoritarian supporters, who were against the negotiations around rehousing and wanted instead to fight for the defense of university asylum (which was then still in force) (Kýklos tīs Fōtiás 2011). Conversely, left supporters viewed antiauthoritarian supporters as disruptive. Both sides, however, while making a practical contribution, appear to have been more focused on their groups and organizations' political objectives than on the practical and social benefits that this action would bring for immigrants.

This can be seen even in a text that is self-critical of the tendency of the supporters to prioritize questions of ideology and consciousness and their failure to build lasting social bonds with immigrants (Vátalos 2011). Despite this critique, the author argues that the law school was the wrong choice of venue, because it was clear that this would entail another university asylum violation. He also insists that the hunger strike was an inappropriate tactic, because the state was only pressured by it on the basis of the humanitarian logic of international human rights laws and institutions, and because it signaled to other immigrants that they could only achieve something by risking their very lives.

While this criticism of the hunger strike is correct, and we could further criticize the fact that the exclusionary institution of citizenship itself remained unquestioned, this would indicate an insufficient understanding of the actual situation of immigrants in Greece. The participants say the hunger strike was used as a tactic of last resort, after the failure of other forms of protest (Fóroum Metanastōn Krītīs 2012). They directly addressed the state, which is the only authority able to solve the problem of clandestinity and continual police persecution in the immediate term. For a part of the population that is treated as superfluous, that is casually dehumanized, that is talked of as a "threat to hygiene," and which is very frequently physically abused by the police, there are probably few alternative ways of demanding things to which Greek citizens are automatically entitled. The degree of violence immigrants without papers face means that a hunger strike may actually be a safer form of action than exposing themselves to riot police in the street. The assumption that three hundred people had a safer option, but they chose to risk their lives in order to evoke sympathy is, perhaps, itself the result of the already identified lack of meaningful social bonds between immigrants and Greek political groups of the left and anarchist scenes.

It should not be surprising that the abjection of immigrants has been repeatedly responded to with a form of action that tries to reaffirm the immigrants' humanity. The hunger strike is a provocation to the witness's sense of guilt and the state's responsibility to keep protesters and prisoners alive. It is a way to disrupt the *exclusionary logic* of citizens' rights and citizens' politics, even though it remains within the logic of rights. The location of the hunger strike in the law school questioned the integrity of university asylum as the privilege of a national citizen. Here were noncitizens, people whose non-Western place of birth is used as an excuse to devalue their lives and labor power,[17] demanding the right to be treated as citizens and to be provided with a space to continue their hunger strike. The state's agreement to negotiate, however mediately, with those it previously treated as a "threat to public hygiene"—that is, as subjectless bodies—questioned the imposition of invisibility and voicelessness on immigrants without papers, even if the ministers' promises were later retracted.

As already mentioned, after the electoral ascent of Golden Dawn in 2012, immigrants, particularly non-Europeans, had to deal with increased levels of racist violence by the state and vigilantes and longer-term incarceration in camps where they also suffered abuse (Omáda Dikīgórōn 2013). In detention, the hunger strike was again frequently used as a tool—as is the case generally for prisoners in Greece—but not exclusively. There was also a series of riots and uprisings in prisons (Nikaia; Komotini) and detention camps (Amygdaleza; Korinthos; Xanthi; Fylakio), too many to mention here analytically. The uprising in Amygdaleza, one of the new camps opened by the New Democrat–led government in 2012, was the most violent. Amygdaleza had been converted from an old army barracks with the simple addition of modified shipping containers, creating miserable conditions for detainees, whose detention was continually extended. On August 10, 2013, after guards trampled on the plates immigrants were meant to eat off of, a large-scale riot broke out, during which prisoners set the containers on fire, attacked the guards, and managed to break through the gates and escape. Out of the escapees, fifty-six were recaptured and imprisoned, further extending the length of their incarceration (To Vīma 2013).

What ought to be questioned in light of the struggles of immigrant detainees is the often presumed contrast between the hunger strike and the riot. Hunger strikes appear more passive and are usually accompanied by a list of demands. Yet these demands, which generally follow a chain of abuse or detainees' deaths due to police violence or medical neglect, do not imply that detainees have a naive faith in the system of negotiations. The hunger strike is an extreme measure, a form of blackmail that puts one's life at risk in response to a degrading situation. Riots seem like a more active response, but while they sometimes offer the possibility of escape, they can also carry the risk of violent retaliation by guards and longer imprisonment if one gets caught. The alternation between the two forms of action in quick succession by the same prisoners in most detention camps suggests that the choice of one or the other form is not ideological but may instead depend on the energy, capacity, and feelings of protesters at each instance. It should be clear to any political critic of immigrants' collective practice that their "options" are made up of forms of action that incur various degrees of harm, with the slight chance of escape carrying with it potentially worse consequences. If immigrants appear passive in the face of cruelty, it is only because their actions are violently restricted and their voices are systematically silenced, often even by their supposed supporters. On this point, it is worth noting the contrast between the heroism typically ascribed to hunger-striking anarchist prisoners by their supporters and the corresponding criticisms by anarchists of the of hunger strikes by immigrants meant to illicit compassion (Vátalos 2011). Perhaps this latter quality is not an objective characteristic of the hunger strike, but rather exists in the eye of the European beholder.

Despite the rise in racist attacks, immigrant self-defense against them did not form a significant wave of action in Athens, demonstrating the fact that immigrants did not have the confidence to contest their marginalized and vulnerable status in urban space. Yet agricultural workers in small towns were able to stage protests despite extreme segregation and violent, hyperexploitative work relations.

Two of these cases became more widely known. The first is the long-running protests by strawberry pickers in Nea Manolada (Ilia Prefecture, Peloponnese). The conflict between workers of various nationalities and bosses in Nea Manolada has gone on for over a decade. It has been covered in the press every so often because of instances of extremely violent abuse and terror against workers (Autonome Antifa 2008; Nodárou 2009a, 2009b, 2009c), which became worse during the crisis, when wages started to be paid less and less frequently. In April 2013, strawberry farm workers collectively confronted their supervisors after having been unpaid for six months; in response, the latter shot and injured thirty Bangladeshi workers (Kathīmerinī 2013). Despite the repeated shock expressed by the media and the Left over these incidents, these workers have been dealing with the situation with little substantive support beyond the limited help by the human rights lawyers of the Council for Refugees. Their perpetual irregular/semi-legal status along with structurally reproduced racism leaves them absolutely exposed to the violence of their employers. It is indicative that, even after international coverage of the case, in court the supervisors only received suspended sentences for the shooting, the employer was acquitted, and the workers did not receive any protection as victims.[18] As a result, many of the workers were detained or deported, while the rest have been "blacklisted" by their former employer (TVXS 2014). Immigrant and antifascist organizations' small protests against this did not have much effect.

The second case is the strike of Pakistani agricultural workers in Skala (Lakonia Prefecture, Peloponnese—a region with a strong far-right tradition). In addition to unpaid wages, these workers faced regular police raids of their accommodations, segregation that prevented them from renting properties and entering shops and public spaces, threats of deportation by their employer, and the risk of vigilante action on the part of Golden Dawn, which paraded in the town in a show of strength (Autónomī Prōtovoulía Enántia stī Līthī 2014a, 2014b). On July 1, 2014, the workers organized a five-day strike and demonstrations in the town center (Zafeirópoulos 2014), their second protest after a two-day square occupation four years earlier, which had temporarily stopped the police raids (Autónomī Prōtovoulía Enántia stī Līthī, 2014b). This action was extremely bold given the circumstances, and it appears to have challenged Skala's racist regime to such an extent that it was followed by a campaign of elimination led by the town's mayor. In a few weeks' time, police began to raid the Pakistani area and carry out arrests, most of which led to detentions for deportation (ibid.). The raids and arrests continued well into 2015, under the Syriza government, and by the time of this writing, few if any immigrant workers remain in Skala (Autónomī Prōtovoulía Enántia stī Līthī 2015). The timing of the strike, which was after Golden Dawn leaders had been arrested, might be related to the lack of interest on the part of the Left in these workers, as we will see below.

There were, nevertheless, a few exceptions to the distance between immigrants' action and the varied political reactions to them by the Left described here. There are groups and communities of activists, as well as political parties, that prioritize building relationships with immigrant groups and organizations. But here, again, it is important to pay attention to the quality of these relationships, which can be illustrated by contrasting two examples: first, the activities of SEK (Sosialistikó Ergatikó Kómma—Socialist Workers' Party), which organized actions in conjunction with immigrant community leaders, and, second, the assembly involving immigrant street vendors and students at ASOEE (Athens University of Economics and Business). Although it is hard to assess the full scale of SEK's collaboration with immigrant communities, a few elements encapsulate the party's relationship to them. In antifascist demonstrations organized by SEK, immigrants carried SEK banners and shouted SEK slogans. In SEK assemblies, according to a Senegalese interviewee (Ī Sfīka 2013), immigrant groups were separated by nationality, each with a representative. Only representatives could speak, while the other immigrants were unable to get to know each other. This contrasted with the relationships between students and immigrants, and among immigrants themselves, in the ASOEE. Relationships developed when students provided a safe space for immigrant street vendors to escape from police raids, and immigrants fought alongside students to keep the police off the campus (Scar 2012). An assembly evolved from these actions, in which students made a conscious effort not to dominate the discussion. Despite the many languages spoken, gradually bonds started to form among the participants (SKYA 2013). Together, they planned small protests and court support and solidarity, as well as larger demonstrations in which immigrants collectively decided on the slogans (Scar 2013, 2015). The contrast between the ASOEE group and the SEK became even more evident after police murdered Babacar Ndiaye;[19] community leaders objected to an immediate demonstration in response to the murder, in favor of a SEK demonstration a few weeks later, which they guaranteed would be "peaceful" (Immigrants-ASOEE 2013). Beyond the ideological differences concerning tactics and the perhaps reasonable effort to protect immigrants from arrests, it is also clear that while the ASOEE environment thrived on facilitating discussion among its members, both SEK and the community leaders thought it safest to keep those voices under control. Yet the ASOEE assembly also reached its limit when the political identity of Greek anarchists became an obstacle for immigrant participants in the assembly. When Syriza initially promised to close the detention camps and provide access to papers for irregular immigrants, anarchists were reluctant to support these demands, for fear of being politically assimilated (Scar 2015).

The distance described here had already begun to deepen when political antifascism reached its own limits after the arrests of Golden Dawn leaders. The same government and media that had defended Golden Dawn, considered political coalitions with it, and accused antifascists of extremism, suddenly seemed to have made a U-turn, appropriating antifascist discourse. But this only seemed to be a paradox and a form of ideological appropriation if one left out of the picture of "antifascism" any lasting change in the *actual* conditions for immigrants. Sadly, this increasingly appeared to be the case for a great proportion of the Left and the anarchist/ antiauthoritarian movement as soon as it appeared as if the problem of Golden Dawn was being dealt with. Once Golden Dawn was out of the way, the problems of immigrants were no longer treated as a priority. Toward the end of 2014, the result seemed to be a certain hierarchy of, or at least a disconnection of campaigns, whereby each left and anarchist group chose their favored turf. This was evident in November and December 2014, when three important hunger strikes coincided with Syriza's election campaign.

First, there was the hunger strike of around six hundred Syrian refugees,[20] women, men, and children, who had occupied Syntagma Square for twenty-seven days demanding papers to travel elsewhere in Europe (0151 2015; Kinimatini 2014). Instead of travel documents, the prefecture eventually promised that it would provide accommodation and asylum. The hunger strikers who refused and insisted on travel documents were evicted violently by riot police at 3:00 a.m. on December 15; fifty-one were arrested, and some were threatened with deportation (Mórfis 2014b). The Syrian hunger-strike occupiers were not supported by the Left in any concerted way, with the exception of ANTARSYA, a small left coalition party (which includes the SEK), and some smaller groups.

Second, a new hunger strike began in Amygdaleza in response to prolonged detention and to the unexplained death of a detainee. Muhammad Ashfaq had been beaten heavily by guards during one of the uprisings in Korinthos detention center, which caused him respiratory problems. The guards refused him access to treatment for over two weeks, and he died during his eventual transfer by the police to a hospital. After four days on hunger strike, thirty detainees were released and another 150 were to be considered for release, which led most detainees to end the strike (Mórfis 2014a). This story, including Ashfaq's death, received only very brief mention in most left media.

Third, a hunger strike was started by Nikos Romanos, a friend of Alexis Grigoropoulos, who has witnessed his murder by the police in December 2008. Romanos had been imprisoned because he had taken part in a bank robbery as an anarchist political act. He had been successful in his exams for university entry while in prison, and he started a hunger strike to demand regular leave to attend classes. Romanos's case was heavily covered by all of the media, and he enjoyed extremely strong support and concern about his well-being from the anarchist scene, as well as the rest of the Left, including Syriza. His hunger strike lasted for thirty-one days, until, with much pressure from Syriza in the parliament, he was permitted leave on the condition that he wear an electronic monitoring bracelet (Psarrá 2014).

It is not surprising that the overwhelming majority of the anarchist and left scene were most moved and mobilized by the case of Romanos. His link to December 2008 sparked the imaginations of anarchists, who occupied the GSEE offices in memory of the uprising (only this time with the support of the GSEE itself, and only for the duration of Romanos's strike) (Katálīpsī GSEE 2014). Syriza could deploy its discourse about the fundamental rights of prisoners and gain favor among anarchists who rallied around a heroic imprisoned comrade. This prioritization, however, also indicated something else. It unequivocally showed that some people's lives matter more than others'. As with Pavlos Fyssas, so with Nikos Romanos, the lives of *Greek* comrades matter the most. There was neither a scandal nor a riot after a whole series of murders of immigrants at the hands of the police and Golden Dawn.

These examples show that it was when immigrants' struggles entered the street, the squares, and privileged university space (the 300; the Pakistani workers in Lakonia; Syrian migrants at Syntagma) that the racism of the state and the "Greek public" was most challenged, even if it was not challenged quite enough. The very presence of immigrants in the country, let alone their demand for equal treatment, is itself a critique of the normalized birthright of citizens, particularly those who are higher in the racialized international hierarchy of labor. These battles, with very little room to move, have had to fight against invisibility. The degree of invisibility of hundreds of Syrian migrants in Syntagma Square, the inconsequentiality of the way in which the square was "swept" for Christmas shopping by the government, while the great majority of former antifascists were passionately focused on a single Greek person's hunger strike, revealed the pervasiveness of an ethnocentric prioritizing of causes among the most politically "progressive" sections of Greek society.

Solidarity in the "Refugee Crisis"

During 2015, after the election of Syriza and the enormous increase in the number of migrants entering Greece, mostly from Syria, Afghanistan, and

Iraq, a shift appeared in the relationship between citizens and migrants. Openly racist discourse against migrants dissipated slightly, and perhaps only temporarily, possibly because of the hegemony of a more humanistic discourse pushed by the government and a degree of recognition of the need of these people to flee not only war but also Greece itself. From the perspective of the rest of Europe, with the temporary exception of Germany, this was not recognized, however. The legal and political distinction between "immigrants" and "refugees" was mobilized to argue that one ceases to be a refugee after the first border crossing. And indeed, these migrants were not merely running from lethal danger but had been fighting their way through the borders of Europe to find somewhere where they could viably settle. This was a scandal, based on the most ideological liberal conception of freedom: entering a labor contract is a choice, and thus to emigrate in order to obtain one, or a better one, is little more than capricious shopping around. From that perspective, to risk one's life and the lives of one's children in order to reach that "better" place is deplorable.

In Greece, on the other hand, despite the fact that Turkey was then formally considered a "safe country," these migrants faced less popular hostility than help and support. Some locals did call for heavier policing, and others rushed to sell migrants basic necessities at overinflated prices. Yet there was also an unprecedented wave of Greek and international support and solidarity, not only from NGOs, newly formed charities, and political groups but also from large numbers of people in the Greek cities and countryside who offered food and other resources, and who opened their homes to migrants. This wave of help, which supported migrants by filling the gap left behind by a bankrupt state, was impressive, considering the strong opposition migrants encountered in other European countries.

Certainly, it played an enormous role that these migrants did not wish to remain in Greece, and thus, until Macedonia closed its border in March 2016, a narrative of competition for resources could not be employed. Solidarity included assistance to move further north to countries whose governments had an extremely harsh stance toward Greece's crisis-ravaged population. Syriza's "failure" to control Greece's borders was often seen as, and likely was, a last-ditch, and eventually unsuccessful, pressure tactic against EU creditors, as well as a simple attempt to avoid hosting refugees under conditions of deep crisis and high unemployment. The weaponization of migrants played a minor role, however. It was more important that it was difficult to construe a million people travelling as families *through* Greece's towns and cities to reach a place outside Greece as a threat to the Greek citizen. It was under such conditions that concern could be legitimately expressed and practiced as solidarity and, in effect if not necessarily ideologically, support for the migrants' struggle to delegitimize these borders and the racist discrimination between Europeans and non-Europeans.

These events have given a new meaning to solidarity with migrants. While previously "solidarity" was strictly separated from "charity" by sticking to notions of "mutuality" and refusing to "give things out," solidarity during the refugee crisis has consisted of the generous offering of resources (Rozakou 2016). Importantly, this also included the offering of housing by occupying buildings in opposition to the state-led management of migrants. Those involved in grassroots immigrant solidarity insisted that their actions were not "charity" (Karyotis 2016), and, indeed, solidarity should not be confused with the specious "mutuality" of exchange relations. These practices have in fact overcome a narrow conception of a "solidarity" that fails to address social and material inequalities on the presumption that the other ought to be treated as formally equal.[21] In this sense, this type of solidarity overcomes the relational and ethnic limits of "solidarity economies" that have been founded upon exchange relations between Greek citizens. Giving under such conditions differs from the "giving" of the state and NGOs and should not be confused with state humanitarianism or redistribution, insofar as it is not part of a strategy to manage a population as a labor resource and as a liability and to maintain their separation from citizens.

The latter has been the strategy of the Greek state since the closure of the northern borders. As is the case every time borders and racial separations are questioned, conservative political forces in Europe led by the Far Right, with very significant numbers of supporters, mobilized to reinforce them. The deal with Turkey, which essentially canceled the rights of refugees, and the UN military patrols of the Aegean minimized migration through that crossing, trapping 57,000 people in Greece and millions in Turkey. If the new processing and detention centers in Greece are demonstrative of how migrants stuck there are to be treated, we can see that the state's "offer" of a roof (usually a tent) and basic living resources is exchanged for segregation and in many cases enclosure in camps far from towns and cities. "Support" is now only permitted by the state and

NGOs who comply with the EU's population control strategies. The possibilities opened up by solidarity have been rapidly shut down and actively policed by the supposedly refugee-friendly state, which rushed to literally destroy solidarity structures on the Greek islands that were functioning beyond its control. At the end of July 2016, in Thessaloniki, three occupied buildings that housed migrants were also evicted in response to a relatively successful No Border camp with migrants fronting its demonstrations (Migrants' Pride) and the creation of migrants' assemblies.[22]

Some Conclusions

Despite state repression and its decline in popularity since the closure of the borders, solidarity for migrants has come a long way since 2014. It has taken very significant steps beyond merely political campaigning, to offer practical support, for which structures preexisted the crisis but are now in much higher demand. Yet there is a lot more to do to help migrants continue to question the increasingly racialized structures that separate them from European citizenry. The flood of support for migrants cannot be unambivalently said to have overcome the separations that existed before the refugee crisis, even if it provided an image of how that might be possible. It is important to now question every tendency to impose different criteria on migrants' action than on that of citizens and to demolish every assumption that this is a battle secondary and peripheral to class struggle or to the integrity of radical political milieus. At a point when a great proportion of the Left across Europe has identified class struggle with the defense of national sovereignty, economic isolationism, and even controls on immigration, it is ever more important to question the racialized exclusionary foundations of citizenship that can also be embedded in political milieus.

This may involve facing ideological contradictions when addressing practical questions in such battles. Migrants are currently *forced* to engage with national and supra-national government to demand asylum, freedom of movement, and access to services, and to organize their lives outside camps equally with citizens. But the legal system they encounter is entirely blocked and increasingly convoluted. Clearly, this system will not free migrants from camps any time soon unless they protest, and solidarity action is aimed at helping *their* voices to be heard. This presupposes facilitating their initiatives by providing access to resources—including, importantly, key information that affects them—and trusting their judgment and their awareness of their own needs instead of imposing leadership. This is a diverse population fighting to meet specific material needs, which will necessarily be ideologically mediated in a variety of ways. Solidarity can collapse in ideological disputes, unless it prioritizes practical and material issues—although I do not mean that criticism is illegitimate.

This is related to another contradiction, which takes us back to the question of the EU and anti-imperialism. Paradoxically, even if the EU is an institution that has built a racialized fortress around its borders, contemporary Eurosceptic politics is largely based on viewing the EU as *too lax* on questions of immigration, because Germany, Greece, and Italy were pushing for a project of distributing refugees among EU countries. For contemporary Eurosceptics, the EU was only good as long as its racialized fortress was holding strong. Now they want their own fortresses along their own national borders. Enter Brexit and its reception by a part of the UK Left as a working-class revolt, and by the Greek Left as some kind of antineoliberal revolt, when in fact the UK rarely ever received any suggestions from the EU on questions of austerity. In fact, Brexit was about a vague notion of British sovereignty and keeping other Europeans—but above all new non-European migrants—out of Britain. As to the left argument that sovereignty is a precondition for the end of austerity, it has to be recognized that the potential dissolution of the EU is not a moment of liberation for proletarians in Europe. It will not dismantle systems of financial governance nor is it the collapse of fortresses. On the contrary, this is a moment when citizens of European countries are one after another deciding that they cannot share "their" resources with "foreigners," already persuaded about the supposed finitude of "money" after years of austerity and about the terrorist threat supposedly brought over by multiply racialized migrants.

Even if the left scenario, the creation of self-sufficient national economies, was possible, it similarly does nothing to challenge international hierarchies and put an end to the "causes" of immigration. On the contrary it is necessarily premised on reinforced national border regimes. This type of commonsense nationalism does not need to be outspokenly racist to encourage racism. It is enough to suggest that the question of sovereignty is so urgent that it justifies the heavier policing and regulation of immigration, even under the strongest anti-immigration regime in Europe and surrounded by xenophobic anti-immigration campaigning.

Again, the stance of some of the British Left on the question of Brexit is a worrying case in point, in arguing that anti-immigration can be solely an economic concern that has only a contingent relation with the question of systemic racism (Todd 2016), and even that "free movement" must now come to an end (Mason 2016). It is apparently fine to define "class" in national terms and want immigrants out, as long as you don't use racist language.

It is then not enough to attribute the recent triumphs of far-right populism in Europe and the USA to immiseration, high levels of immigration, the delegitimation of mainstream parties, or the desire of a "precarious" section of the population to punish elites. It is also not enough to expose the Far Right as the "long arm" of the repressive state apparatus or to be appeased by the notion that democracy is the ideal political form for capitalist reproduction. far-right populism is an expression of the aforementioned popularity of a fetishistic anticapitalism that is embedded in the political traditions of both Right and Left. Oppositional discourse from both sides has been against "cosmopolitan elites" and "international financial capital," projecting the problem outward in the name of a suffering people. But elite theory oversimplifies capitalist abstract domination by personifying it, thus leading to the conclusion that it can be gotten rid of by setting oneself free from its human representatives. And if these human representatives are agents of a "globalized elite" that enslaves national citizens and erodes their privileges by importing migrants, then nationalism is the most fitting response to it.

As a result, for a great interclass—but nationally homogeneous—section of proletariat and lower middle classes, the most attractive answer has emerged as a domestic autarkic and isolationist capitalism, perhaps with a "social" face. *Citizen* proletarians' alienation from class identity, their experience of being not only objectified but also treated as superfluous by capitalist reproduction, has not translated into questioning capitalist reproduction but has found a host of other targets instead. This has proven not to be a temporary mistargeting of discontent but the most dominant ideological framing of social opposition in the crisis.

Yet the problem posed here is not that of ideological mediation standing in the way of the true dynamic of struggle. Instead, it must be posed in terms that break with the distinction between real material relations and social practice, on the one hand, and their ideal interpretation, on the other. This means that the fetishism of the nation and the violence of racism that comes with it is unlikely to be undermined by ideological campaigns against the Far Right, or even by texts like the present one. Instead, the most likely promise lies in migrants' own fight to pull down racializing borders and camp walls, access spaces, and acquire a voice currently reserved only for citizens.

Notes

1   The concept of "antipolitics" has been used in political science to refer to abstention from and critical attitudes toward formal politics (parties, elections, unions, etc.). Such attitudes can be associated with democratic as well as authoritarian orientations (Stocker and Hay 2012). In the crisis, we saw *mass action* that rejected formal politics and created new forms of organization, yet the rejection of formal politics alone cannot be taken as inherently democratic or radical.

2   This was not the first pogrom against immigrants in Greece. Another notable case was the pogrom against Albanian immigrants in September 2004, after Greece lost a football match against Albania.

3   The expression "indignant citizens" (*aganaktismenoi polítes*) has a history of being used by the Far Right to present themselves to the media without revealing their political identity, when staging protests against immigrants, Roma people, and squatters. Perhaps as a result of this coincidental connotation of the Greek translation of the Spanish word *indignados*, the more conservative wing of the movement preferred the word "aganaktismenoi" to describe the movement, while the left wing preferred to call it "the Movement of the Squares" or to use the slogan "real/direct democracy now."

4   The "300 Greeks" was an organization that attempted to summon patriotic pride against the humiliation of being nationally indebted and the corruption of politicians. The number 300 is a reference to the heroism of Leonidas's 300 Spartans in Thermopylae. The idea was that Greek citizens would unite and reempower their country in an orderly and lawful way.

5   This discourse often referred to Cornelius Castoriadis's work, particularly that which has valorized and idealized the image of ancient Athenian democracy—a much-needed boost for a humiliated Greek national identity.

6   These percentages refer to the electoral results of the June 2012 repeat elections.

7   Pavlos Fyssas (aka Killah P.), a thirty-four-year-old antifascist rapper, was murdered by members of Golden Dawn on September 18, 2013, in Keratsini, Athens.—Ed.

8   An example is the strongly anti-imperialist tone of the call for a demonstration to the German embassy organized by anarchist, communist, and antifascist groups (Rouvikōnas et al. 2015).

9   The most common slogan representing this is "EAM, ELAS, Meligalas: this is the way for people's victory," a direct reference to a well shaft in the town of Meligalas, where, in September 1944, the corpses of defeated Security Battalion soldiers of the collaborationist Ioannis Rallis government were thrown after

their defeat by the communist forces of EAM-ELAS. Golden Dawn organizes an anniversary pilgrimage to the location every year to commemorate the victims.

10   One form of backlash against left nationalism and its commonplace antisemitism was the relative empowerment of a theoretical current that is influenced by German "anti-Germanism." The journal *Terminal* 119 has represented this antifascist tendency, whose prime target is antisemitism. *Terminal*'s anti-German/anti-Hellenic stance is not, however, antinationalist, because its antifascism insists on a principled defense of Israel, failing to question the nation-state as such.

11   Although it is not always, despite the sophistication of its authors on broader philosophical issues. One example is Giorgio Agamben's proposal for a Southern European "Latin Empire" against the North, which, he argues, is trying to impose its Protestant work ethic on freedom-loving southerners (Agamben 2013).

12   This is more or less the program of parties to the left of Syriza like ANTARSYA and KKE, as well as Syriza's anti-EU contingent, which has now formed the party Popular Unity.

13   See Sotiropoulos et al., 2013, 182–99, for an alternative Marxist analysis of the euro crisis that opposes theories of dependency and, like Bonefeld (2013), emphasizes the abstract disciplinary role of the monetary union.

14   Consider the demonstration in protest of Angela Merkel's visit to Athens on October 9, 2012, which featured a vehicle carrying Nazi flags and unionists dressed as Nazi officers (Wearden 2012).

15   As Moishe Postone (1983) has pointed out, it is the personification of this most abstract form of capital, finance, that, about eighty years ago, brought together the national-socialist valorization of industry and the drive to exterminate those (the Jews and other immigrants) whose very presence challenged everything concrete (the blood and soil).

16   The immigrants also demanded "that residence permits are no longer connected to work credits; that all of those who lost their permits for the above reason are re-legalized; the vindication of everyone whose application was rejected in 2005, after their application had originally been accepted and after they had been forced to pay thousands of euros each; the establishment of a permanent and open procedure for complete legalization, which will process applications continually; an end to the criminalization of our comrades in solidarity with us, who have been treated as suspects of criminal acts by the authorities" (Anoichtī Prōtovoulía 2011a).

17   The "devaluation of lives" could not be expressed here in a more precise way. The phrase is not emotive but instead it is the most literal way to describe the fact that non-Western immigrants are typically killed or are left to die with impunity.

18   According to the Greek Council for Refugees, which brought the action to court, a labor trafficking case should have examined the situation of the 119 or more employees who were protesting, not only that of those who had been injured by the shooting: "According to the legislation, a trafficker is a person

who, while having every opportunity and obligation to provide some form of protection to his workers, never pays the agreed wages and enforces the continuation of the supply of labor with threats of violence and use of firearms, taking full advantage of the absence of the State for his own profit and at the expense of defenseless people—for all purposes—his slaves" (Greek Council for Refugees 2014).

19 Babacar Ndiaye, a street vendor from Senegal, was killed on February 1, 2013, after an aggressive pursuit by municipal police on the Electric Railway lines in Thiseio, Athens.—Ed.

20 I am using the word "refugees" because these migrants were clearly fleeing war, despite the fact that they did not seek asylum in Greece.

21 See also Rozakou (2016) for a discussion of this phenomenon from an anthropological perspective.

22 See Karyotis (2016) for more details on the evictions.

References

0151. "Synénteuxī me Treis Gynaíkes prósfyges apó tī Syría" [Interview with three women refugees from Syria]. *0151*, December 15, 2014, at 0151.espivblogs.net/2014/12/15/.

Agamben, Giorgio. "The 'Latin Empire' Should Strike Back." *Libération*, March 26, 2013. http://www.voxeurop.eu/en/content/article/3593961-latin-empire-should-strike-back.

Anoichtī Prōtovoulía Allīleggýīs stous 300 Metanástes Apergoús Peínas. "Hunger Strikers' Assembly Decision: 21/02," February 22, 2011b, https://allilmap.wordpress.com/2011/02/22/.

———. "Message by the Assembly of Fifty Hunger Strikers in Thessaloniki to the Mayor and the Members of the City Council," February 14, 2011a, https://allilmap.wordpress.com/2011/02/14/.

Autonome Antifa. "Péftontas apó ta sýnnefa (gia kamiá dekariá chrónia): Manōláda" [Bursting our bubble (for about ten years): Manolada]. *Autonome Antifa* 9, no. 6 (2008).

———. "Tésseris méres pou den (thélei na) tis thymátai kanénas" [Four days nobody wants to remember]. *Autonome Antifa* 22, no. 6–7 (2011).

Autónomī Prōtovoulía Enántia stī Līthī [Autonomous Initiative Against Forgetting]. "Ī orgánōsī tōn metanastōn eínai to móno prógramma diásōsīs tous apó ton ellīnikó voúrko" [Immigrants' organization is the only program to rescue them from the Greek mire], February 13, 2015, at skalalakonias.wordpress.com/2015/02/13/.

———. "Ī Sýntomī Istoría Tīs Pakistanikīs Koinótītas Stīn Lakōnía" [The short history of the Pakistani community in Lakonia], *0151*, no. 3 (2014b): 4–8.

———. "Mia prōtī katagrafī tīs syzītīsīs me tous Pakistanoús metanástes stīn Skála Lakōnías" [An initial record of the discussion with Pakistani immigrants in Skala Lakonias], July 23, 2014a, at skalalakonias.wordpress.com/2014/07/23/.

Bonefeld, Werner. "European Integration: The Market, the Political and Class." *Capital & Class* 26, no. 2 (July 1, 2002): 117–42. http://journals.sagepub.com/doi/abs/10.1177/030981680207700105?journalCode=cnca.

———. "Human Economy and Social Policy: On Ordo-Liberalism and Political Authority." *History of the Human Sciences* 26, no. 2 (March 26, 2013): 106–25. http://journals.sagepub.com/doi/abs/10.1177/0952695113478243.

Eleutherotypía. "Dénoun ta stoicheía gia to chrysaugítiko pogkróm to 2011" [Evidence on the Golden Dawn pogrom of 2011 adds up]. *Eleutherotypía*, August 26, 2014.

Fóroum Metanastōn Krītīs. "Apó tī synénteuxī týpou prōīn apergōn kai allīléggyōn tīn Pémptī 26/1 gia ton éna chróno apó tīn Apergía Peínas tōn 300" [From the press conference of the former strikers and their supporters on Thursday, January 26, 2012, on the first anniversary of the hunger strike of the 300]. January 26, 2012, at fmkritis.wordpress.com/2012/01/26/.

———. "Deltio typou: 4 mīnes fylakī kai 1.500 eurō próstimo" [Press release: 4 months imprisonment and a €1,500 fine]. November 16, 2014, at fmkritis.wordpress.com/2014/11/16/.

Geōrgiádou, Vasilikī. "Ī eklogikī ánodos tīs Chrysīs Augīs: Psīfos-reváns tōn episfalōn kai nées politikés eukairíes" [The electoral ascent of Golden Dawn: Revenge voting of the precarious and new political opportunities]. In *2012: O Diplós eklogikós seismós*, edited by Giánnīs Voúlgarīs and Īlías Nikolakópoulos, 185–219. Athens: Themélio, 2014.

Greek Council for Refugees. "Press Release. Manolada: The Chronicle of a Judicial Failure." *Greek Council for Refugees*. August 7, 2014, at www.gcr.gr/.

Ī Sfīka. "Synénteuxī me metanástī mikropōlītī apó tīn Senegálī" [Interview with immigrant street vendor from Senegal]. *Ī Sfīka* no. 5, September 2013. https://skya.espiv.net/2013/09/09/συνέντευξη-με-μετανάστη-μικροπωλητή/.

Immigrants-ASOEE. "Schetiká me tī dolofonía tou metanástī mikropōlītī Babacar Ndiaye sto Thīseío" [About the murder of the immigrant street vendor Babacar Ndiaye in Thiseio]. *Synéleusī Metanastōn & Allīléggyōn ASOEE*, February 3, 2013. http://immigrants-asoee.espivblogs.net/2013/02/03/.

Karyotis, Theodoros. "Criminalizing Solidarity: Syriza's War on the Movements." *Roar Magazine*, July 31, 2016. http://roarmag.org/essays/criminalizing-solidarity-movement-refugees-greece/.

Katálīpsī GSEE. "Līxī tīs Katálīpsīs GSEE" [End of GSEE occupation]. *Katálīpsī GSEE: apeleutherōménī GSEE gia tīn allīleggýi ston Níko Rōmanó*, December 10, 2014. http://katalipsigsee.espivblogs.net.

Kathīmerinī. "Migrant Workers Shot by Bosses in Manolada Farm." *Kathīmerinī*, English Edition, April 17, 2013. http://www.ekathimerini.com/150459/article/ekathimerini/news/migrant-workers-shot-by-bosses-at-manolada-farm.

Kinimatini (@kinimatini). *Synénteuxī Sýriou prósfyga sto Sýntagma* [Interview with a Syrian refugee at Syntagma]. Twitter. November 25, 2014.

Kýklos tīs Fōtiás. "Allīleggyī ston agōna tōn 300 metanastōn-ergatōn apergōn peinas" [Solidarity with the struggle of the 300 migrant workers on hunger strike]. *Maúrī Sīmaía* no. 59 (May 2011). http://squathost.com/a_deltio/gr/d59_300.htm.

Lapavitsas, Costas. *Crisis in the Eurozone*. London / New York: Verso, 2012.

Linardīs, G. "Ī asýmmetrī apeilī tīs athróas eisvolīs lathrometanastōn stīn Patrída mas" [The asymmetric threat of mass illegal immigrant invasion into our fatherland]. *Chrysī Augī*, June 5, 2015.

Mastoras, Níkos, and Stelios Vradelīs. "Mazikī apergía peínas apó 300 paránomous metanástes" [Mass hunger strike by 300 illegal immigrants]. *Ta Néa*, January 25, 2011.

Mason, Paul. "Britain Is Not a Rainy, Fascist Island—Here's My Plan for ProgrExit." *Guardian*, June 25, 2016. https://www.theguardian.com/commentisfree/2016/jun/25/britain-rainy-fascist-island-progrexit-brexit.

Mavroudeas, Stavros. "To ellīnikó krátos kai to xéno kefálaio stīn oikonomikī krísī" [The Greek state and foreign capital in the economic crisis]. Paper submitted to the conference *Krátos kai Díkaio ston 210 aiōna*, Law Department, Panteion University, Athens, 2011.

———, and Dimitris Paitaridis. "The Greek Crisis: A Dual Crisis of Overaccumulation and Imperialist Exploitation." In *Greek Capitalism in Crisis: Marxist Analyses*, edited by Stavros Mavroudeas, 153–75. New York: Routledge, 2014.

Milios, John, and Dimitri Dimoulis. "Commodity Fetishism vs. Capital Fetishism: Marxist Interpretations Vis-à-Vis Marx's Analyses in Capital." *Historical Materialism* 12, no. 3, August 2004. https://www.researchgate.net/publication/238428261_Commodity_Fetishism_vs_Capital_Fetishism_Marxist_Interpretations_vis-a-vis_Marx's_Analyses_in_Capital.

Mórfis, Tásos. "O Mocháment Asfák épasche apó ásthma. Den ton pīgan poté se nosokomeío, gi'autó péthane" [Mohamed Ashfaq died of asthma: He was never taken to hospital, that is why he died]. *Popaganda*, November 21, 2014a. popaganda.gr.

———. "Ti apéginan oi Sýroi prósfyges tīs plateías Syntágmatos?" [What happened to the Syrian refugees at Syntagma Square?]. *Popaganda*, December 17, 2014b. popaganda.gr.

Nodarou, Mákīs. "N. Manōláda: Típota den állaxe sta fraoulochōrafa tīs ntropīs" [Nothing has changed at shameful strawberry fields]. *Eleutherotypía*, March 23, 2009a.

———. "Fōtiá stous Kataulismoús tīs ntropīs: Fráoules kai aíma" [Set fire to the camps of shame: Strawberries and blood]. *Eleutherotypía*, June 4, 2009b.

———. "'Kou Kloux Klan' stī Manōláda" [Ku Klux Klan in Manolada village]. *Eleutherotypía*, June 20, 2009c.

Omáda Dikīgórōn gia ta Dikaiōmata Prosfýgōn kai Metanastōn. "Kéntra krátīsīs metanastōn—Apothīkes psychōn kai sōmátōn" [Immigrant detention centers—warehouses of souls and bodies], August 14, 2013, at omadadikigorwn.blogspot.co.uk/2013/08/.

Papadiochos, K.P. "Kérdī kai zīmíes metá tī Nomikī" [Gains and losses after the law school occupation]. *Kathīmerinī*, January 30, 2011.

Postone, Moishe. "Anti-Semitism and National Socialism: Notes on the German Reaction to 'Holocaust.'" In *Germans and Jews Since the Holocaust: The Changing*

Situation in West Germany, edited by Anson Rabinbach and Jack D. Zipes, 302–14. New York: Holmes & Meier, 1983.

Psarrá, Anta. "O Níkos más édōse anáses eleutherías" [Nikos gave us a breath of freedom]. *Ī Efīmerída tōn Syntaktōn*, December 11, 2014.

Rancière, Jacques. "The Concept of 'Critique' and the 'Critique of Political Economy'" (from the 1844 Manuscript to Capital). *Economy and Society* 5, no. 3 (1976): 352–76.

Rouvikōnas, Kokkinī Grammī, Antifasistikó Métōpo Kallithéas-Moschátou, Anarchikī Syllogikótīta Néas Filadélfeias, Laikī Antepithesī, Thryallida, K* VOX, & Sýntrofoi/ Syntrófisses. "Poreia pros tīn Germanikī Presveia, 23/05/2015" [Protest march to the German embassy]. *Indymedia Athens*, May 23, 2015. https://athens.indymedia.org/event/56807/.

Rozakou, Katerina. "Socialities of Solidarity: Revisiting the Gift Taboo in Times of Crises: Socialities of Solidarity." *Social Anthropology* 24, no. 2, May 2016. https://www.researchgate.net/publication/303669334_Socialities_of_solidarity_revisiting_the_gift_taboo_in_times_of_crises_Socialities_of_Solidarity

Scar. "Apó tīn Ntáka éōs to Ntakár apénanti stous Ntángka eímaste mazí" [From Dhaka to Dakar against the Danga we are together]. *Ī Sfīka* no. 5, September 11, 2013.

———. "Koinoí agōnes ntópiōn kai metanastōn (kai pank katastáseis stīn ASOEE)" [Common struggles of locals and migrants (and punk situations in ASOEE)]. *Ī Sfīka* nos. 2–3, June 10, 2012.

———. "Viōmata kai sképseis apó ton koinó agōna ntópiōn kai metanastōn stīn ASOEE kai tis kinīseis enántia sta kéntra krátīsīs" [Experiences and thoughts on the common struggle of locals and immigrants at ASOEE and the actions against detention centers]. *Ī Sfīka* no. 8, July 12, 2015.

SKYA. "Synenteúxeis me metanástes mikropōlītés" [Interviews with migrant street vendors]. *SKYA*, June 22, 2013, at skya.espiv.net/2013/06/22/.

Sotiropoulos, Dimitris P., John Milios, and Spyros Lapatsioras. *A Political Economy of Contemporary Capitalism and its Crisis: Demystifying Finance*. London: Routledge, 2013.

Stocker, Gerry, and Colin Hay. "Comparing folk theories of democratic politics: stealth and sunshine." Political Studies Association (PSA), 62nd Annual International Conference, Belfast, April 3–5, 2012.

Sunderland, Judith, et al. *Hate on the Streets: Xenophobic Violence in Greece*. New York: Human Rights Watch, 2012.

To Éthnos. "Kataulismós lathrometanastōn ī Nomikī" [The law school has become a camp for illegals]. *To Éthnos*, January 25, 2011.

To Vīma. "Exégersī metanastōn, sovará epeisódia kai syllīpseis stīn Amygdaléza" [Immigrants' uprising, serious incidents and arrests in Amygdaleza camp]. *To Vīma*, August 10, 2013.

Todd, Joseph. "Building a progressive majority: Left strategy after the Brexit vote." *Red Pepper*, June 27, 2016. https://www.redpepper.org.uk/building-a-progressive-majority-left-strategy-after-the-brexit-vote/.

TVXS. "Apeláseis ergatōn gīs sta fraoulochōrafa tīs Manōládas" [Deportation of land workers in the strawberry fields of Manolada village]. *TVXS*, March 17, 2014.

———. "Pogkróm katá metanastōn sto kéntro tīs Athīnas" [Pogrom against immigrants in the center of Athens]. *TVXS*, May 12, 2011.

Vátalos, Symeōn. "Gia tīn apergía peínas tōn metanastōn . . ." [On the immigrants' hunger strike]. *SKYA*, May 10, 2011, at skya.espiv.net/2011/05/10/.

Wearden, Graeme. "Merkel visits Greece as 50,000 people protest," *Guardian*, October 9, 2012. https://www.theguardian.com/business/2012/oct/09/eurozone-crisis-angela-merkel-visits-greece.

Zafeirópoulos, Kōstas. "Ī Manōláda tīs Lakōnías" [The Manolada of Lakonia]. *Ī Efīmerída tōn Syntaktōn*. July 9, 2014.

SEVEN

Imperialism and Internationalism in Neoliberal Modernity

Panos Drakos

We cannot be calm until Europe, all Europe, is in flames
—Jacques Pierre Brissot, Girondin leader,
French National Convention, 1792

"Omnia in Unum"[1]

Any discussion on a contemporary definition of *proletarian internationalism* must begin with the effort to clarify how we perceive the notion of *imperialism* in the era of neoliberal modernity. Namely, it cannot but begin with a general overview of the hierarchical structures and oppressive social relations nurtured by neoimperialism, as well as of the driving forces behind its manifestation as a component of the reproduction of the market economy system. It would be a first-order theoretical misstep to approach neoimperialism as an independent expression of domination that does not pertain to the level of the molecular clashes and class contradictions developing in the field of social struggle. Even in the case of classic imperialism, as it was formulated and described by Lenin (1999), imperialist disputes linked to the competition between the national elites of developed capitalist countries should not be interpreted as a social phenomenon that is separate from class struggle, but rather as another expression of social antagonism between classes.

This does not mean we embrace the perspective of Arrighi, Hopkins, and Wallerstein (2011: 66), according to which anti-imperialism at the level of interstate relationships is the embodiment of class struggle at a higher level. There is no doubt that this opinion has been used as an ideological pretext by anti-imperialist regimes in order to impose a compulsory social uniformity in the domestic sphere, mercilessly suppressing any autonomous expression of class struggle turning against their rule. But this does not mean we should completely abandon any attempt at (class) analysis of the social forces and the class interests that anti-imperialist regimes embody, as well as of the role the latter might play in the field of *social struggle.*[2]

The national elites of the interwar period found themselves at the helm of state-centered capitalist formations. Through their imperialist campaigns, they affected the development of social struggle in societies of both the center and the periphery, on which they exercised direct or indirect political control. The imposition of a militaristic ideology (attacked with any available means by the anarchists of the time), the increase of "national" wealth through the expropriation of the natural resources of subjugated populations, and the subsequent capitulation of the working class of the developed countries in the name of "increasing the pie" were only a few of the harmful consequences of imperialism in the face of social struggle in the metropoles of the center. At the same time, the colonies suffered the violent adaptation of social subjects to the barbaric conditions of colonialism, as well as the disruption of the social structure of local communities and their utter control by foreign centers of political and economic power. Therefore, from the viewpoint of liberating social theory, an interpretation of imperialism and colonialism as strictly geopolitical phenomena with no class origins and consequences would be insufficient.

The problem with the modern anarchist conception that rejects the distinction between imperialism and anti-imperialism as constructed and "ideologized"—that is, as a distinction that does not express existing social forces and contrasts—is that it regards as static and unaltered notions that are dynamic and historically defined, notions that acquire new features during each historic period. Analytical terms such as "capitalist accumulation" and "class struggle," as well as the very way in which we conceptualize terms such as "national" and "international," must be redefined according to the prevailing conditions created by the evolution of the market economy system, if we want them to conserve their value as methodological tools for a class analysis of social reality. For example, we would be blinded by dogma if we were to remain attached to the notion of intra-imperialist contradictions in the way that Lenin used it almost one hundred years ago—as the threshold to widespread war between the developed capitalist countries—at a time when the internationalization of capital has advanced to such an extent that it is heading toward global capitalist unification. To prove the point, all we have to do is observe how France and Germany, the "eternal enemies," have gone as far as to contemplate holding common meetings of their Councils of Ministers!

Therefore, it follows that any war between the closely interdependent capitalist metropoles of the center is, in our day, almost inconceivable. Instead of ritually repeating traditional Marxist definitions that refer to a period when imperialism was an inseparable part of the national spheres of influence, we should reflect on how it is possible that imperialism has survived until today, despite the significant degree of internationalization of capital and the subsequent unification at the field of interests, social functions, and the logic of domination expressed today by the once nationally distinct systemic elites. If interstate competition was the engine behind the appearance of imperialism in its classical form, the same could not occur in the era of globalization. Today, intra-imperialist contradictions have receded, giving way to a decentralized mechanism of power, the supranational elite, which handles the fate of the system in its totality (Fotopoulos 2009: 88–97).

From this point of view, the inherent expansionism of the internationalized market economy system (the constant tendency toward the universalization of its institutions at all levels) cannot but be the result of the dynamic developed by inherent systemic factors that are crucial for the smooth reproduction of the heteronomous totality of capitalism as the hierarchical organizational system of society. I am not referring to the dynamic of "development or death" that pertains to the institutional framework of the market economy but to the class brewing through which this dynamic turns into praxis and acquires operational social forms. Therefore, systemic imperialism can be defined as the expansive activity of the elites that aspires to a mechanistic transplant of the class model of social organization of the Global North to the subjugated societies of the Global South (Drakos 2016: 184). The way to accomplish this goal includes various heteronomous forms of institutionalizing power, from military invasion and occupation to economic subjugation and the imposition of a regime of supervision. In any case, it always includes acts of pure coercion that de facto negate the possibility of individual and collective self-determination.

At this point, I will venture into describing the content of the structures of heteronomy linked to systemic imperialism by referencing the formula of the alchemists of the Middle Ages to describe the unity of matter and the unified structure of the world that surrounds us. "What is below is the same as what is above" (Sadoul 1982: 37): This is the codified message that is included in one of the main texts of Islamic and Western alchemy. This means that the principles that contribute to the unity of the organic matter of infinitesimal particles are exactly the same—though, obviously, at a larger scale—in the most massive natural formations, such as astral formations. Likewise, the example of hierarchical stratification that institutionalizes the unequal distribution of power among the different social monads is the same for all levels of organization of the heteronomous social paradigm. Thus, crystallized hierarchical structures supervene in the internal organization of each separate social group (bureaucratic professional trade unions), as well as in the institutional framework that regulates the relations between social groups (a hierarchical social distribution of labor within capitalism) but also between the different heteronomous totalities (relations of dependence between the metropolis/center and the periphery).

Just as the proletarian "subclass"[3] depends for its survival on the privileged social groups that own and control the entirety of the means of production, so the subjugated societies of the periphery depend on the developed economies of the center for the provision of know-how and the influx of direct or indirect productive investments, as well as the import of ready consumer products with which to cover the basic and nonbasic needs of their populations. This relation of dependence also exists between the wealthy strata and the lower-ranking social groups in the hierarchy of the subjugated society. A fundamental qualitative characteristic of this relation is that the societies of the periphery are obliged to purchase from the capitalist metropoles even those products they themselves produce, in the form of ready consumer products that have been processed by Western industries and returned to their "place of origin." Therefore, the conservation of the living standards of privileged sectors is linked more to the continuation of the exploitation of the local society and the deepening of the ties of dependence that guarantees the supremacy of the economies of the center, rather than to any process of autonomous development of local economies.

The Internationalization of Domination

In the context of liberal political theory, anti-imperialism cannot but start from admitting the obvious: namely, that isolated states relate to each other at the level of international relations. To the extent that the latter are not institutionalized in a context of equality and the equal distribution of political and economic power, interaction between the states inevitably leads to the emergence of informal hierarchies and structures of heteronomous domination. The model is the same. The heteronomous societies construct hierarchical totalities with an institutional articulation that crystallizes and establishes the unequal distribution of all forms of power between social groups and subgroups (which, in turn, might constitute new heteronomous subtotalities that are hierarchically articulated). Likewise, in the field of the permanent give-and-takes between states, informal hierarchical forms of organization are constructed that define the model of class stratification that emerges in each separate society.[4] This realization, of course, cannot lead to the assumption that the fundamental class contrast during the period of neoliberal modernity is the contrast between powerful and powerless states participating in the international system. It is obvious that the nation itself, as a fundamental monad of political organization, is fragmented by class divisions and constitutes a heteronomous hierarchical totality that cannot be conceived as a unified social monad with uniform interests and perceptions.

This assertion could apply, to a certain extent, to the state-centered phase of modernity, where the main organizational unit of the market economy system was, indeed, the nation-state, and relations of heteronomy at the international level were expressed mainly through the direct military occupation and annexation of territories, with the goal of instituting national spheres of influence and zones of exclusive economic exploitation. Colonialism was such a model of economic exploitation, which due to its ethnocentric nature inevitably led to the settlement of the differences that emerged between the nation-states in the field of economic competition through armed conflict, culminating in two disastrous world wars. Indeed, it is no coincidence that a big part of the working class of Europe's superpowers abandoned, at the moment of crisis, their internationalist outlook and frantically embraced the violent nationalism stirred up by the European elites, sacrificing class solidarity in the name of national unity and the mobilization of the forces of the "nation." A telling example of this opportunistic tendency that subconsciously linked the well-being and improvement of living conditions for a country's proletariat with the development of a powerful national capitalist economy was that of the leader of Austrian social democracy Friedrich Adler. His treacherous stance regarding the participation of the Austrian workers in the First World War has been repeatedly referenced in the work of renowned internationalist Bolshevik leaders, including Trotsky (1921). Yet another example is that of the French Communist Party (PCF), which refused to assist the Algerian people in their struggle for national independence and self-determination against French colonialism.[5] Finally, it is not easy to overlook the ease with which the German proletariat—so "developed" in what regards class consciousness, in the words of Daniel Guerin (1994)—succumbed to the ideological charms of Hitler's National Socialism.

In this sense, perhaps it is better to speak of the existence not of an integrated international system of political and economic domination during the statist phase of modernity but of multiple antagonistic systems articulated around the dominant national capitalist market economy of each given moment. That said, during the neoliberal phase of modernity, the increasing internationalization of the market economy (the continually intensifying process of opening and organically articulating national economies) is a fundamental element. In developed capitalist countries, this leads to a tendency of the organic sectors to merge and become interdependent; in what concerns the interaction of center and periphery, it inevitably leads to the institutionalization of relations of dependence and subjugation between monads with unequal economic development.

The main unit of economic development during the period of neoliberal modernity is no longer the nation-state but the gigantic multinational corporations that have grown since the mid-1970s and now control the biggest portion of global production and distribution. The organic process of the emergence of multinationals as an engine of development within the internationalized market economy and the systemic character of the phenomenon have been described in detail by Takis Fotopoulos (2008: 88–96). For lack of space, we will not repeat here the entire historical path of evolution of the market economy system that led us to the present situation.

On the contrary, more important for the purpose of the present analysis are the effects of the rise of multinational corporations on the model of capitalist exploitation, the internationalized mechanisms of drawing surplus value, the geographic distribution of wealth, and the restructuring of the hierarchies of the system of the market economy at a global scale. The main ingredients of this intensifying (supranational) economic activity of multinational corporations were the natural decentralization of one part of the production into units located in countries of the capitalist periphery and semiperiphery and, finally, the creation of supranational commercial flows and integrated chains of production in more than one country. These resulted in the exercise of "objective" economic pressures upon the national political elites so that they would adopt measures imposing the complete deregulation of the markets of capitals, commodities, and services. These policies involved the cessation of social controls—in the broader sense of the words—imposed on the markets by the national elites in order to protect both the weaker sectors of the country's capital from the consequences of international competition, as well as one part of the organized proletariat from the destructive effects the operation of the market economy had on the weaker social groups.[6]

The increasing internationalization of the capitalist economy inevitably led to a process of gradual erosion and undermining of the economic sovereignty of the nation-state and to a progressive shift of political, economic, and cultural power into the hands of an informal supranational elite. The latter became entrusted with the task of creating and reproducing, at a global scale, an institutional framework and a system of rules that would guarantee the smooth operation of the global capital and commodity market. The only reason we speak of an "informal" elite is that the global superstate is not yet a reality. But the voices of systemic ideologists (such as standing *Financial Times* columnist Gideon Rachman) that ask for the imposition of official supranational institutions of power that will enable a centralized global governance are, distressingly, ever more frequent. In this sense, it is not inappropriate to compare the current situation with the historical process of the emergence of national capitalist markets, which was necessarily accompanied by the political institution of the heteronomous form of social organization spearheaded by the power mechanism of the contemporary nation-state.

For the elites and the privileged social strata that make up the classes of the supranational elite (and originate mostly in the capitalist metropoles of the world): "The best way to guarantee their privileged position in society is not through securing the reproduction of some kind of nation-state imaginary but, on the contrary, through ensuring the global reproduction of the system of the market economy and of representative 'democracy'" (Fotopoulos 2009: 89). Therefore, the new type of imperialism cannot acquire in the market economy system the form of a territorial expansion of a dominant nation-state or of an annexation of territories through the use of military force. On the contrary, neoimperialism manifests itself through the artificial creation of social conditions that allow for the class model of organization of central developed capitalist countries to be transplanted into the societies of the periphery. This, at the same time, entails the transmission of all the pathogenic features of such a process of political, economic, and cultural "rape" of local societies and nondeveloped countries. I speak of pathogenic features because interaction between unequally developed—in productivity and technology—capitalist economies within the market economy system is based on antagonism. This can only lead to the reproduction of the hegemonic position of the powerful economy, to the creation of ties of absolute dependence and heteronomy between the two parts, and to the essential distortion of the productive model of the social totality that belongs to the periphery of the global capitalist system. It is precisely these formal hierarchical relations and structures of power concentration that are reproduced within the subjugated social totality: the incorporation of the local economy into the internationalized market economy and the modification of class power relations (in relation to class articulation as well as to the power concentrated in the hands of each social group). They, in turn, lead to the alteration of the nature of class subjects, that is, of the historical role of each social subject in the creation of the political, economic, and social content of the heteronomous social totality but also of the position the latter occupies within the global capitalist hierarchy.

Let us look at some examples of the role of the bourgeoisie in countries of the center and of the periphery. The European bourgeoisie operated, to a certain extent, as an agent of political liberalization and democratization of the authoritarian monarchies of the eighteenth and nineteenth centuries. On the contrary, the bourgeoisie of twentieth-century Latin America, under the weight of the relation of subjugation with the already overdeveloped US capitalism, was an agent of imposition of the most ruthless and criminal military dictatorships in the countries of the region. This was the ideal regime for the defense of its interests and the reproduction of its institutionalized privileges. Furthermore, Europe's corporate class, through its unlimited commercial activity, has ensured global technological and economic supremacy for European countries. At the opposite pole, Africa's new corporate class, educated in the universities of the West and having completely assimilated the power dogmas and principles of dominant neoliberal orthodoxy, cannot but operate as an agent of heteronomy for African societies. It imports ideological perceptions and cultural values that do not spring from an autonomous historical evolution of African societies, while at the same time implementing basic parameters of an outgoing model of economic "development." In this sense, the bourgeoisie of nondeveloped countries plays a crucial role in the destruction of the self-sufficiency of their societies and in the deepening of the material ties of subjugation and dependence from the capitalist metropolitan centers.[7]

Therefore, the main goal of the neoimperialism of supranational elites is the institutionalization at a global level of the conditions that will allow for the unhindered flow of capitals, commodities, and services from one domestic market to another. This creates the necessary institutional framework for multinational corporations to expand their activities in time and space, incorporate new investment destinations into their business plan, develop economies of scale, and, ultimately, impose an informal but perfected capitalist division of labor with supranational geographic and social characteristics. The natural outcome of this tendency—which originates from the "objective" development dynamic of the market economy system—is the massive subsumption of domestic economies to the unmediated rule of supranational centers of economic power. The violent restructuring of their edifice of production and consumption takes place in such a way that it smoothly becomes incorporated and serves, thereafter, the needs of a specific section of the internationalized chain of production, as defined each time by the dominant monads of the economic system; that is, by transnational corporations. In this sense, it is no coincidence that the protection of international commerce and the adoption of measures for the promotion of "open" economies was once again included in the fundamental geopolitical goals of the US strategic dogma, as was expressed in the speech war criminal Barack Obama gave at West Point Military Academy in 2014.[8]

"De Principis"[9]

"The poor are the blacks of Europe."
—Manuel González Prada

It is clear that social struggle is a structural element of heteronomous societies. In this sense, the political constitutions that define the institutional framework of the operation of an oppressive regime are but the terms that regulate the cessation of hostilities between different social groups. They are the crystallization and legal codification of the balance of power between opposing social groups at a specific historical moment and according to the outcome of social struggles. Therefore, it is clear that there is no real difference between social relations determined by the class model of social organization, on the one hand, and the relations of dependence and submission that spring from a regime of direct military occupation of one country by another, on the other. In both cases, the political constitution of heteronomous societies codifies relations of unequal distribution of power between social groups. Military occupation is merely the social condition with the highest concentration of power in the hands of the supreme authority; namely, the highest possible form of heteronomy, through the imposition of a regime of integrated heteronomy on an occupied people and the abolition of their right to self-determination. In fact, in its most extreme authoritarian version, the typology of domination in a classist social totality can acquire a form analogous to that of a society under foreign occupation.

The political character of the constitution of domination (liberal, social democrat, authoritarian, dictatorial, etc.) corresponds to the width of the social coalition that makes up the bourgeois power bloc in each heteronomous formation. In this sense, the rule of the conquerors—at least in the first phase of imposition of the occupation regime—is always despotic. This is due mostly to the extreme social isolation immediately affecting the forces of occupation; it does not occur because of the qualitative difference between the system of militarist rule of a society and an authoritarian representative "democracy" or a domestic military junta. In addition, the more multifarious the bourgeois power bloc, the more it incorporates assorted/heterogeneous social groups at its core, the more the heteronomous form of social organization that establishes it as dominant will focus on the cession and protection of individual rights by the state, on the incorporation of institutional mechanisms of income redistribution, and on the establishment of a true possibility of social mobility between the different ranks of the social hierarchy.

As Fotopoulos (2000) rightly points out, it is this "significant degree of social mobility that offers a motive to the subaltern [social] monads to tolerate the entire system [of social stratification]." But the preconditions for the conservation of social mobility are undermined by the inherent tendency of the market economy system to concentrate more and more power into fewer and fewer hands. That is why the political form of the heteronomous social totality steers toward coercion and tends to acquire increasingly authoritarian characteristics. In other words, there is a disturbance of the balance between the ideological legitimization of the social system among the lower strata—which is achieved when they internalize the hegemonic imaginary of the elites—and their coercion into fulfilling the social roles that are imposed upon them from above, through the state's organized physical violence. As Fotopoulos mentions:

> The degree of stability that can be attained by a specific authority always depends on the extent to which it can be accepted as justified by the subjugated social monads. That is, the true foundation of any power within a hierarchical totality is not the hierarchical organizations itself but the habits, opinions, values and overall imaginary meanings that unite the members of a totality under a common acceptance of hierarchical structure, as well as the mental processes that create the psychological backdrop for submission to authority and to the decisions made by others. (Fotopoulos 2000)

In this sense, military occupation as a system is similar to any classist social formation with regard to the basic parameters that constitute its foundation. The difference lies in the fact that, in the quantitative gradation of the factors that make up the social paradigm of heteronomy, the extreme parameter of physical violence prevails in military occupation. This, of course, does not exclude the possibility that the occupying army might find allies and bridgeheads within the classes of the social formation upon which it has imposed its rule. According to the aforementioned, one could arguably claim that armed imposition equals the explosive moment in which the heteronomous social totality is conceived. This type of political "big bang" necessarily accompanies the creation of the particular economic and social conditions that contribute to primitive accumulation. That is, it shapes the basic material preconditions that sustain the reproduction of the market economy as a heteronomous system of organization of social totality. Hence the fact that military conquest is the political form par excellence adopted by classical imperialism, with which it is continues to be, until today, compatible as a political, economic, and social structure of domination.

Polanyi (2001) was right in arguing there were many common features in the ways in which the domination of the Western elites was constructed during the period of what we call primitive accumulation and the era of colonialism. The same inhumane methods were used to guarantee the class hegemony of the elites both upon the people who were under the brutal rule of colonialism and upon the subaltern groups of their own countries during the initial formation of the basic parameters of the heteronomous social totality. On this, he wrote:

> Now, what the white man may still occasionally practice in remote regions today, namely, the smashing up of social structures in order to extract the element of labor from them, was done in the eighteenth century to white populations by white men for similar purposes....
>
> The analogy was all the more striking as the early laborer, too, abhorred the factory, where he felt degraded and tortured, like the native who often resigned himself to work in our fashion only when threatened with corporal punishment, if not physical mutilation. The Lyons manufacturers of the eighteenth century urged low wages primarily for social reasons. Only an overworked and downtrodden laborer would forgo to associate with his like in order to escape from that state of personal servitude under which he could be made to do whatever his master required from him. Legal compulsion and parish serfdom as in England, the rigors of an absolutist labor police as on the Continent, indentured labor as in the early Americas were the prerequisite of the "willing worker." But the final stage was reached with the application of "nature's penalty," hunger. In order to release it, it was necessary to liquidate organic society, which refused to let the individual starve. (Polanyi 2001: 172–73)

The goal of neoimperialism—or, better, a sufficient precondition for the imposition of a regime of brutal capitalist exploitation—is always the dissolution of extra-institutional networks of mutual support, collective structures of solidarity, and collectivist value systems in indigenous societies, so that the cultural hegemony of the heteronomous capitalist imaginary can prevail. In the system of the market economy, the only type of socialization and interaction tolerated between social groups is the conventional relationship; a type of impersonal relation that obeys certain formal legal norms and is protected by the state. In the same spirit, in the context of a fully commodified society, the only organizational authority of the rational social activity of individual or collective subjects can be the principle of profit, insofar as it guarantees: a) the sustainability of the activity, that is, the autonomous reproduction of its existence through the raising of funds for its own financing, and b) the social utility of the activity. Of course, utility—according to neoliberal ideological orthodoxy—depends exclusively on the activity not putting an economic burden on those who are outside it and not operating antagonistically toward another similar activity or service that one can find on the market in the form of a commodity. This, essentially, is how the fragmentation of the existing social body is accomplished, as well as the "recomposition of the economic system within its coordinates, so that each one can become incorporated into the part of the system where it was more useful" (ibid.: 176).

The parallel drawn by Polanyi between two historically distinct and apparently heterogeneous phases in the evolution of the capitalist system (primitive accumulation/colonialism) is even more timely in our day, mainly in terms of the way in which the power-driven mechanisms of neoimperialism expand but also in the objective functions they fulfill. Chronologically, as well as historically, in the order of succession in the development of the market economy, colonialism certainly follows the period of primitive accumulation. Furthermore, the sociological characteristics, the processes set in motion, as well as the changes in the historical setting caused by each phase differed from one case to the other. Classic imperialism used the societies of the enslaved periphery as trophies to be looted and as a source of unskilled laborers. For the colonial bureaucracies there was never an issue of creating a separate model of capitalist development for the colonies that could gradually contribute to the rise of a national social formation—even in terms of subjugation—within the international division of labor. That was, in good part, due to the fact that there was no optimized division of labor at the international level yet, as the nation-state remained the basic unit of development of the market economy system during neoliberal modernity.

Given that the state was the epicenter of capitalist social formations, the international division of labor was multileveled and fragmented.

Nevertheless, even India—the "crown jewel" the English would boast about—had an underprivileged role in the broader colonial plans of the empire. It was an immense natural reservoir of cotton and spices, as well as a source of millions of unskilled and destitute workers. In the words of Noam Chomsky:

> British officials, merchants, and investors "amassed vast fortunes," gaining "wealth beyond the dreams of avarice" (Parker). That was particularly true in Bengal, which . . . "was destabilized and impoverished by a disastrous experiment in sponsored government"—one of the many "experiments" in the Third World that have not exactly redounded to the benefit of the experimental subjects. Two English historians of India, Edward Thompson and G.T. Garrett, described the early history of British India as "perhaps the world's high-water mark of graft": a gold-lust unequaled since the hysteria that took hold of the Spaniards of Cortes' and Pizzaro's age filled the English mind. Bengal in particular was not to know peace again until she has been bled white." It is significant, they remark, that one of the Hindustani words that has become part of the English language is "loot." The fate of Bengal brings out essential elements of the global conquest. Calcutta and Bangladesh are now the very symbols of misery and despair. In contrast, European warrior-merchants saw Bengal as one of the richest prizes in the world. (Chomsky 2015: 15)

The endogenous capitalist changes that took place in the colonies were arguably the outcome of the long-term rule of advanced capitalist countries. They occurred as secondary consequences of a destructive economic policy that certainly did not prioritize the needs of the colonies and reflected an already crystallized power relation between the colonies and their respective European metropoles. On the contrary, the incorporation of local societies into the system of rule of internationalized capitalism during neoliberal modernity takes place through their violent adaptation to the neoliberal models of the wealthy societies of the North—always from a subaltern, less favored position. The imposition of the neoliberal social paradigm is completed through the adoption of an extrovert model of capitalist development. One could schematically claim that, in the first case (colonialism), underdevelopment is the symptom and a result of a crystallized condition of rule. But in the second case (neoliberal modernity), dependence and poverty originate from a dynamic process that creates and establishes the preconditions for the reproduction of the economic rule of the metropoles of the center, through the objective influence of the forces of the globalized market on the regional economy.

As a result of this process, the internationalized market economy system creates, within the heteronomous social paradigm, a fundamental contradiction. On the one hand, it is incapable of convincingly combining the universalization of its basic institutions with the nationalist ideology in its classical form. On the other hand, the nationalist imaginary continues to exist within the core of the imaginary creation of the statist form of social organization. Thus, the incorporation of a society—from a position of inferiority—into the economic hierarchies imposed by internationalized capitalism is not generally compatible with a traditional nationalist narrative. Namely, it does not correspond to a small-town, old-style nationalism that would unite the different ranks of the social hierarchy under a unified cultural or racial imaginary community.

The extroverted model of "development" that is imposed by the market economy system does not create the appropriate social conditions for regional elites to ideologically legitimize their power through praising an artificial "grandeur of the nation." Within the institutional framework of globalization, their politics brings the exact opposite results, for it does not allow for the implementation of a certain degree of social justice in the domestic sphere that could give a material dimension to the imaginary notion of the symbolic national "community." On the contrary, the elites and the privileged groups that embody the rule of internationalized capitalism in the societies of the periphery play a catalytic role in deepening material ties of dependence and subjugation of local communities in their relation with the capitalist metropoles. They also display a cultural heterogeneity with regard to the lower classes, for the world vision, habits, way of life, interests, moral principles, and, of course, material interests they defend do not correspond to the values and principles of the dependent strata; on the contrary, they are completely separated from them. Lieros has described this privileged multinational minority as follows:

> The cohesion of all under the rule of capital is accomplished through a condensed circulation of images, digitized information, capitals, commodities, but also *humans*: executives constantly move within a circuit whose basic nodes are relatively homogeneous. Indeed,

airports, five-star hotels, big highways, expensive malls or restaurants are more or less the same in New York, London, Shanghai, Sao Paolo, or even Lagos. . . . The global elite seems to have unlimited power and share the same values, the same way of life, and the same culture. Without any—"cosmic" or other—epiphany, these "nomads" speak the same language: English. (Lieros 2012: 46–51)

In other words, the hegemonic culture and living conditions of the neobourgeois class are cosmopolitan. They are more likely to turn their well-intentioned interest toward the unfortunate victims of an earthquake in Nepal or to the victims of the heinous Darfur genocide than to show some elementary consideration for the poor and disadvantaged that live in the same country as they do. This, of course, is no coincidence, for, as Bauman (2005: 57–63) has shown, a display of humanitarian spirit toward the popular strata of a "national" capitalist regime could easily cause concepts that are damaging for the privileged social groups to surface, concepts such as "social justice," "redistribution," and "the welfare state," which neoliberalism has put a lot of effort into dissolving and banishing from public discourse.

Dependence and Class Rearticulation in Greece

They make a desert and call it peace.
—Tacitus

There has been a lot of discussion in recent years of the relation of dependence between the Greek economy and the advanced economies of the markets of the capitalist center. But the content of the term has not been sufficiently specialized and analyzed from the scope of autonomist political theory, neither have its consequences for the choices and strategy of the contemporary antagonistic movement been meticulously assessed. It is important that such analysis be attempted, for the interpretation of the relations of unequal power distribution between two market economies that are at different levels of development is not only an academic issue. It is also crucial for the understanding of the ideological orientation and political profile of social groups in Greece, of the agents that influence the balance of power between the classes, as well as of the framework within which the Greek capitalist economy is reproduced, on the one hand, and the inherent limits of this reproduction, on the other.

The Greek economy is undoubtedly part of the underprivileged periphery of an internationalized economic structure that ranks local economies in a hierarchical system of stratification on the basis of the productive needs that each economy is destined to satisfy within the overall division of labor in globalized capitalism. This means that the trigger of possible social unrest and destabilization of domestic heteronomous institutions can easily come from the "outside." This, in fact, is what happened in the mid-1970s, when the rhythms of economic development during the seven years of the military junta slowed down because of the crisis of stagnant inflation in the capitalist center (Fotopoulos 2010: 42). It also occurred in 2009, with the bursting of the financial bubble in the USA, the turning of the financial crisis into a public debt crisis, and the enormous sums invested by the Greek state in order to prevent the collapse of the banks (Fotopoulos 2009: 70–101). Furthermore, the social changes and class shifts that have been taking place in recent years in Greece at a tectonic scale (such as the impoverishment of a big part of the middle class and the proletarization of small business owners) is the outcome of measures that have been greatly dictated by international capital with the goal of entering the Greek market under privileged terms and winning complete control over the domestic economic activity, eradicating any factor that might stand in the way of its despotic rule. The fate of small business owners is decided in the corridors of the European Commission building, turning them into "collateral losses" of the overall plan of restructuring the Greek capitalist model. Hence the increased "radicalization" displayed by the GSEVEE (Hellenic Confederation of Professionals, Craftsmen, and Merchants), as well as the fiery communiqués issued from time to time by the institutional body of small business owners against the policies of the Brussels dictatorship.

This, of course, does not imply that retailers must immediately be considered potential allies of a libertarian movement for antisystemic change. What the retailer wants, above all, is to protect his property. Therefore, he would certainly be more willing to support a nationalist conservative government that promises measures for the protection of the material conditions of reproduction of the retail class, rather than join a radical, antistate movement that questions the very concept of private property. The tension between small business owners—as an active branch of the economy—and government policy has to do with different strategic approaches to the issue of economic "development" within the institutional framework of the market economy and not with the abolition of the system of the market economy itself. To the extent that the smooth reproduction of the market system demands the dissolution of small businesses and the proletarization of the retail class by salami-slicing, the petty bourgeois businessman will ultimately opt for being absorbed by supranational capital and becoming a wage laborer, rather than break with all the parameters on which the neoliberal social paradigm is founded. And this is so because he has the aspiration to someday be able to go back to the individual regime of limited "autonomy" of the retailer, provided that, as a proletarian, he "works enough" to gather the required amount of money.

But the tendency toward the systematic decimation of the traditional middle-class strata and their replacement by a new small bourgeois class (which owes its prosperity and material conditions of existence to the direct assimilation of the domination of multinational corporations and the expansion of their activity) is the result of the dynamic of the market economy system. This is a dynamic of continuous concentration of power at all levels—that is a characteristic feature of the dependent capitalist economy in the neoliberal period of modernity. Thus, the great mass of petty bourgeois and retailers that constituted the main bloc of Greek society's class structure, a class whose professional and social constitution was linked to economic activities oriented toward the domestic market, is on the verge of extinction. The division between ruling and subjugated social strata is objectified and consolidated at the highest level, and privileged groups climb up the hierarchy, groups that are either directly employed by the multinational corporations or perform labor that is complementary and utterly incorporated into the cycle of accumulation of supranational capital (wage laborers employed by the private sector, subcontractors of corporate activities, importers of consumer products, etc.), that is, oriented toward the external, international capitalist market.

The electoral rise of Golden Dawn is but a desperate effort of the big mass of petty bourgeois to resist the visible threat of their collective impoverishment and the sharp rise of the neoliberal bourgeoisie. Despite the fact that, in the political literature of the anarchist space, the figure of the "petty bourgeois" is considered the embodiment of the most alienated and repulsive anthropological type among all those living within the market economy system and, at the same time, is attributed the role of an "objectively" reactionary social force, I believe the popularity of Golden Dawn among the petty bourgeois should not be interpreted as an inherent tendency of the latter toward conservative positions and opinions. In fact, I consider it is important to see that precisely because of their social positioning between the subaltern and higher social strata, the petty bourgeois are an unstable subtotality that can at times turn into the raw material of heteronomous ideological currents but can also ally with popular movements aiming at the radical transformation of society. Therefore, their turn to Golden Dawn should not be interpreted through easy references to the inherent reactionary mentality of the petty bourgeois and their instinctive enmity toward autonomy. It is above all the result of the political inability of the antagonistic movement to effectively question, through its class force, the institutions and structures of power of the heteronomous social system.

It appears to be a general norm that in every historical moment when a possible class polarization and escalation of social struggle takes place the petty bourgeois tend to join the side that has the best chance of prevailing. During the Spanish Revolution (1936–1939), when the organized proletariat proved powerful enough (at least at the beginning) to impose a regime of labor self-administration on the Catalan industry, the class of retailers responded energetically to the revolutionary call and proceeded to socialize the productive branches under its control. At this point it is worth mentioning the example of the socialization of bakeries, hair salons, and ophthalmic instrument laboratories that were united and reorganized from their foundations, following anarcho-syndicalist models, to create modern and far more efficient productive units (Dolgoff 1982).

On the contrary, in 1968 France, the alliance between the students in revolt and the workers failed to deliver the coup de grâce to the de Gaulle regime, which until that moment awkwardly observed the escalation of class struggle. As then young activist Daniel Cohn-Bendit observes:[10]

> This phase, short though it was, showed up the political vacuum in French society and created a new historical phenomenon: a duality of non-authority. From 27 to 30 May nobody had any power in France. The government was breaking up, de Gaulle and Pompidou were isolated. The police, intimidated by the size of the strike, and exhausted by two weeks of fighting in the streets, were incapable of maintaining public order. The Army was out of sight, conscripts could not have been used for a cause in which few of them believed. (Cohn-Bendit 1968: 124)

The revolt seemed to gradually retreat as the general strike of ten million workers proved incapable of implementing an antisystemic program for the creation of large-scale institutions of self-administration, even though it had de facto dissolved institutionalized heteronomous powers. De Gaulle was then able to reclaim the initiative of movements and the petty bourgeois participated massively in the huge concentration organized by the regime in order to prove it had not irrevocably lost the support of the popular strata. "Then petty bourgeois, racist, nationalist, reactionary, Fascist, religious, Catholic, Protestant or Jewish, France gradually shook off the dust and marched sprucely down the Champs Elysées, shouting support for the old general" (ibid.: 128).

The oscillation of the petty bourgeois between conservative and radical social conceptions was the characteristic that defined capital's model of class hegemony in Greece during the period following the military junta. But the social power bloc on which the neoliberal social paradigm is based is much more homogeneous and solid in its interests and opinions and, for this reason, a lot more monolithic and authoritarian in the way it imposes its rule. Indeed, the arithmetical supremacy of small holders in Greece's social stratification had, until recently, left some space for political agreement between sectors of the antagonistic movement and the radical elements at the fringes of the petty bourgeois. On the contrary, the new model of class domination crystallizes the hegemony of an elite that draws its power from the unified supranational economic sphere following the rise of the internationalized market economy. Under this elite we find, in a subsidiary role, the privileged social classes of the new bourgeois. Their dependence on internationalized capital for their affluence does not allow them to internalize or mediate their relations with the subaltern social classes on the basis of a small-town nationalist imaginary or to define themselves as vessels of an alternative vision for the "rebirth" of the Greek nation-state. In addition, dependence on the centers of economic power of the metropolitan capitalist countries had, from the outset, a distorting effect on the social subjects who would later become the agents that transplanted capitalist domination into the Greek territory. As Kondylis writes:

> The dependence of commercial/non-industrial activity on capitalism from abroad helped the domestic patriarchal labor and social relations to survive, for the economic product of these relations

could increase and be absorbed in a market that does not care about its social origin; namely, its increase and absorption did not demand the restructuring of the domestic economic sphere and the overturning of its own social preconditions. (Kondylis 1995: 16)

One cannot but smile in the face of the contradictions that the waged advocates of neoliberalism are forced into when trying to reconcile the incorporation of Greece into the New International Order—in terms of enslavement and subjugation—with a narrative of the "modernization" and "progress" of the "backward" Greek society. Thus, political science professor Nikos Marantzidis (2014) goes as far as to express his disappointment that Germany, the leading force of the European sector of the supranational elite, does not seem to have the necessary experience in imperialist governance techniques to skillfully and efficiently manipulate political developments within the Greek protectorate. The power-thirsty invention of neoliberal pseudo-cosmopolitanism has no room for interclass, unifying narratives of an alleged "general interest" of the social classes.

The traditional, Greek-centered "thousand-year Greek Christian civilization" (Kondylis 1995: 30–37) cannot fit into the core of an ideology that defends the absolute heteronomy of the Greek economy by the internationalized market economy and serves to theoretically substantiate the need for an unconditional submission of the human, natural, and material resources of the local society to the needs of capitalist globalization. Indeed, the social mobility between verticalized levels of social organization during the social democratic period of modernity (1920–1975) has been replaced by the possibility of a horizontal mobility within the globalized economy for privileged social groups only. In advanced sectors of the international market economy, when the neoliberal model of class organization is not capable of adequately reproducing itself under the objective and subjective conditions of domestic society, this is achieved by professional nomadism or the search for work even outside national borders.

The very dynamic of the extroverted model of development of the market economy contributes to the absolute extinction of any notion of local self-sufficiency and the utter dependence of the domestic economy on price fluctuations, the ups and downs of the overall level of economic activity, and the shifts and rearrangements that take place in the international market. Indeed, who can forget the example of Uruguay during the 1950s and 1960s, when the sudden plunge in the international prices of meat and wool—pillars of the domestic capitalist economy—caused the drastic limitation of government revenues with which the state financed the country's social democratic model of development? The result was consecutive currency devaluations, the growth of external lending, and, finally, the state's incapacity to pay the salaries and pensions of public servants on time, leading to generalized social unrest and the uprising of the state-dependent middle classes and the militant proletariat (Antisystemic 2012). Furthermore, this type of economic development in an economy that depends on the global market cannot respond to a program of "national" productive reconstitution. It can only acquire the form of fragmented and isolated islets of "development" in sectors of the economy that are one-sidedly handpicked by the supranational capital on the basis of their profitability. For example, during the seven-year military junta in Greece, when there was a flow of direct investments from the capitalist center to the regional economies, the interest of international capital in the Greek economy focused mainly on the chemical industry, the extraction of aluminum, and oil refineries, without, however, proceeding with investments in the metallurgic sector, which was vital for the development of a "national" economic edifice (Fotopoulos 2010: 43).

In other words, the opening of an economy to the international markets and the subsequent outgoing "development" can never lead to the creation of an integrated capitalist economy with national characteristics.[11] Analyzing the mechanisms of economic rule developed by US imperialism in order to obtain surplus value and squeeze the wealth out of Latin American countries, Cuban revolutionary Armando Hart showed that the control exercised by the US metropolitan capital spread over the totality of the productive branches of the true economy of Latin American countries (industry, processing, credit, distribution, farming) and was not simply limited to the capitalization of the "comparative advantages" of overdeveloped US capitalism (Gerassi 1971: 494–97). This means that a developed market economy is a Leviathan, an integrated structure of heteronomy and rule that naturally reproduces the relations of unequal power distribution as its preferred way of interacting with the dependent regional economies at all levels. For example, we observe that while Greek governments deceptively talk of tourism as the engine of "development" in the Greek protectorate and celebrate the fact that approximately sixteen million tourists visited Greece, the corresponding number of visitors in only one of the metropoles of the capitalist center, London, was as high as fifteen million in 2014.[12] This data confirms the claim that the capitalization of "comparative advantages" does not establish the supremacy of the dependent economy in any sector in which it might conserve a relative superiority while, for neoliberals, it constitutes a suitable method for the achievement of development within the system of the market economy. It simply objectively urges it to occupy its subaltern position in the hierarchical division of labor within international capitalism.

Therefore, it is reasonable for the well-paid propagandists of the rule of multinational and domestic merchant capital to debase ideological references to the country's "national grandeur" and recur to the pseudo-cosmopolitan imaginary of the elites that administer the European Union. This way, they defend the legitimization of the power that is exercised by the supranational elite on the heteronomous strata of the new poor European periphery. As they have no promise left to make to the proletarians on the fulfillment of their desires and the satisfaction of their material needs, they bombard them with sermons on the blessings of labor ("lazy Southern Europeans")[13] and the need for political stability (respect for "democratic" institutions), which they invest with ritual calls to the supranational boogeyman of Islamic terrorism. Along this line, for example, we find the reference by Theodoropoulos (2014): "Located where the western world meets a region . . . riven by the barbarity of a murderous Islam that hates democracy and all it involves, Greece must always remember that the values of democracy are not to be taken for granted." This is the pseudo-cosmopolitanism of the forces of domination and exploitation that we must rid ourselves of in order to establish true proletarian internationalism based on equal relations of autonomy, integrated mutual dependence, and solidarity between the strata of the oppressed, both in the domestic sphere and in the subjugated people of the periphery.

Antinomies of Internationalism

> *War to the castles, peace for the peasant homes.*
> —Slogan of the French Revolution

Systemic imperialism leads to the fragmentation of the social body, the imposition of hierarchies, the absolute heteronomy of the proletarian strata, and the institutionalization of cannibalistic competition between social monads. In this sense, proletarian internationalism as a political practice and worldview of the subaltern classes should concentrate on the exact opposite. Notably, it should explicitly pursue the abolition of the basic institutions of heteronomy: representative "democracy" and the market economy. Therefore, it becomes clear that nationalism is no longer the only political tendency par excellence that opposes internationalism; it is mainly systemic neoimperialism, assisted by a cosmopolitan ideology focused on the dogma of "humanitarian" military interventions, the limitation of national sovereignty, and a constitutional chauvinism of postmodern origins (Fotopoulos 2003: 52–58). A telling example is today's Great Britain, which has turned into a police state. Under the rule of a cold-blooded parliamentarian "dictatorship," it ruthlessly suppresses any attempt at organized resistance by the nonprivileged social classes. But its official ideology does not recur to a small-town, old-line English nationalism; on the contrary, it is completely in line with the ideological commands of the globalized capitalist economy.

Organizations such as the neofascist British National Party and the disruptive, deplorable far-right English Defence League have been banished to the margins of politics and are scorned by the advocates of domination and the political analysts in charge of shaping public opinion.[14] In the best of cases, such as that of Greece's Golden Dawn, neofascists play the role of the "useful idiot" for the elites holding economic and political power. They are mobilized as a subsidiary mechanism from above in order to reinforce the foundations of the heteronomous social formation, as a counterweight to the centrifugal political and social forces that threaten to destroy it in times of crisis. Yet the fascist extreme right fails to act as an independent and potentially dominant political force. This is so because the institutional framework of the neoliberal social paradigm is by no means compatible with the centralizing economic measures of the traditional program of fascism as a political movement. Hence the ideological transformation of the Austrian Freedom Party when it participated in a coalition government in 1999 or the subtle but steady shift of the French National Front toward the political center, with the abolition of the most extreme positions from its official ideology as it comes closer to winning state power (Hainsworth 2000).

But while the supranational institutional framework of the neoliberal social paradigm is defined one-sidedly through different political lines as the decadence and withdrawal of the rule of the nation-state, the narrative of a false internationalism does the same for itself. The EU has incorporated this mythology on neoliberal internationalism into its political vocabulary unaltered. In fact, it is accustomed to deploying the ideological prestige that comes with this "progressive" identity in order to delegitimize any protest against its authoritarian policies. For this reason, it cautions all opposing forces, claiming they signal a sad relapse of the isolation and bigotry of a dated nationalist imaginary. Yet the EU is a ruling political organization with supranational characteristics that is in no way related to the revolutionary alternative proposal of internationalism.

The goal of an internationalist proposal is the complete dissolution of hierarchical relations, the creation of economic structures of integrated interdependence and mutuality, and the establishment of the autonomy of the social monads that make up its organizational model. On the contrary, the EU is an artificial union of states whose main unifying element is coercion. The debasement of the sovereignty of the nation-state within the institutional framework of the EU does not entail an emancipating perspective. Quite the opposite: it includes a process of transferring political and administrative competencies from the domestic to the supranational sphere. The fact that the bureaucratic administrative mechanism of the EU is made up of a multinational class of officials and technocrats does not means it is not a social stratum that has privileges and interests of its own, as well as an independent class awareness of its social role and mission. This cosmopolitan bureaucracy becomes necessary, for the cornerstone of "unity" within the EU is the system of the internationalized market economy. While the latter can nurture bonds of mutual dependence between the economic monads, this interaction is based exclusively on the driving force of competitiveness. It incorporates them into informal hierarchies between economies that exist at different levels of technological evolution, structural cohesion, and productivity. Therefore, the main mission of this vast army of technocrats is the reinforcement and reproduction of the capitalist hierarchy with a parallel conservation of formal equality between the member-states. Devoid of nationalist prejudices, they openly asseverate their allegiance to the cosmopolitan European "ideal."[15]

Each heteronomous social totality, notably, each form of social organization that is based on the unequal distribution of power between its members, needs a central political authority that will oversee and provide for the maintenance of law and order. This is because the cohesion of the social totality greatly depends on the effectiveness of strategies used to force the subaltern members to follow and materialize the commands of the higher levels of the social hierarchy. Malatesta (1994) once wrote on the heteronomous society: "It was still association and cooperation, outside which there is no possible human life; but it was a way of cooperation, imposed and controlled by a few for their own personal interest."

From this standpoint, the European Commission is nothing but the supranational government that looks out for the collective interest of European capitalists, the central agent that organizes the collective force of the European elites against the antagonistic supranational capitalist blocs. Of course, this does not mean the European Commission and the vast bureaucratic mechanism that is under its command is "neutral" with regard to politics and class, that it is a group of technocrats in charge of performing simple technical tasks. Anyone who plays the role of the collective capitalist must be utterly imbued by the capitalist values and perceptions, embrace the "supremacy" of the system of the market economy, understand its basic laws of movement, and have an invested interest in maintaining and reproducing its basic structures. In this sense, not only is the collective capitalist not "neutral" politically or economically; he is, rather, the most entrenched and unremorseful advocate of the systemic establishment.

But while the EU is a cosmopolitan, power-driven teratogenesis that does not in the least fulfill the basic requirements of an international organization, this does not mean that analogous hegemonic political forces in the anti-EU pole, such as the National Front in France or UKIP in Great Britain, should be credited with the role of providing some sort of emancipating orientation to Europe's working classes. The truth is that anti-EU nationalists of all colors have incorporated in their programs mostly conservative demands for the restoration of social "injustices" and the "salvation" of the proletarian strata, which has been irreparably affected by the marketization of all aspects of social life and is now treated by the elites as an excess segment of the population. This nationalist ideological expropriation of the demand for social justice is feasible only because the impoverished popular strata are incapable of collective self-determination and of defining the general subjective and objective terms of their own social existence.

The degradation of living standards in the countries of the European semiperiphery is but a symptom of the strengthening of the ties of subjugation under and dependence on the dominant elites of the metropolitan center; notably, of the tendency to concentrate economic and political power into even fewer hands, a tendency that is innate in the system of the market economy. In this context, it is easy for nationalists to claim they defend the return to a preexisting right of the popular classes to self-determination. But in essence, they spread propaganda on the virtues of going back to a nation-centered model of capitalist economy, in which the working classes will, undoubtedly, occupy a subjugated position in the social hierarchy.

It is no coincidence that the Eurosceptic parties that tilt toward the right are flourishing, mostly in the "wealthy" countries of the European North (England, France, Scandinavian countries), that is, where the organic interlacing of the national economies within the context of the globalized economy occurs in terms of bidirectional penetration and mutual dependence, and the element of the "national economy" (to wit, partial self-sufficiency of sectors of the bourgeoisie) allows for the conservation

> of the economic and political power/force of the state in defining the terms and forms of economic operation in its area of jurisdiction. Thus, in what regards the element of interdependence/dependence, these relations are expressed today mainly at the level of relations between the states and the multinational corporations that operate on their soil. (Fotopoulos 2010: 94–95)

Furthermore, the political and economic elites of the South long ago lost any independence from the dominant forces of the North and are incapable of playing an autonomous role in the international political scene. That is why, in said countries, resistance against the social steamroller imposed by the EU acquired more militant characteristics and was partly expressed in terms of rebellion and rupture-from-below toward the dominant social paradigm. But this resistance, insofar as it is successfully mediated by systemic political institutions, has been expropriated by the program of "radical" parties of the systemic Left, such as Syriza in Greece or Podemos in Spain.

One could reasonably argue that political nationalism is the embodiment of the collective demand of the bourgeois minority for independence from its competitors. On the contrary, internationalism is the expression of the demand of the majority and heteronomous proletarian strata for self-determination and confrontation with the new bourgeoisie.

The bourgeois class is not productive. Its reproduction and subsistence depend on the effective assimilation by the working classes of the goals and operation of the economic forms that serve the continuation of its rule. That is why the bourgeois class has no other choice but to recur to the nationalist imaginary in order to forge symbolic ties of "unity" with the masses it exploits and suppresses.

That said, the proletarian strata—which includes all of society's productive classes—have no other choice but to attack and question the nationalist imaginary, if they want to rid themselves of the guardianship and command of the capitalists. This process undoubtedly includes, if not the total disappearance of the concept of the nation, at least its radical transformation (as concerns the way the social members are linked through language, common origins of culture and civilization, and proximity of beliefs, traditions, and values). All beliefs and values that pertain to the heteronomous tradition—and are, therefore, contrary to the ideal of ecumenical liberation and universal class solidarity from the outset—must be eradicated through their delegitimization in the consciousness of the insurgents. In relation to this, the anarchist Gregori Maximoff writes:

> The right to be oneself ... is a natural consequence of the principles of liberty and equality. ... International freedom and equality, world-wide justice, are higher than all national interests. National rights cease to be a consequence of these higher principles if, and when, they place themselves against liberty and even outside liberty. (Schmidt and Van der Walt 2009: 310)

The reshaping of international relations and their adaptation to the principles of proletarian internationalism will surely not come about through the prevalence of well-intentioned instincts in the psyche of the lower classes. Neither will they come effortlessly after a sudden revelation of the virtuous nature of the proletariat, contrary to the innate "evilness" of the power-thirsty systemic elites. Internationalist solidarity is itself an antisystemic political project, and its prevalence presupposes the rupture with what exists. It also entails the redefinition of the life of insurgent communities around a social paradigm that expresses a liberating democratic morality, the hegemonic values of autonomy, but also the institutions/processes of equal distribution of political and economic power that materialize the principles of complete interdependence and self-determination.

Historically, the aspiration to a global implementation of the principles of proletarian internationalism has come up against the very real limits imposed by the way in which the heteronomous system organizes and fragments social life. Furthermore, it led the movements that could have been its exponents not only into political contradictions but also into the wavering institutional forms that would constitute the political expression of the internationalist movement. Thus, political commentators often blame Stalin for having turned the internationalist Russian Revolution into an increasingly isolated and nationalist regime. But anyone who wants to precisely pinpoint the moment the Bolsheviks withdrew from their political proposal and failed to observe the internationalist commitments that were at the core of their ideology should go back to Lenin signing the peace treaty of Brest-Litovsk. At that moment Stalin had barely begun to emerge from the unknown world of the illegal mechanism set in place by the party in Baku (Deutscher 1984: 193–95).

Indeed, what was the internationalist class duty of the Russian workers in the face of the wild beast of German militarism? Surrender to the powerful German imperialists, putting an end to the war and, thus, protecting the fortunes and survival of the proletarian revolution within the country? Or continue to fight, supporting the German working class, which was at a point of revolutionary turmoil and was ready to launch its own attack against the kaiser? The satisfaction of the needs of the soldiers in revolt, the insurrectionist working class, and the millions of impoverished farmers in the countryside commanded capitulation. The end of the war had also been one of the main demands that brought a critical mass of Russian proletarians to the side of the revolution. Yet this did not stop the German Spartacists from talking about what was, essentially, their abandonment by the Bolshevik revolutionary regime as a movement of "erroneous strategic calculation," thus expressing—in quite a reserved fashion, it must be said—their bitterness with regard to this deviation of the Russian revolutionaries from the principles and values of the internationalism they claimed to defend. On this, Rosa Luxemburg wrote:

> Psychologically, we can understand that in their situation, the Bolsheviks feel the need to believe, in the fundamental question of peace, that their policies are crowned with success and present it in that way to the Russian people. But when we look at things with calm, they are presented under another light. The most direct

result of the cessation of war (or ceasefire) in the East will be only to see the German troops head from East to West. But what I am saying? They are already there. Trotsky and his comrades can give themselves and give the Soviets the satisfaction that they wanted to succeed, as a condition of the ceasefire, to oblige the Germans not to attempt movements of their armies in order not to capture the Western forces from behind. For this statement, German army officers can laugh under their whiskers, knowing very well what this means.... Still warm from the scenes of brotherhood with the revolutionary Russian soldiers, the common group pose in front of the photographer, the songs and the great hooray in the sounds of the International, the German "comrades" are now thrown with sleeves raised in the fire of massive heroic acts to crush, as much as they can, the French, English and Italian proletarians. (Prudhommeaux 1981: 132–33)

This original sin accompanies almost all revolutions from the moment of their outbreak, for obvious reasons: revolutions a) take place in a specific time and place and have to do with the redistribution of power between social groups that preexist in social formations that are aligned with a territorial definition of their existence and b) are surrounded by hostile social totalities that have the force of preventing, with their own mechanisms of domination, the spreading of revolutionary turmoil within their own borders (Halliday 1999: 207–34). In fact, very often the political, economic, and diplomatic isolation of the insurrectionist society is followed by violent military action in order to crush the revolution where it began. Therefore, it seems that the retrenchment of the victorious revolution is a necessary measure of self-defense and self-conservation and has to do, mainly, with the hostile reaction at the international level and less so with the class correlations within the side revolting. No matter how internationalist the origins of a revolutionary political theory might be, as soon as the latter manages to express the interests and desires of the proletariat and materialize their hegemony in society, it will find itself up against the structural features of the international system of rule and will be forced to take into account the material limits it imposes upon its political practice.

For example, if an anarchist commune is quick in declaring it does not recognize the political border of nation-states (and it would have every right to do so on the basis of its political theory of liberation), this would automatically give the "external" enemy forces a pretext for armed intervention. This, of course, would be preceded by references to the threat that the "revisionist" border-related tendencies of the newly formed revolutionary republic represent for their own territorial integrity. Thus, arguably, the de facto recognition of the limits of an artificial political space (borders) within which a revolution is born could possibly favor its existence, at least in its initial stages. Of course, this does not in the least mean that the community revolting should necessarily slip toward its "self-definition" in the (heteronomous) terms of the nationalist imaginary. The institutions, structures, and processes of self-administration within the autonomous social totality will be created through the alterations in the social conditions and whichever imaginary meanings prevail during the revolutionary process, but they will not necessarily bear the artificial characteristics of the abstract legal notion of "citizenship." Furthermore, the measure par excellence for the definition of a true proletarian internationalism in our days is the extent to which it can include the domestic multinational proletariat (immigrants) within the community of insurgents, as well as within the society it dreams of constructing. In other words, internationalism begins from within the heteronomous social totality and has to do, above all, with the terms through which the antagonistic social subject is politically expressed and articulated.

In her chapter of this book, Dimitra Kotouza attempts to point out this problematic relationship between the domestic antagonistic movement and the masses of immigrants, as expressed in the context of the social struggle that has been taking place in Greece since the signing of the first memorandum. She also refers to the material limits of the movement's invocation of the ideal of proletarian internationalism and its subsequent failure to overcome, in practice, its underlying nation-centered foundation and forge true class ties with immigrants as a separate social monad. Despite the differences of the theoretical framework within which they interpret social reality, these two chapters have a way of complementing each other due to the fact that liberating social theory has been stagnant for years. Although it expresses a militant antiglobalization discourse, it often falls back to a defensive nationalism as the last line of defense of the proletariat (Terzakis 2015). On the other hand, while it is right in focusing on the multinational composition of the proletariat, antinationalism with a "class consciousness" completely obscures the new systemic structures of supranational rule and their role in shaping the balance of power between classes and social groups. Furthermore, the anti-imperialist approach, while pointing out the mechanisms of concentrating power at the supranational level, runs the risk of succumbing anew to a nation-centered perception of the basic parameters that make up a social totality. At the other end of the scale, stale antinationalism avoids falling into nationalist traps but it does not incorporate internationalized rule in its analysis, while it also gives in to statist "necessary" solutions, thus confirming the force of institutionalized heteronomy. The contradictory political results of this "consequent" ideological course were displayed in full color, for example, by the English antifa movement on the issue of Brexit. It emphatically supported the "remain" side, obviously driven by a will to oppose the domestic far-right forces that, in their majority, opted for "leave." So, we have here (to use a favorite Marxist word) a fetishization of the EU that is elevated, wrongly in my opinion, to a bulwark against nationalism, racism, and xenophobia.

The same occurs with the apparent "antistatism" of the antinationalist approach, unlike statist tendencies that, according to this specific critique, are innately anti-imperialist. Kotouza is right in criticizing the way in which the antagonistic movement projected its own political goals in its interaction with the struggles of immigrants and rarely took into account the needs and interests of the latter. Nevertheless, the content of the immigrants' protests never went beyond the self-evident demand for their political recognition by the state's legal system and the granting of their basic rights to facilitate their permanence in the country and put an end to the systematic police persecutions and legal prosecutions. Unlike the antinationalist opinion that such a development could undermine the force of the heteronomous institutional framework, I do not believe the incorporation of the immigrants into the system will challenge the class organization of heteronomous totality. On the contrary, immigrant populations are assimilated through their formal "legalization." In other words, instead of leading to a de-hellenization or deconstruction of the state's national constitution, it is the immigrant element that is, somehow, "nationalized," in the sense that it is assimilated by the system's structures as a subject of civil law with specific legal rights and obligations. But this results in a renewed reinforcement of the state form, given that the rights—as inseparable elements of the state form—turn individuals into participants in the imaginary institution and reproduction of the heteronomous society, for they legitimize a power from which they are allegedly protecting us.

Besides, it is no coincidence that even PASOK (Panhellenic Socialist Movement) of the era of "antiauthoritarians in power"[16] voted a short-term law that granted political rights to all (second-generation) immigrants who fulfilled certain formal preconditions.[17] Discerning the impending shattering of its electorate as a result of the austerity imposed by the era of memorandums, the socialist party set in motion a preliminary plan to expand its nepotistic network beyond the limits of the traditional composition of the Greek electorate. This initiative from above met with the approval of part of the anarchist sphere. As anarchist philosopher Murray Bookchin wrote (1969), however, class struggle in the developed market economies of the North historically acquired the role of a structural element of the system that ultimately served as a mechanism for the assimilation of the working class and contributed to the unity of capitalism, rather than being a starting point for widespread social war from below against the totality of heteronomous institutions, outside and beyond the field of production.

It must also be pointed out that although post-Marxism claims to be the highest advocate of the interests of the proletariat, it displays an unprecedented indifference toward issues related to the constitution of the material conditions of life of the "submission." One could argue that the notion of "productive reconstitution" can turn toward a more procapitalist content and adopt the form of an assertion of capital in other terms—in terms of an alternative, dominating administration of the system of the market economy. But what is more troubling in this approach is the refusal to examine this issue through a libertarian lens, given that libertarian communism requires specific material terms and preconditions in order to acquire tangible forms of social institution through the self-determination of collective subjects. Furthermore, the international market economy system imposes its rule precisely through a process of continuous and multilevel fragmentation of its social surroundings, as well as of its restructuring in social totalities and subtotalities that are hierarchically ordered and in a relation of antagonism. It follows, therefore, that the revolutionary plan—that is, the antisystemic program that the heteronomous proletarian strata will be called to materialize from below—will have to negate, by definition, all structural inequalities and hierarchical dependencies that consolidate the unequal distribution of power and the rule of one segment of the society over the rest. To reject the need to constitute the material foundation of communism in terms of the self-determination of the popular strata in the name of a cosmopolitan, allegedly "ecumenical" perception conceals the classist nature of the cosmopolitan ideal itself. That is, it conceals the fact that cosmopolitanism does not advocate world solidarity but, above all, world solidarity between the privileged social strata that belong to the new international bourgeoisie.

In other words, it is the ideological banner of the social imaginary of the new bourgeoisie. It ideologically confirms the possibility of horizontal social mobility from one country to another, of the new professional strata of cutting-edge sectors of the globalized capitalist economy that has to a great extent replaced the vertical social mobility of the social democratic period. Consequently, cosmopolitanism expresses, in Orwellian terms, the "nationalism" of the new bourgeoisie against the subaltern social classes that are struck by the social conditions imposed and reproduced by the system of the international market economy. In other words, it is a representative sample of the solidarity of the rich toward the social strata that threaten their way of life.

Besides, we should not forget that the internationalist anarchists of the Iberian Peninsula did not hesitate to tackle issues related to the productive reconstitution of the domestic social formation, well aware that a victorious social revolution in Spain would most probably face—from the very first day—complete commercial embargo and absolute isolation by Europe's great capitalist powers (Puente 1932). Just like the Russian workers before them, the Spanish proletarians could not afford to place their hopes on the possibility of an uprising of the working class at a European level to safeguard the necessary preconditions for the survival of their revolution. Of course, in the case of the Russian Revolution, it was the Russian workers who denied their German brothers their help, contributing to the creation of the necessary conditions for their entrapment.[18] Given the aforementioned, if the proletariat of the developed European countries—constantly praised by the educated migrant leaders of the Bolsheviks for their class consciousness, discipline, and high degree of organization—failed miserably in rising to the challenge and saving the Russian Revolution from its isolation, one wonders what other choice was left to the Russian workers but to put all their energies into reinforcing the power of the USSR, so that it could one day save the proletariat of the countries of the West.

There are two paths to such a goal: on the one hand, the export of the revolution through military force (expansion of the Soviet influence in Eastern Europe); on the other hand, the subjugation of the international communist movement to the priorities of the Soviet national interest through a centrally administered bureaucratic mechanism (Comintern).[19] In this sense, it is no exaggeration to claim that the paradoxes that emerge on the surface of history when a state entity tries to put internationalism in practice exist because it is contradictory by definition for a state-based heteronomous form of social organization to try to enforce policies identified with the ideals of the tradition of autonomy. A telling example is the one referenced by Halliday (1999: 116–24) regarding the fatigue and discontent of the people of socialist Cuba when a military envoy was sent to faraway Angola in 1975 to aid the socialist revolutionaries in their armed struggle for independence. Although the people of Cuba were indoctrinated with a socialist culture and internationalist ideals, they were incapable of understanding why their youth had to die on the other side of the world for the independence of a country that hardly any Cuban had ever visited or could locate on the world map. Furthermore, the fact that the states of the former socialist bloc were never capable of institutionalizing an alternative way of coexistence based on equality and mutual assistance is also exemplary of the deep antinomy governing the theory and political practice of internationalism.

On the contrary, most were assimilated and obediently adapted to the strict hierarchy imposed by the centralized interstate structures of the USSR-ruled Eastern Bloc. Yet others fell as low as to display selfish and antagonistic behaviors, adopting the reference point of a so-called national interest and even engaging in open war, such as in the case of the Chinese-Soviet conflict or the three-day armed clashes between Laos, Vietnam, and Cambodia.

Consequently, the second main element of the social forms expressing their commitment to the ideals of proletarian internationalism is their stateless, anti-hierarchical character. The antistate element is strongly visible in the historical form acquired by the class struggles for self-determination and social justice in Zapatista Chiapas and in the autonomous region of Rojava in Syrian Kurdistan but also in the horizontal forms of organization adopted by the corresponding social movements in the countries of the Global South.

Finally, reference must be made to the obvious historical paradox that there have been many cases of internationalist political movements placed at the head of campaigns for the attainment of the self-determination or national independence of a people under direct military administration and occupation. From the Greek EAM and the French communist resistance militia to the Latin-American internationalist revolutionaries of the 1960s and 1970s, the adoption of the principles of proletarian internationalism did not seem to be in line with an active participation in struggles of national liberation. The extent to which internationalism can, indeed, walk hand in hand with nation-centered versions of a heteronomous institution of society can be seen through the posterior authoritarian evolution of anti-imperialist regimes. But even at their most authoritarian, when they were already turning into monolithic party dictatorships, these regimes had conserved some of the internationalist solidarity from their previous revolutionary role. Thus, Algeria under Ben Bela was the first state to offer political asylum to the exiled leaders of the Black Panthers when they were forced to leave the US to escape being captured by the US government (Cleaver 1979: 134–65). There is also the example of Baathist Syria: on the one hand, it implemented neoliberal reforms, slowly but steadily undermining the economic foundation of the regime within its borders; on the other, it never stopped providing weapons and military know-how to Hamas and Hezbollah so that they could continue their armed conflict against the barbaric occupation of Palestinian territories by Israel.

This type of internationalism is obviously part of a web of geopolitical interests and expediencies at the level of the internationalized system of rule. But an internationalism that has not been fully severed from its geopolitical backdrop and the material conditions for shaping of relations between different people will not be able to operate as an agent of change or overturn of the existing balance of power. It will be no more than an ideological abstraction that bears very little relation to reality, one that will be hardly capable of producing tangible results in the field of international politics, the field that proletarian internationalism mostly aspires to reform.

Notes

1 Everything from one.
2 The emphasis is placed on *social struggle* as a separate and broader notion than that of class struggle that, according to the orthodox Marxist approach,

refers mainly to relations of production and the capital/labor opposition. On the contrary, *social struggle* refers to the social antagonism that is expressed in all fields of social organization where relations of unequal power distribution prevail. It is multifaceted and denotes relations of mutual dependence and influence between the social fields, without regarding certain spheres of social reproduction and organization as a priori superior.

3   As Rosalyn Deutsche and Cara Gendel Ryan (1984: 96) have explained:

> The term *underclass* is used with predictable contempt and callousness by neoconservatives to characterize the lower classes. Their explanations for the existence of such a category run the gamut from the biological to the cultural, from the economic to the social, but, in the final analysis, they believe that many members of this class are socially and economically irredeemable because of their inability to assimilate bourgeois values and behavior. Edward Banfield presents the most distorted version of this view of the underlying conditions of poverty: "Most of those caught up in this culture are unable or unwilling to plan for the future, or to sacrifice immediate gratification in favor of future ones, or to accept the disciplines that are required in order to get and to spend.... Lower-class poverty is 'inwardly' caused (by psychological inability to provide for the future and all that this inability implies)" (Banfield, *The Unheavenly City*, cited in Murray Hausknecht, "Caliban's Abode," in *The New Conservatives*, Lewis A. Coser and Irving Howe, eds. [New York, New American Library, 1976], 196).

4   Thus, the collapse of actually existing socialism and the incorporation of the countries of the former Eastern Bloc into the internationalized market economy system marked the transition from a hierarchical model of social organization—where political and economic power was the result of the position the members of the elite held in the party bureaucracy—to an equally hierarchical social system that is based on structures of unequal distribution of economic power, in which the same elites have conserved their privileged position, securing the ownership and control of the means of production. For more on this, see Fotopoulos 1990.

5   Only a small minority of communist combatants organized networks of subsidiary support outside the supervision and against the will of the PCF (known as the Jeanson network) in order to assist, on French metropolitan soil, the Algerians in their struggle for national liberation.

6   On the consequences of the system of the market economy on society and the erosion of the social fabric caused by the rampant forces of the market, see Polanyi 2001.

7   The neoliberal ideals and elitist mentality impregnating the Westernized African "new leading class" are characteristically portrayed in the program *Tutu's Children*, broadcast by *Al Jazeera* on a weekly basis.

8   "Transcript of President Obama's Commencement Address at West Point," *New York Times*, May 28, 2014, https://www.nytimes.com/2014/05/29/us/politics/transcript-of-president-obamas-commencement-address-at-west-point.html?mtrref=www.google.ca&assetType=nyt_now.

9   *On First Principles* was the title of a work by Origen, written in Alexandria, Egypt, between 212 and 215 CE.

10 Daniel Cohn-Bendit, also known as "Danny the Red" for his activity and participation in anarchist groups in May 68, is today a leading figure of the European Green Party. Together with Guy Verhofstadte, he is also at the head of the Spinelli Group, a tendency within the European Parliament that aims at creating a postnational European federation.—Ed.

11 In practice, this amounts to the creation of an economy with powerful ties between its different branches, where each sector of production supplements the rest, and all industries have equal levels of technological development and effectiveness.

12 On this, see http://www.forbes.com/pictures/ehlk45iehm/2-london/#5d13cdde38d2.

13 For a sociological analysis of the capitalist ethics of work as an instrument of disciplining and control of the subaltern social strata, see Bauman 2005.

14 The British National Party was founded in 1982 and achieved its greatest victory in the 2009 European elections, wining 6.2 percent and two seats (with Nick Griffin then head of the party). The English Defence League is an English anti-Islamic street protest organization.—Ed.

15 In this sense, the choice of Greek bureaucrat Margaritis Schinas as the chief spokesperson of the European Commission is highly symbolic at a time when the EU is leading, with mathematical precision, a formally independent member-state toward political enslavement and economic destruction through the program of structural adjustments included in the third memorandum. On the Commission's new spokesperson, see the relevant article in *Enet*, September 10, 2014.

16 In the words of (the then prime minister and PASOK president) Giorgos Papandreou in the Council of Ministers of September 10, 2010. The author refers to the specific period of the country's governance by PASOK (2009–2011).—Ed.

17 The Ragousis bill (N.3838/2010) granted citizenship rights on the basis of birth or schooling. It was in force for two years (2010–2012) and was revoked by the Greek Council of State as unconstitutional. It was modified and re-implemented by Syriza in 2015 (N.4332/2015).—Ed.

18 This does not mean that the Russian army was capable of launching a large-scale counterattack and chasing off the imperial army that had reached the outskirts of Petrograd.

19 Following the victorious Russian Revolution, the Third International (union of national communist parties) or Comintern, also known as the Communist International, was founded by Lenin and Trotsky in 1919 in Moscow. It denounced the previous Second (socialist) International for its stance during the First World War. It was officially dissolved by Stalin in 1943.—Ed.

References

Antisystemic. "Ο Ακήρυχτος Πόλεμος των Τουπαμάρος" [The undeclared war of the Tupamaros]. *Antisystemic*, November 6, 2012. https://antisystemic. wordpress.com/2012/11/06/o-ακήρυχτος-πόλεμος-των-τουπαμάρος/.

Arrighi, Giovanni, Terrence K. Hopkins, and Immanuel Wallerstein. *Anti-Systemic Movements*. London: Verso, 2011.

Bauman, Zygmunt. *Work, Consumerism and the New Poor*. New York: Open University Press, 2005.

Bookchin, Murray. *Listen, Marxist!* New York: Anarchos, 1969. https://www. marxists.org/archive/bookchin/1969/listen-marxist.htm.

Chomsky, Noam. *Year 501: The Conquest Continues*. Chicago: Haymarket Books, 2015.

Cleaver, Eldridge. *Soul on Fire*. London: Hodder & Stoughton, 1979.

Cohn-Bendit, Daniel, and Gabriel Cohn-Bendit. *Obsolete Communism: The Left-Wing Alternative*. New York: McGraw-Hill, 1968.

Deutsche, Rosalyn, and Cara Gendel Ryan. "The Fine Art of Gentrification." *October* 31 (1984): 91–111.

Deutscher, Isaac. *Stalin*. Middlesex: Penguin Books, 1984.

Dolgoff, Sam, ed. *The Anarchist Collectives: Workers' Self-Management in the Spanish Revolution, 1936–39*. Montreal: Black Rose Books, 1974.

Drakos, Panagiotis. *Ενάντια στο Κράτος* [Against the state]. Thessaloniki: Nautilos, 2016.

Eleutherotypia. "Ποιος είναι ο νέος εκπρόσωπος Τύπου της Κομισιόν Μαργαρίτης Σχοινάς" [Who is the new spokesperson of the European Commission, Margaritis Schinas]. *Enet*, September 10, 2014. http://www.enet.gr/?i=news.el.article&id=446817.

Fotopoulos, Takis. "The Catastrophe of Marketization." *Democracy & Nature* 5, no. 2, (July 1999): 275–310. https://www.democracynature.org/vol5/fotopoulos_marketisation.htm.

———. "Class Divisions Today—The Inclusive Democracy Approach." *Democracy & Nature* 6, no. 2 (July 2000). http://www.inclusivedemocracy.org/dn/vol6/takis_class.htm.

———. *Παγκόσμιος Πόλεμος κατά της Τρομοκρατίας* [The global war on democracy]. Athens: Gordios, 2003.

———. *Η Ελλάδα ως Προτεκτοράτο της Υπερεθνικής Ελίτ* [Greece as the protectorate of the supranational elite]. Athens: Gordios, 2010.

———. *Περιεκτική Δημοκρατία: Δέκα Χρόνια Μετά* [Inclusive democracy: Ten years later]. Athens: Eleutheros Typos, 2008.

———. *Η Παγκόσμια Κρίση, η Ελλάδα και το Αντισυστημικό Κίνημα* [World crisis, Greece, and the antisystemic movement]. Athens: Koukkida, 2009.

Gerassi, John, ed. *Towards Revolution*, vol. 1. London: Weidenfeld & Nicolson, 1971.

Guerin, Daniel. *The Brown Plague: Travels in Late Weimar and Early Nazi Germany*. Durham, NC: Duke University Press, 1994.

Hainsworth, Paul, ed. *The Politics of the Extreme Right: From the Margins to the Mainstream*. London: Pinter, 2000.

Halliday, Fred. *Revolution and World Politics*. London: Macmillan, 1999.

Kondylis, Panagiotis. Η Παρακμή του Αστικού Πολιτισμού [The fall of bourgeois civilization]. Athens: Themelio, 1995.

Lenin, Vladimir Ilich. *Imperialism: The Highest Stage of Capitalism*. Sydney: Resistance Books, 1999.

Lieros, Giorgos. *Σκέψεις για την άμεση δημοκρατία* [Thoughts on direct democracy]. Athens: Ekdoseis ton Synadelfon, 2012.

Malatesta, Errico. *Anarchy*, 1891. https://theanarchistlibrary.org/library/errico-malatesta-anarchy.

Marantzidis, Nikos. "Το σφάλμα της Γερμανίας" [The mistake of Germany]. *Kathimerini*, December 28, 2014. http://www.kathimerini.gr/797477/opinion/epikairothta/politikh/to-sfalma-ths-germanias.

Polanyi, Karl. *The Great Transformation*. Boston: Beacon Press, 2001.

Prudhommeaux, André, ed., *Σπάρτακος: Η Κομμούνα του Βερολίνου 1919*, μτφρ. Ελεάνα Β., Σπυρόπουλος Βασίλης, Διεθνής Βιβλιοθήκη, Αθήνα, 1981.

Puente, Isaac. *Libertarian Communism*, 1932. https://libcom.org/library/libertarian-communism.

Sadoul, Jacques. *Ο Θησαυρός των Αλχημιστών* [The treasure of alchemists]. Athens: Divres, 1988.

Schmidt, Michael, and Lucien Van Der Walt. *Black Flame: The Revolutionary Class Politics of Anarchism and Syndicalism*. Oakland: AK Press, 2009.

Terzakis, Fotis. "Τι θα κάνουμε με το κράτος" [What to do with the state?]. *Koursal* 4 "Κοινωνικός Αναρχισμός" [Social anarchism], 33–57. Thessaloniki, 2015.

Theodoropoulos, Takis. "Δεσμώτες του Ιλίγγου" [Captives of vertigo]. *Kathimerini*. December 28, 2014.

"Transcript of President Obama's Commencement Address at West Point," May 28 2014, *New York Times*. https://www.nytimes.com/2014/05/29/us/politics/transcript-of-president-obamas-commencement-address-at-west-point.html.

Trotsky, Leon. *The Defence of Terrorism*. London: Labour Publishing, 1921.

EIGHT

Crisis and Negativity: On the Revolutionary Subject in Times of Crisis

Katerina Nasioka

The Proletariat against (and beyond?) the Working Class

For capital, crisis is the disturbance of what was, until that moment, a more or less smooth reproduction of the pattern of (class) relations between capital and labor; namely, of the position of capital as capital and that of the working class as working class in their articulation within the existing social antagonism. For labor, crisis is not only the tension of the external antithesis between two classes, of labor against capital (which it is, of course) but also the internal material questioning of all collective bodies that constitute a revolutionary perspective and of their political narratives. It is the moment that allows us to recognize the totality of the capitalist assault and domination, and our own limits as the vessels of its reproduction. It is precisely what reveals the possibility of breaking it. When Marx (1971: 250) mentioned that "the real barrier of capitalist production is capital itself. It is that capital and its self-expansion appear as the starting and the closing point," he was not conceding to economicism or to a positive teleology of revolution but rather emphatically stressing the contradiction that pervades the very subjectivity participating in the production of the social relation. And this is so because social production based on the production of value, such as the capitalist one, simultaneously (re)produces a particular subjectivity. For Sergio Tischler (2013: 33): "the commodity form of social relations produces a process of totalization and a type of reified subjectivity that makes abstraction of the human drama that constitutes capital."

The articulation of the capital-labor relation in the twentieth century (Fordism) also created an image that legitimized social conflict in the form of a unified subject, the labor movement, which was mainly represented by the political identity of the party and the trade union and based its activity on a program. *Programming* had to do with practices of struggle whose short-term goal was to confirm and reinforce labor (accomplishing a more advantageous position for labor within capitalism through the satisfaction of labor demands),[1] while the long-term—revolutionary— horizon aimed at replacing the society of capital by the society of workers. By the nineteenth century, developed capitalism promoted a systematic organization against itself, including demands for political and economic rights, the recognition of trade unions, and participation in new institutions of representation (Williams 1973).

With the twentieth century comes the peak of systematized anti-capitalism, on the one hand, and the introduction of Keynesian policies that promised the construction of a fair world, on the other. In essence, Keynesianism tried to contain the momentum of the rebellions and revolutions of that time by correcting the system's self-destructive tendencies. Postwar restructuring was successful in channeling social protest into demands—"putting more money into the hands of the consumers" (Holloway 2003: 82)—and in increasing the institutional interdependence between the state and trade unions (corporativism). As the salary (and the linking of salary and productivity) became a central element in social struggles, the crystallization of class struggle in the form *labor movement–Keynesian policies* highlighted the fetishistic character of the anticapitalist movement. The struggles became essentially systemic, as their demands—insofar as they were part of the circuit of capitalist reproduction—remained enmeshed in capital's logic and mode of production.

In what was an (admittedly ungracious) generalization of form, the collective subject that was constituted and established during the twentieth century as the labor movement in all its different historical expressions around the world—the bureaucratized, centrist, and productivist socialism of the former Soviet Union, the popular national anti-imperialism of the colonized world, trade-unionism in the West—drifted away from the (revolutionary) horizon of the subversion of capital. Its incorporation into the system of reproduction of the capitalist relation destroyed, to a great extent, the possibility of envisioning an anticapitalist society.

From the mid-1970s onward, it became obvious that what was, until then, defined as class relations and class struggle (Keynesian policies, the social state, deep corporativism) could not contain social antagonism within its norms. On the one hand, the new organization of labor led to increased alienation and insubordination of workers (industrial mass production, repetitiveness and productivity, the repressive and discipli- nary nature of labor, etc.). On the other hand, the expansion of the state and the close interconnection of the political and the economic revealed the "intensification of capital's socialization" "at a global level" and the subsequent "intensification of social alienation" (ibid.). Furthermore, the institutionalization of social struggles in the form of trade union demands meant, at the same time, that the Keynesian contract was finding it increas- ingly difficult to extract surplus value "not because the rate of exploita- tion has decreased, but because exploitation was becoming increasingly expensive for capital" (ibid.: 91). Consequently, capital's onslaught on labor after the 1970s (neoliberalism) targeted the balance that had been created through the linking of salary and productivity; that is, the wage relation itself. Today's dissociation (between the reproduction and circulation of capital and the reproduction and circulation of the labor force) hinders the overall cycle of reproduction of the capitalist relation, because the latter is reproduced through the production not only of commodities but also of the labor force itself as a commodity. Namely, through the process that, according to Marx (1965 [1867]: 577), incessantly hurls the laborer back on to the market as a vendor of his labor power, with the capitalist as its purchaser.

The social conflicts of the 1970s revolved around the rejection of labor as a way of breaking with capitalist survival, which forbids all poetic dimensions to life. As abstract labor, the essence of value (Marx 1990 [1867]: chapter 1), reproduced the normality and ennui of the individual that is subjugated to measurable time (the socially necessary labor time), rebellion against the tyranny of the "social factory" repelled the abstrac- tion of the social equivalent (money) that turned society as a whole into the articulation of production, into a factory operation (Tronti 1962: 20; Cleaver 1992). "Never work!" Guy Debord declared, proclaiming the nega- tion of labor as a project of emancipation for the overturning of bourgeois society. This project essentially concentrated the multiplication of social experiences that had been placed under the rule of capital not only within but also outside the spaces of work and production (real subjugation).

Antilabor, as well as the diverse negations of the proletariat against all expressions of submission that were being naturalized and normalized by the society of capital, denoted the universalization of the dialectic of class war (Workers of the Negative 2005). In this context, social "defeats" within the factory, that is, the labor movement's "failure" to destroy the capitalist machine at the production level, also reflected the "defeat" of the workerist project to the extent that the workerist form of struggle constituted the confirmation of labor.

Therefore, crisis appears as the crisis of the revolutionary subject who, through her activity, confirmed labor within capitalism and acquired an identity through the labor movement. This process of subjectivization was not the result of bad intentions or erroneous strategies on the part of the labor struggles. The issue was that this specific content of revolutionary proposals allowed the counterrevolution to turn the revolution against itself. While the increasing commodification of all aspects of everyday life revealed labor's extensive alienation, a revolutionary project that confirmed labor (labor as the new social context in the form of the "labor society") became more and more part of the totalization of life under the rule of value; to wit, it reproduced capitalist normality. Furthermore, antilabor slogans today seem to be materialized more from the side of capital. The latter's increasing tendency to exclude labor in its effort to expand value tends to simultaneously create surplus populations that the subsequent economic development fails to absorb. The unemployed, the precariously employed, the "illegal" immigrants, and other members of the excluded "subclass"; those who cross national and international borders as a cheap labor force in an effort to access the basic means of subsistence through any kind of labor; those who work without getting paid; those who live in tents, who are abused or murdered, who find it difficult to envision themselves as incorporated in, or identified with, the collective demands of the "citizens" in relation to salaries or welfare, as Dimitra Kotouza mentions in her article. Today's image of the world is an inverted picture of the utopian plans of May 1968, when violence and desperate rage constituted the foundations of social explosion.

The new form of class struggle necessarily places the category of *class* at the center of critical theoretical analysis. The rejection of class (the end of class struggle, just like the end of history) has become the theoretical buzzword of the neoliberal wing, and anticapitalist theory has also made many efforts to sketch the present and understand the new players in the field of the revolutionary perspective. The critique of the Leninist tradition of taking power and turning the state into an instrument of emancipation has taken different paths since 1970. Generally speaking, two tendencies emerged. Certain theoretical approaches focused on the inadequacy of class to interpret social reproduction and opted for abandoning it and adopting a more pluralistic version of the collective subject, such as the *multitude* or the *commons*. Others insisted on maintaining class as a critical (and not positive) category, that is, on reinterpreting it. On this conversion, Tischler points out:

> Globalisation is a phenomenon of class struggle, of breaking the limits that the working class had imposed on capital in the form of the welfare state in the central countries of capitalism, and in the form of development and populism in Latin America. Hence a first idea: the so-called end of history is not the end of class and of class struggle, but rather a constitutive moment of a new form of class struggle and a different hegemonic plot. (Tischler 2004: 107)

These efforts toward a critical renewal of class (a critique of "constitutive subjectivity") can be comprehended as a theoretical shift in the conceptualization of *working class* (or perhaps laboring class would be more accurate) and *proletariat* as categories that are not necessarily synonymous (Nasioka 2017). The working or laboring class that became linked to a specific form of articulation of class struggle, as it is usually presented in the practices of the labor movement, aimed at the reinforcement of the class condition within capitalism in order to establish the labor society. That is, the laboring class was the positive, self-affirming subject of class, steering the possibility of rupturing the class contract itself toward an impasse. On the contrary, the crisis of the labor identity and of the practices of the labor movement allows for a shift in the category of proletariat as an act of questioning the class condition itself, as a de-identification of working class.[2] The *proletariat* now turns into the negative imprint, the movement-against class determination (self-negation), and, therefore, into rupture with the *working or laboring class*. In this context, the proletariat can be conceived of as the process of subjectivization that moves *in, against, and beyond* the working class, *in, against, and beyond* all classifying definitions: "We are a question, an experiment, a scream, a challenge. We need no definition, we reject all definition, because we are the anti-identitarian power of creative doing and defy all definition" (Holloway 2006).

At this point, we will insert a theoretical parenthesis and return for a while to the concept of the subject, negativity, and ... Adorno.

A Critique of Constitutive Subjectivity

The Leninist tradition that pledged loyalty to the positivized figures of the party, the vanguard, and the revolutionary state is deconstructed by critical theory. In critical theory, the subject is conceived in negative terms, as a moving contradiction that is dialectically "threatened" by the surplus object, the objective that is not identical with subjective conceptualization. In his *Negative Dialectics* (2006), Adorno rejects the notion of idealistic dialectics in the Hegelian philosophic tradition, arguing that the effort to conciliate subject and object in the form of the Absolute Spirit has failed. Furthermore, he denounces the empiricist version of historical materialism, which dogmatically shaped orthodox Marxist thought.

However, the conception of the subject as a movement—a negative one, for that matter—can already be found in Hegel's *Phenomenology of Spirit* (1977) and is the source on which Marx (systematically in *Grundrisse*) builds the concept of *form* and, through it, the critique of the commodity fetishism. In the preface to *Phenomenology of Spirit* (1977: 10) Hegel refers to the notion of the subject that unfolds, doubles itself as negativity, and comes to contradict itself. That is, he criticizes the classical notion of identity as pure tautology. More specifically, he says in reference to the true subject: "This Substance is, as Subject, pure, *simple negativity*, and is for this reason the bifurcation of the simple; it is the doubling which sets up opposition, and then again the negation of this indifferent diversity and of its antithesis." Yet the dialectic of subject/object in Hegel is conceived as a purely subjective movement, as "subjective constitution." According to Adorno (1973: 7): "The fundament and result of Hegel's substantive philosophizing was the primacy of the subject, or—in the famous phrase from the introduction to his *Logic*—the 'identity of identity and nonidentity.'" Therefore, subjectivity, in light of Hegelian thought, turns into a *deceptive construction*, the so-called constitutive subjectivity (ibid.: xx), that is, the one that constructs reality (objectivity, society) on the basis of itself, the *concept*, and thus limits (and ultimately demotes) the object to a *concept*, an *object of thought*.

Unlike transcendental subjectivity, which completely absorbs the object, Adorno turns to the element of negativity, of what is not identical in the object and mediates even in the deepest expression of subjectivity, which, suffering, resists it: "For suffering is objectivity that weighs upon the subject; its most subjective experience, its expression, is objectively conveyed" (ibid.: 18). But he argues that renouncing the supremacy of the subject cannot lead to a simplistic realism or to an idea of imaging according to which "the subject is bound to mulishly mirror the object" (2014 [1966]: 205). Thus, critical theory resists the core of orthodox Marxism, which stresses the definition of social reality through the inherent laws of the economy and limits the subjectivity and consciousness of the subject to their reflection/ideology (identity).

According to the orthodox Marxist tradition, subjectivity can escape its reified condition (fetishism of the subject) only if it acquires the form of a *privilege*. Indeed, for the Leninist norm, the working class is a revolutionary subject only insofar as it opposes capital as the economy (subject) through its political struggle, defined by the revolutionary party as organized class consciousness. According to Tischler (2013: 100), however, "the Leninist theses on organization, class consciousness and the party imply the basic idea that inside capital it is impossible to produce class consciousness." In the Leninist strategy, the figure of the party as a legitimate authority that embodies the "spirit" of the state presupposes that the revolutionary subject comes "from the outside" to act in the political sphere as an autonomous social subject. At the same time, this reflects the historical reality that once a revolution becomes the state it not only reproduces the bourgeois categories of power; the bourgeois form itself is constitutive of the revolutionary process. Thus, class acquires an instrumental, objectivist character, while its organization and consciousness are perceived as external to class struggle, as forms of an objective knowledge that are imposed on it so as to express it, ensuring the creation of a communist society in terms of evolution and progress.

For Adorno, this direction grants the object a specific existence, turning it into something static and allowing it to remain unhindered, beyond all criticism. On the contrary, when analyzing Marx's commodity fetishism, he claims that, despite the prioritization of the object, the reified character of the world is as real as it is apparent, even if it is objectively produced through the exchange process; it is, at the same time, true and false. If, for Hegel, truth is the indicator both of itself and of falseness, for Marx, falsity (the reified character) is the indicator of truth. Reflection (consciousness) on the object cannot dissolve its socially produced, fetishized (false) character. But it allows for the critical observation of the object that mediates in subjectivity and thus insists on opposing the naturalization of social relations; it refuses to capitulate (antagonistic movement).

An important critique of the rule of the *object* (economic laws) upon the *subjective* can be encountered in Lukács's analysis and in the category of reification. In *History and Class Consciousness* (1972) Lukács returns to Hegel and claims that commodity fetishism constructs the social relation in all the forms of subjectivity and objectivity. This viewpoint negates the automatism of the development of the productive forces as a happy and unavoidable end to bourgeois society. Therefore, revolution can only be conceived in terms of possibility, the crucial point being the subjectivization of the proletariat through class consciousness. Lukács makes a distinction between the reified consciousness of the proletariat (class *in itself*, the proletariat as an object) and the revolutionary, de-reified consciousness of the proletariat (class *for itself*, the proletariat as the subject of history). This distinction is the basis of the argument that the proletariat itself—to the extent that it becomes aware of its capacity to understand historical developments (capitalism) as a totality—is "capable of overcoming the separation of subject and object and the antinomies of bourgeois existence; unfold its practical discourse in relation to the constitution of a world that is its own, through which it constitutes itself freely in the course of history" (Meyer Forbes 2013: 81). According to Lukácsian theory, capitalist totality can be overcome through the produced unity of subject/object that is embodied in the proletariat as a revolutionary class. Consciousness, as the mediation of the new condition, places totality on critical foundations to the extent that it is perceived as the unified knowledge of a fragmented and contradictory world.

But there are two points in Lukács's theory that turn it into a positive confirmation of class. First, class consciousness constitutes the proletariat as the identical subject/object of history, capable of opposing capital precisely because it is itself a type of alternative totality, a new composition. Does this concern the entirety of the proletariat? While, for Lukács, all the proletariat can, in theory, acquire revolutionary consciousness, objectively it is only one enlightened part that is capable of attaining it. Yet the subject is demoted here to an organizational form (class, party, state) that is necessarily separated and autonomized from the struggle. The subject that is conceived of in terms of organizational composition (organicism) turns into a new totality that submits the social to the supremacy of the political and class consciousness to the vanguard-form.[3]

Second, and as a result of the aforementioned, if revolution is a matter of consciousness, and subjectivity is relegated to consciousness (Jay 1985; Meyer Forbes 2013: 90) revolution remains an epistemological issue. In this sense, the problem does not only lie in the subjectivity that is limited to consciousness but also in the fact that the process of fetishization is perceived as "false consciousness," as the false appearances of a true world. This viewpoint suggests that the essence of the proletariat is divided and maintains an external relationship with its *appearance*, as the pure rebelliousness of the proletariat cannot be damaged or affected by its reified apparentness. The problem of idealistic ontology can be overcome, according to Lukács, through the construction of a materialist ontology: "the self-consciousness of the proletariat as an identical subject/object, that is, the destruction of the illusive veil" (ibid.: 98). Totality appears as ontology (the ontology of labor), as a positivized category that must come into being.

The Unfortunate Self-Valorization of the Working Class...

The same theoretical thread (of *essence* against the *appearance* of the proletariat) runs through the analytic arguments of certain theorists of autonomy. In the autonomist version, however, the revolutionary perspective of the state or of the political mediators of the working class has been inverted. More specifically, Hardt and Negri suggest a certain type-figure of subjective liberation that begins from an epistemic subject that, in the new "biopolitical production" of immaterial post-Fordist labor, manages to become autonomized and attain self-valorization. By 1988, in the first part of his book *Revolution Retrieved: Writing on Marx, Keynes, Capitalist Crisis and New Social Subjects*, Toni Negri analyzed the reform of the Keynesian state and insisted on the idea that the potentially autonomous working class is progressing toward its self-valorization. The process of autonomization, according to Negri, was the result of the crack opened up by the Russian Revolution, in the face of which capital was forced to reorganize itself in order to maintain the movement of the increasing socialization of labor within the sphere of its own interests. After the 1930s and the Great Depression, capital's response to the trade union movement—a result of the soviets and the workers councils—was the turn of the state toward interventionism: "Working class struggle has imposed a movement of reformism *of* capital. . . . [Keynesianism] is forced to recognize that the working class is the driving motor of development . . . and that the system functions not because the working class is always inside capital, but because it is also capable of stepping outside it" (Negri 1988: 28). All the measures adopted by capital aimed at forbidding the working class to act outside capital.

This approach has clear theoretical and political consequences. How is the category of *class* perceived through the approach of an epistemic subject that is being autonomized? For Hardt and Negri (2004, 2009) *class* is not constituted on the basis of the separation between the producer and the means of production or of the reproduction of the wage relation. Its constitution is defined by the conflicts between the different social strata or the different classes. In *Multitude* (2004: 103–7) the authors refer to the classes that are constituted as social classes through an infinite number of different paths such as race and economic class. The "biopolitical transformations" of the multitude define a new type of connection between the social groups on the basis of which "what it shares in common and what it produces in common against the imperial power of global capital" (2004: 101) is activated: the force of the workers who translate into a creative multitude, into "singularities that act in common" (2004: 105). The multitude transcends the notion of working class to the extent that the latter is linked only to inclusion or exclusion with regard to productive labor. That is precisely why it is capable, according to the authors, of acting inside as well as outside capital.

This process also defines the dynamic of its autonomization. Acting outside capital, it encounters the path toward its own self-valorization. The autonomization and self-valorization of class implies the twofold perception that the *essence* and the *image* of class are different and can be potentially separated. It implies that the autonomy of class is a type of liberation of class's *true situation* from its incorporation into the capitalist mode of production. Thus, labor is sought for in its *liberated* form, to the extent that labor can also be something else beyond its historically defined form as social abstract activity (abstract labor). But how is this liberation achieved? How is the "autonomy of class" attained?

For Hardt and Negri (2004, 2009) there are two sides to this course of liberation. On the one hand, the increasing collectivization/socialization of labor reinforces the dynamic of autonomy (biopolitical production) in the form of general intellect, the common capabilities unleashed by developed capitalism. This can be attained precisely because "capitalist accumulation today is increasingly external to the production process (2009: 137) and "the extraction of value . . . is increasingly accomplished without the capitalist intervening in its production" (ibid.: 141). On the other hand, the critical negation of political mediations as practices of class within capitalism reveals and liberates the "revolutionary nature" of the proletariat. The *multitude* represents this twofold reform in political terms.

The globalized movement of capital creates a *common* world where, through "an organization project to construct an alternative on the immanent plane of social life" (ibid.: 16), *the multitude* (the democratic prince) will learn "the art of self-rule and inventing lasting democratic forms of social organization" (ibid.: viii). The basis of the *common* as the socialized productive force and capacity of self-valorization is, for the authors, a focal point of contemporary struggles. Thus, according to the authors, the questions posed by contemporary social movements revolve around the way in which common resources can be ensured, so that they are not privatized but organized around an axis of common structures.

Immaterial labor and general intellect are conceived here partially as the positive movement of the productive forces of capital that almost automatically operates in a liberating way. Hardt and Negri discern something positive in the movement of capital itself, given that the possibility of social change (*exodus* from capitalism) lies in the very acceleration of the biopolitical capitalist mode of production. On the other hand, their critique focuses on the distinction between productive/nonproductive labor and not on the category of labor itself. Therefore, value (and, consequently, the relations of exploitation) as an antagonistic movement is abandoned. Nevertheless, "it is strange to speak of an 'end of work' when temp agencies are among the largest employers in the US" (Dauvé 2008). In this sense, the autonomous confirmation of the multitude on the basis of the positivization of the increasing socialization of labor in capitalism overlooks the fact that the latter precisely implies the increasing incorporation of the reproduction of the proletariat in capital's reproduction cycle; that is, the autonomization of class is a contradiction: it is itself capital's movement of reproduction (Théorie Communiste 2010: 58).

This biologized revolutionary subject necessarily puts aside the *contradiction* in order to confirm the *difference*, while, correspondingly, antagonism is perceived through the lens of *antinomy*. But the confirmation of *difference* is also the confirmation of *hegemony*, that is, of the symbiosis of a hegemonic social form with forms that are subjugated to hegemony or resist it.[4] The notions of *multiplicity* and *multitude* are formulated in such a way that they abstain from the dialectic; as a consequence, their objects lack their inherent antagonistic character (Bonnet

2007: 51). The abandonment of the antagonistic perspective and the emphasis put on the inherent forces of social life unavoidably lead us to understand the transition to an emancipated life in terms of political organization. Struggle acquires a secondary role and is limited—in what concerns its creative practice—to the organization and establishment of new democratic institutions of the commons (radical democratization). Therefore, autonomization does not question capital but political media-tions, confirming the separation of the economic and the political, given that political mediations are considered external in relation to the "true situation" of the proletariat and not a constitutive element. This is one way of perceiving revolution; however, it is precisely the way through which revolution is perceived as impossible (Théorie Communiste 2010: 59). For Bonefeld, Negri's argument on the autonomous subject (*multitude*) that fights against capital for its self-valorization means that we are talking of

> human particles and similar forms of biopower [that] have already "escaped the grip of capitalism" without capitalism even having noticed. Could this be a somewhat inaccurate caricature of his work? Negri's perception of autonomy as a sort of naturalization of the human being (biopower) is rather unclear. He attempts a creation of an alluring resource for anticapitalist struggles on the basis of the naturalization of capitalism, of human social practice. Instead of being "valorized" by capital, labor is hailed as a power that is self-valorized. What a misfortune! (Bonefeld 2013: 314)

... And the Metaphysical "Essence" of the Revolutionary Class

If we do not want to fall into the trap of a metaphysical approach, the prole-tariat cannot be perceived in terms of a dichotomy between the *is* (essence) and its apparent form of existence (appearance). The proletariat takes part in capitalism and is defined within it. Its constitutive condition is that of class; however, the activity of class expresses two points of view. The proletariat is a class within capitalism—class as objective existence, according to Tischler (2004: 114)—but it can, at the same time, question its existence as a class within capitalism—class as a subject.

This dimension can be perceived through the twofold character of social relations within the capitalist mode of production as *forms*[5] (use value—exchange value). This means that, on the one hand, *essence* and *appearance* are innately and inseparably linked, constituting the unique "mode of existence" of social phenomena (Gunn 1992). We do not have a point of observation that is beyond capitalist forms, as traditional historical materialism suggested. Neither do we have a *theory of society* and a *theory of history* that can guarantee a happy ending. The commodity is the *social form* that connects "my" activity to "yours," and it is the only one existing between these two activities. In other words, *essence* and *appearance* cannot be separated: we live in *one world*, and this world is *real*.

On the other hand, this point could turn into something unfathomable. When it comes to the perspective of overturning the existing system of exploitation, did we not view *existence* not as something static but as a dynamic process, as constant movement? According to Gunn (1992: 19), the *appearance* of human (social) practice in the capital relation as true abstraction is a "determinate abstraction—abstraction capable of practical and particular existence." While, according to Gunn, appearance can be conceived as a "mode of existence" of reality, existence acquires meaning only when perceived "as existence or ek-stasis or ecstasy, i.e., in an active way" (1992: 21).[6] This means that if social relations in capitalism appear as relations between things (fetishism) and if subjectivity appears as objectivity and class, then relations are what they are, but, at the same time, they are also their contradiction; subjectivity is constituted as class (objectivized existence) and is, at the same time, its contradiction. Likewise, concrete labor is not the essence (the true content) of abstract labor but its contradiction within the same social form.[7] The contradiction allows us to think that the capital relation is constituted as a perversion (Bonefeld 2004, 2013, 2014) to the extent that capitalist forms appear as things in themselves (within the social relation of capital), as well as subjectivities for themselves and against themselves (against and beyond the social relation of capital). Capital subjugates, but it remains a prisoner to its dependence on the transformation of human capacity into a producer of value. The proletariat produces capital but, at the same time, urges against its exploitation. Capital rules, the proletariat revolts. In this case, the dialectic between the proletariat as class and against its constitution as class is, according to Adorno, an asymmetrical dialectic, nonidentitarian and negative, a dialectic in constant conflict.

Through the category of *form*, it becomes clear that the capital relation is constituted in its foundations as *struggle*, because the confirmation of the contradictory existence can never be fully materialized—the proletariat as class (subjectivity) can never attain the confirmation of its autonomous existence as class. Therefore, there is no "inside" and "outside" capitalism (capitalist/noncapitalist relations) as the theories on biopolitics and certain perceptions of the *commons* sustain, but an "in," "against," and "beyond" capitalism, according to John Holloway (2002). In this sense, equality in capitalism does not appear as nonequality but rather as contradictory equality; neither does freedom appear as non-freedom (absence of freedom) but rather as contradictory freedom, as "Freedom, Equality, Property and Bentham" (Marx 1965: 176), that is, as "unfree freedom" (Cleaver 1992: 29). This means that freedom, or the classless condition, are already experienced in their contradiction, they exist *in the mode of being denied.* If that were not so, it would be impossible for us to think of how we can find our way to a condition of freedom from a situation of nonfreedom, or of what steps must be taken for its realization, given that the attainment of this specific freedom would mean we are walking blindly toward something we do not even know.

In this line of thought, *class* is not "a category of consciousness. It is a category of a perverse form of social objectification" (Bonefeld 2014: 114). If, therefore, we think of the subject in nonidentitarian terms—as self-contradiction—and the proletariat as a "living contradiction" (ibid.: 107), *totality* is not something that can be materialized, as Lukács suggested, but what we are fighting to overcome (detotalization). This presupposes the abolition of the proletariat as a class within capitalist totality. Class, therefore, is not only *in itself* and *for itself* but also *against itself*: "The society of human purposes can be defined in negation only. In the struggle against the negative world nothing is certain, except misery itself" (ibid.: 226).

Is this the dynamic that appears in recent social struggles? If the content of post–Second World War struggles can be perceived as the empowerment of the working class, as the confirmation of the identitarian movement of the proletariat as a class within capitalism, today's struggles display a different dynamic. Today, the proletariat finds itself increasingly incapable of attaining its self-confirmation as a class within capitalism.

Limits and Questions of Collective Subjectivizations

Sweet Nothing
—pop song title

Since the 1970s, capital—in its effort to reconstitute its profitability—has been walking more and more along the line of credit expansion and the monetization of the economy. Credit expansion (in the form of bank loans) has been the answer of the states to the escalation of social protest and wage-related demands. According to Holloway:

> The last years of the post-war boom were sustained by a rapid expansion of debt. In the late 1970s, after the crisis of profitability had made itself felt in the richer countries and monetary auster-ity had been proclaimed, the flood of money moved south, particu-larly to Latin America, offering itself to governments looking for a way of containing social tensions, and converting itself into debt. (Holloway 1995: 134)

The chain of financial bubbles and bankruptcies began in Latin America at the end of the 1970s; when these economies collapsed, the bubble moved to the United States of America in a game of musical chairs, shifting the weight of surplus capital and debt from one bubble to another (and then to the European periphery and to Greece) once one bubble bursts and while waiting to see which bubble comes next.

The debt crisis is internally linked to the policies of austerity and state repression, as Panagiotis Doulos mentions in his chapter. One is legitimized in the name of the other. At the global level, the brutality of capital's onslaught amounts to increased repression, generalized unem-ployment, abrupt proletarization, devaluation of labor power, abolition of labor and welfare accomplishments of the labor movement, marginali-zation, heavily indebted households. The process of exclusion from wage labor, which is mediated in social reproduction, is intensified. As a result, the gap between the worker and the labor market widens, and the pursuit of a "normal working life," a "normal job," a "normal salary," a "normal subsistence" seems ever more distant. That is, the edifice of the relations that constituted "being part of" the labor movement is crumbling (Théorie Communiste 2009). The new reality is characterized by the loss of the material objectivity with which the proletariat reproduced itself; it is labor as noncapital perceived negatively, as Marx mentions:

> As such it is not-raw-material, not-instrument of labor, not-raw-product: labor separated from all means and objects of labour, from its entire objectivity. This living labor, existing as an *abstraction* from these moments of its actual reality (also not-value); this com-plete de-nudation, purely subjective existence of labor, stripped of

all objectivity. Labor as *absolute poverty*: poverty not as shortage, but as total exclusion of objective wealth. (Marx 1973: 295)

Here, Marx historically analyzes how labor in capitalism and the proletariat as laboring class within the capitalist mode of production are constituted on the basis of a unifying condition. Therefore, the relation of exploitation is not only the relation of fragmentation of workers into units (individuals) but a relation that simultaneously defines the way in which the workers come together and acquire their identity as workers, as a class (wage labor). The fact that this specific relation is today undergoing crisis, leading to the transformation of labor[8] into noncapital, means that the proletariat is excluded from objective wealth, which appears in the form of the commodity. This *lack* is not a condition that is external to labor and capital; it does not define an automatic autonomization of labor from capital (labor as subject, as activity). The labor form is today a type of *incorporation through exclusion* from all that this embodiment has meant until now (Blaumachen et al. 2013): the relation of the proletarian to wage labor becomes more uncertain, the previous dividing lines between employment and unemployment are dissolved, the proletarian who produces value today receives a salary that is not enough for her subsistence (that is, the reproduction of her labor power) and might, tomorrow, find herself unemployed and with no benefits, conditions that used to be fundamental in defining the labor norm.

But while the proletariat is expanding qualitatively as well as quantitatively, the form in which it became unified in the past—its practice and identity as working class—is weakening. The process of proletarization is intensified but placed outside the traditional working condition: the proletariat increases as a reserve, as deprived and displaced populations, as the cursed stockpile that capital tries to rid itself of. In today's reformed conditions, the horizon of class struggle and the context that previously gave meaning to the struggle have changed. The proposals of the labor movement, which place the wage relation at the center of its demands, do not in the least correspond to the increased mass of surplus population, they do not define the stakes of class struggle. For the new proletariat that is now entering the labor market, the working future is simply to struggle for unemployment benefits: for the student, it is to try to repay student loans in order to get an education that will, most probably, not lead to employment; for entire rural communities the future consists in resisting extinction in the name of "development"; for immigrants it is to try to save their own lives from the onslaught of the state through the deployment of police and army; while for the worker in the *maquiladora* the future amounts to an everyday struggle to escape her abuse, humiliation, rape, and murder.

In this new context, a convergence emerges between a negative (destructive and with no demands) practice of struggle and a positive (assertive) form of social protest. In fact, during the past years we have witnessed an explosion of "suicidal" struggles and protests (of the unemployed, the precariously employed, the *sans papiers*, those who are structurally excluded from the labor market), but, at the same time, there has also been an increase in struggles with specific demands for a social salary, an increase in the price of labor power, for the defense of labor rights conquered through struggles of the past. These two practices came very close to each other and even met on the streets during the social mobilizations of recent years, but they did not achieve much. The assertive struggles strongly protested against the disappearance of the social state and were mainly linked to the idea that the crisis increases "injustice" within the capitalist system. But this "defensive" character is not in itself very telling, nor is it a criterion for "qualitative" distinction, considering that these struggles have necessarily found themselves at the center of violent clashes and brutal repression. Maybe what renders the defensive character of assertive struggles more relevant is their interclass nature—not because of their composition, but because of the fact that the latter was not overcome. That is, prevailing social and class definitions were not fractured. The partial confirmation of social roles (instead of their abolition) resulted in the stakes of the struggle shifting toward state-related distribution. The struggles that have taken place since 2011 have greatly highlighted the capitalist experience as a relation of unequal distribution of social wealth (and not, above all, of exploitation) and have moved the center of gravity toward the mitigation of contrasts between the rich and the poor. The famous Occupy Wall Street slogan "We Are the 99%" expresses precisely this viewpoint. Therefore, as the problem is conceived in terms of justice and distribution, the answer to the question "Who is to blame?" or "Who has failed?" is: "the state." The state appears as the one responsible for the problem but also as part of the solution, and this underlines the concentration of contradictions in the *capitalist state* form: national state, social state, democratic state.

The delegitimization of political and institutional mediation, which was not capable of deterring the implementation of austerity measures, meant for many the return to the category of "the people" and the demand for "national unity" against international economic and political power centers. The peripheral zones that are excluded by economic activities that are vital for international competition due to globalization and their demotion within the international hierarchy search for the culprit "outside," beyond national borders, either in other powerful states or in the invasion of any "non-national" element that "takes advantage" of "domestic" resources (immigrants). This led to the emergence of a popular, nation-centered identity capable of spearheading the struggle of "us against the others"; this from a racist, xenophobic extreme Right, as well as from an anti-imperialist/patriotic institutional and extra-institutional Left that was even borderline anarchist.

In the European periphery (Greece, Spain, Portugal), massive mobilizations against the austerity measures and the Movement of the Squares displayed many signs of identifying with "the people," "popular (national) unity," and the defense of a national economy in the face of the collapse of the state. Furthermore, while the demand for "direct democracy" displayed a vast array of creative practices and endeavors against state democracy—as Giorgos Sotiropoulos mentions in his chapter—it was not capable of overcoming the bourgeois categories of *citizen, civil society*, and *entitlement* as forms of exclusion; that is, it did not question the central role of the state as the regulator and guarantor of social life.

The national democratic characteristics, which focused on demands for the equal distribution of wealth through the reinforcement of the state's legitimizing role in order to guarantee social cohesion, placed limits on the struggles (statism of the movement).[9] Even the endeavors that touched on the issue of production and emphasized the need to change relations, roles, identities within the productive process came up against their own contradictions. Instead of spreading their practices across the entire social sphere, many of the (cooperative) initiatives of the social and solidary economy abandoned—under the weight of the crisis—the *idea of overturning the old world and looked for private salvation*, operating in a way that complements the capitalist economy. Therefore, bestowing hope on a left-wing government cannot be interpreted in terms of incorporation or betrayal. While it is true that in many cases (not only in Greece) there has been a link between left-wing governments and social movements that goes both ways, the tendency to state-ify social resistances reveals that the state was already part of the protocol of many anticapitalist endeavors, either as the outright horizon of social change or as hope for the constitution of a hegemonic identity of the rule of "the people."

Thus, while the anticapitalist movement in Europe seemed unable to break the imaginary of the parliamentary illusion, the possibility of temporarily containing austerity was enough for a broad social basis to gather around the hope of a left-wing government. The promise of creating a rudimentary safety net for the social strata that had been hit the most by the recession set the scene for the neo-Keynesian hope of a left-wing, more moderate capitalism. In Greece, Syriza won the 2015 elections with a radical rhetoric of putting a stop to the implementation of further austerity measures (and a promise to tear up the memorandums), without, however, breaking ties with the European Union and the Eurozone. Somewhere along the way, when negotiations did not produce the desired outcome, the horizon shifted toward the pursuit of a strange balance between what had been arranged with the European elites and a minimal satisfaction of the basic needs of the low social strata, mainly in the form of humanitarian aid. But there was no success there either. For one part of the militant Left that was looking forward to a significant rupture with neoliberal policies, Syriza's failure to negotiate with the EU and reach a political solution amounted to a complete refutation, as it became clear that all political forces that go through the mill of political power come out equally fragmented. Despite the widespread disappointment, there was a broad social base that still viewed Syriza as the only defender of the wage relation.

Therefore, although the outcome of the referendum of July 5, 2015 expressed a widespread rejection of European austerity policies to the tune of 62 percent, Syriza, by now their main champion, won the elections once again only two months later. The referendum was the last—albeit small-scale and fundamentally ideological—*event* of conflict and rebelliousness (post-2012). It went beyond its defined institutional framework, breaking the fear of economic and social disaster that was implied if the European agreements were disrupted. The class vote of "No," vague and unclear, cannot be perceived as the expression of hope or as a simple denunciation of left-wing politics, but rather as class rage, as an inarticulate scream of hate against the pattern of relations of domination that are at the heart of financial capitalism. The inversion of the result and the passing of the third memorandum was a harsh reality check. But the apparent limits of collective subjectivizations in recent anticapitalist struggles leave no room for conceiving the prevalence of Syriza as *yet another Left that came to do the dirty job*. It is the specific content of class struggle that limits the action of the proletariat to the role of recomposing the state from its crisis. The delegitimization of the workerist form of struggle and of its practices did not spearhead social rage against capitalism but was expressed as a protest against the loss of all that the labor movement stood for: full employment, social security, national identity, working stability.

The dynamic of class struggle seems to increasingly acquire the form of a global counterrevolution: wars, the rise of fascism, clashes between states, the construction of an "external enemy" through terrorism, military interventions in defense of security, which is elevated to a paramount social good. As for their "level of democracy," the states shield their authoritarian policies, both within the country—against the workers and the unemployed, criminalizing all forms of protest—as well as outside, in their relations with other states, closing borders or making agreements that put the lives of thousands of migrants at risk every day. Furthermore, national economies around the world are characterized by stagnation and generalized instability, a situation that does not exclude the possibility of a new recession and consecutive credit crunches. This pattern, called a "holding pattern" by Endnotes (2015), presupposes the intensification of the attack against labor power and an increasing proletarization. The worker is constantly under the threat of unemployment and, therefore, weak and subdued. The social reality resulting from the retreat of the 2011–2012 movements and the failure of the left hope to reverse the deterioration of living standards leads to a deepening of the crisis and to generalized instability. These are the conditions that lead us to think that, despite the ugly guise of pragmatism and realpolitik that the world has donned, the dreams of those who defend the possibility of a technocratic administration of the capitalist market with a steady, deep, and uncontested exploitation are not very feasible.

Nevertheless, the drift away from previous forms of collective struggle makes the discussion of the refutation-despair that emerges from poverty, proletarization-without-labor, and the crisis of the state utterly urgent. Can a new, reverse dynamic emerge, a potential radicalization of the struggle? And how can critical thought face today's reality beyond the simple denunciation of left-wing politics in the continuation of the restructuring? The questions formulated by a fetishistic anticapitalism stand critically before us. It is obvious that the ever-repeated proposals that insist on the reconstitution of the working-class identity—through the attainment of class consciousness—are more likely to confirm that state-ification of the movement or, in the most innocent of cases, look nostalgically to moments of past grandeur. On the other hand, the fragmentation or disappearance of the labor identity and the questioning of the workerist norm cannot be theoretically constituted as a negative teleology of class struggle with a happy ending, in replacement of the positive teleology of the labor movement. For critical thought, it is crucial to look with eyes wide open at the way in which the social antagonism of capital and labor is produced today compared to previous forms of collective struggle and understand the limits of our actions in order to break free from the hopelessness that looms over the present.

In putting aside all efforts to define the revolutionary subject—except that its social constitution will depend on all those who take the side of human emancipation in the constant clash with capital and its state (Bonefeld 2013: 311–12)—we cannot but insist on thinking of the subjectivity that is produced today as the questioning of class determination, as negativity; that is, not as the *Universal Subject of History* or as the subject *within history*, but as the subject that moves against its own history, a history that is leading us to extinction.

Notes

1   On the constitution of the *programmatic action* of the labor class during the twentieth century, see *Théorie Communiste* (2008).
2   We are not referring here to crystallized identities that are completely fragmented because of *conjuncture*, because of the specific contradictions displayed by capital in this specific period. On the contrary, there is reference to continuous *procedures/movements* of identification/de-identification that are perceived as flows of struggle. In this sense, Richard Gunn (2015: 157–58) is right in criticizing the Althusserian category of "conjuncture": "There is nothing outside the contradiction that could define the contradiction itself." If the conflictive conditions of the crisis activity clear the path for the questioning of the capitalist relation, it is the ek-static dimension of the struggle of the proletariat that allows (or not) for the critical production of prefigurative practices against (and beyond) capital.
3   On this, see the critique in the chapter in this book by Panagiotis Doulos.

4   On the issue of hegemony, see the insightful observation in the chapter by Theodoros Karyotis in this book.
5   For an analysis of the category of *form*, see *Open Marxism*, vol. 2 (1992).
6   We can envision this if we think of the different forms of ek-static existence of the butterfly (or the fly, which also transforms in this way) from caterpillar to chrysalis (in the cocoon) and then to butterfly.
7   At the beginning of *Capital*, vol. 1 (2002: 55ff), Marx mentions that in the capitalist mode of production the labor included in the commodities has a twofold character (useful or concrete and abstract labor) and that abstract labor prevails. This is obvious for Marx, if we take into account the forms acquired by labor in other historical periods, for which he uses terms such as "human labor," "indiscriminate human labor," or, simply, labor, "a process of labor in its essential elements." We can accept that the notion of human labor is used by Marx to facilitate analysis; that is, it is an empirical abstraction (and not a defined one, as Gunn mentions). However, it points toward a hyper-historical approach to labor. How certain are we that labor is "the everlasting Nature-imposed condition of human existence, and therefore is independent of every social phase of that existence, or rather, is common to every such phase" (1965 [1867]: 184) or "an eternal, nature-imposed necessity, without which there can be no material exchanges between man and Nature, and therefore no life." (1965 [1867]: 42–43)? This deserves further analysis. In any case, the discussion on useful or concrete and abstract labor is very vast and cannot be analyzed in the present article. On this, see for example Postone (1993), Rubin (1994), and Gunn (1992).
8   Conceived negatively, labor as an object and not as activity, according to Marx.
9   On this, see the analysis in the chapter in this book by Leonidas Oikonomakis.

References

Adorno, Theodor W. *Negative Dialectics*. New York: Continuum, 1973.
Blaumachen and friends. "Η ανάδυση του μη-υποκειμένου" [The emergence of the non-subject]. *Blaumachen* 6 (2013): 76–83.
Bonefeld, Werner. *Critical Theory and the Critique of Political Economy*. New York: Bloomsbury, 2014.
———. "El principio esperanza en la emancipación humana: acerca de Holloway." *Herramienta* 25, April 15, 2004. http://www.herramienta.com.ar/revista-herramienta-n-25/el-principio-esperanza-en-la-emancipacion-humana-acerca-de-holloway.
———. *La razón corrosiva*. Buenos Aires: Herramienta, 2013.
Bonnet, Alberto. "Antagonismo y diferencia: la dialéctica negativa y el posetructuralismo ante la crítica del capitalismo contemporáneo." In *Negatividad y Revolución*, edited by John Hollaway, Fernando Matamoros, and Sergio Tischler, 37–72. Buenos Aires: Ediciones Herramienta, 2007.
Cleaver, Harry, "The Inversion of Class Perspective in Marxian Theory: From Valorization to Self-Valorization." In *Open Marxism*, vol. 2, edited by Werner

Bonefeld, Richard Gunn, and Kosmas Psychopedis, 106–44. London: Pluto Press, 1992.

Dauvé, Gilles. "Love of Labor? Love of Labor Lost." *Endnotes* no. 1, October 2008. https://endnotes.org.uk/articles/12.

Endnotes. *Αθλιότητα και αξιακή μορφή*, Φίλοι του κεραυνοβόλου κομμουνισμού, [Misery and value form, friends of unexpected communism]. *Endnotes* no. 2, April 2010. https://2008-2012.net/2016/11/17/endnotes-2-misery-and-value-form/.

Εργάτες του Αρνητικού [Workers of the Negative]. "Μηχανολογία και ταξικός ανταγωνισμός: Βιομηχανική επανάσταση—φορντισμός—υπερτεχνολογικοποιημένος καπιταλισμός" [Mechanical engineering and class antagonism: Industrial revolution—Fordism—ultratechnologized capitalism]. *System Failure Acceleration* no. 2 (2005). http://ratnet-blog2.blogspot.mx/2010/03/blog-post_29.html.

Gunn, Richard. "Against Historical Materialism: Marxism as First-Order Discourse." In *Open Marxism*, vol. 2, edited by Werner Bonefeld, Richard Gunn, and Kosmas Psychopedis, 1–46. London: Pluto Press, 1992.

———. *Lo que usted siempre quiso saber sobre Hegel y no se atrevió a preguntar.* Buenos Aires: Herramienta Ediciones, 2015.

Hardt, Michael, and Antonio Negri. *Commonwealth*. Cambridge, MA: Harvard University Press, 2009.

———. *Multitude*. London: Penguin Books, 2004.

Hegel, G.W.F. *The Phenomenology of Spirit*. Oxford: Oxford University Press, 1977.

Holloway, John. *Change the World without Taking Power: The Meaning of Revolution Today*. London: Pluto Press, 2002.

———. "Global Capital and the National State." In *Global Capital, National State, and the Politics of Money*, edited by Werner Bonefeld and John Holloway, 116–41. London: Palgrave Macmillan, 1995.

———. *Keynesianismo, una peligrosa ilusión*. Buenos Aires: Ediciones Herramienta, 2003.

———. "We Are the Crisis of Abstract Labor." Speech in Rome, 2006 http://libcom.org/forums/thought/john-holloway-we-are-crisis-abstract-labor-14042006.

Lukács, György. *History and Class Consciousness*. Cambridge, MA: MIT Press, 1972.

Marx, Karl. *Capital*, vol. 1. Moscow: Progress Publishers, 1965.

———. *Capital*, vol. 3. London: Lawrence & Wishart, 1972.

———. *Grundrisse: Foundations of the Critique of Political Economy (Rough Draft)*. Harmondsworth, Penguin Books, 1973.

Meyer Forbes, Eric. "Que el propio educador debe ser educado . . . Indagaciones sobre la dialéctica del cambio social." Master's thesis, Instituto de Ciencias Sociales y Humanidades "Alfonso Vélez Pliego," BUAP, Puebla, Mexico, 2013.

Nasioka, Katerina. *Ciudades en Insurrección: Oaxaca 2006/Atenas 2008*, Cátedra Interinstitucional-Universidad de Guadalajara-CIESAS-Jorge Alonso, Guadalajara, 2017.

Negri, Antonio. *Revolution Retrieved: Writings on Marx, Keynes, Capitalist Crisis and New Social Subjects*. London: Red Notes, 1988.

Postone, Moishe. *Time, Labor and Social Domination.* Cambridge: Cambridge University Press, 1993.

Rubin, I.I. "Abstract Labor and Value Theory." In *Debates in Value Theory*, edited by Simon Mohun. Houndmills: Macmillan, 1994.

Théorie Communiste. "The Glass Floor." In *Les Emeutes en Grèce*, Paris: Senonevero, 2009. http://www.riff-raff.se/wiki/en/theorie_communiste/the_glass_floor.

———. "Much Ado about Nothing." *Endnotes* no. 1, October 2008. https://endnotes.org.uk/issues/1/en/theorie-communiste-much-ado-about-nothing.

———. "Για την ιστορική καταγωγή της Théorie Communiste" [On the historical origins of Théorie Communiste]. *Blaumachen* no. 4 (2010): 55–85.

Tischler, Sergio. "La crisis del canon clásico de la forma clase y los movimientos sociales en América Latina." In *Lucha = Clase*, edited by John Holloway, 103–27. Buenos Aires: Herramienta Ediciones, 2004.

———. *Revolución y Destotalización.* Guadalajara: Grietas Editores, 2013.

Williams, Raymond. *The Country and the City.* New York: Oxford University Press, 1973.

NINE

Anti-Epilogue

John Holloway, Katerina Nasioka, and Panagiotis Doulos

It is customary to add an epilogue or conclusion. An epilogue comes to summarize. It is the ending that unfolds the conclusions, homogenizes the arguments, and ensures the smooth flow of the questions. It highlights the most important issues, records the basic axes that traverse the texts of a book, and reveals the aspects that shape the points of communication between them. In this sense, the conclusions totalize the questions and the answers and shape the common place to which they are all heading.

But we did not want to write such an epilogue or draw any conclusions. We only want to comment on why this is not an epilogue. The issues raised by each writer have their own dynamics, their own melody, and they are unfolding at their own rhythm. An epilogue means that we should give priority to some paths over others, assume the position of a final judge who would draw a line, no matter if it is straight or diagonal, that would suggest to the reader a certain way of reinterpreting these paths. Since this book is more like hiccups (this hiccup that catches you when things do not work well or when you feel awkward or maybe when you feel great enthusiasm), we thought it would be best to let the dance of the texts unfold its questions freely, without any restrictions. Do not squeeze the criticisms that are analyzed into a homogenized narrative, which certainly does not exist. We let the dialogues and the debates maintain their own energy.

Or perhaps we just want to break a habit. It is the habit that often leads us when we are reading a book to look first at the conclusion, to make sure we have understood the correct interpretation, that we have found the answer. In this case, we don't have answers. Maybe it's better that way. This book is a question that remains open. We only know that we do not like the world as it is. We want something else beyond this one.

When we say that under capitalism the subject is contradictory, we are not talking about people observed from some type of glass sphere or the screen of a "smart" device. We ourselves, like all others in the capitalist world, are contradictory. This is our scream against the capitalistic barbarity. A contradictory "no" to that which negates us, to that which eliminates us, to all that says that this is how the world is, that it does not change. If for the representatives of the bourgeois class our negations mean that we are immature and insane, then we are proud of it. We already know that history does not come to an end, that its movement can't be prejudged. The society we live in can appear as painting gray on gray. In real terms, this society is nothing more than the unfolding of a constant bloodshed in the continuous movement of social antagonisms and contradictions. Gray is the color of this monotonous and boring grammar of a world that constantly murmurs the monologue of the dominant logic.

The concerns that have created the need to express ourselves are still here. Maybe with more rage. Like a river that continues to inflate and press on its banks in order to break them; the agony, in other words, to break the gray wall of the capitalist reality that is crushing us. As the social resistances-and-rebellions have no epilogue against the generalized injustice, we also think that this book cannot have any conclusions. The question remains: What is beyond the crisis? What do we envision as a horizon against and beyond capitalist barbarity?

Contributors

Panagiotis Doulos completed his PhD studies in sociology at the Instituto de Ciencias Sociales y Humanidades "Alfonso Vélez Pliego" of the Benemérita Universidad Autónoma de Puebla, Mexico. He teaches in the Department of Social Anthropology in the Universidad Autónoma de Tlaxcala. His research interests concern issues such as violence, antiviolence and social resistances, and critical theory.

Panos Drakos received a degree in Politics, Government and Philosophy from the University of Kent in Canterbury and at the same university completed his postgraduate studies in European studies and international relations. He has devoted his writing activity to enriching the political theory of social anarchism.

John Holloway, professor in the Posgrado de Sociología, Instituto de Ciencias Sociales y Humanidades "Alfonso Vélez Pliego," Benemérita Universidad Autónoma de Puebla, has written widely on anticapitalist resistance-and-rebellion and on Marxist theory. His books include: *Change the World without Taking Power* (Pluto Press, latest edition 2019), *Crack Capitalism* (Pluto Press, 2010), and, with PM Press, *In, against and beyond Capitalism: The San Francisco Lectures* (2016) and *We are the Crisis of Capital: A John Holloway Reader* (2019).

Theodoros Karyotis is a sociologist, a translator, and a member of grassroots movements practicing direct democracy, solidarity economy, and the defense and self-management of the commons. He is currently a doctoral researcher on housing and citizenship at the University of Ghent, Belgium. He coordinates www.workerscontrol.net, a multilingual resource on workers' self-management, and sits on the advisory council of the Transnational Institute of Social Ecology.

Dimitra Kotouza is the author of *Surplus Citizens: Struggle and Nationalism in the Greek Crisis* (Pluto Press, 2019). She lectures in sociology and politics at universities in and around London and is an editorial collective member of the journals *Mute* and *Endnotes*. She is a contributor to *Biopolitical Governance*, edited by Hannah Richter (Rowman and Littlefield 2018), and the forthcoming *What Is to Be Done under Real Subsumption* edited by Anthony Iles and Mattin (Mute Books). Her writing has also appeared in academic journals and radical publications in English and Greek.

Katerina Nasioka received a doctorate in sociology from the Instituto de Ciencias Sociales y Humanidades "Alfonso Vélez Pliego" of the Benemérita Universidad Autónoma de Puebla, Mexico. She is the coauthor of *Gender and Journalism in Greece* (2008) and the author of *Ciudades en Insurrección. Oaxaca 2006 / Atenas 2008* (2017) and of various articles and chapters on the social struggles in Greece (e.g. "The Proletariat versus the Working Class: Shifts in Class Struggle in the Twenty-first Century," in *Open Marxism* vol. 4, 2019). Her research interests center on space, critical theory, subjectivity, and social struggles.

Leonidas Oikonomakis is a COFUND Junior Research Fellow in the Department of Anthropology at Durham University. He was awarded his PhD from the European University Institute's Department of Social and Political Sciences and has taught at the University of Crete and the Hellenic Open University. He is also a rapper with Greek hip-hop collective Social Waste and a member of *ROAR Magazine*'s editorial team. He is the author of *Political Strategies and Social Movements in Latin America: The Zapatistas and Bolivian Cocaleros* (Palgrave Macmillan, 2019).

George Sotiropoulos holds a PhD in political theory from the University of Kent. He is teaching at the International School of Athens and he is also a visiting researcher at the Department of Political Science and International Relations of the University of Corinth. He has been active in various movements, groups and collective projects and he is a member of the Void Network collective. His publications cover a wide range of themes, including democratic theory and contemporary social movements. He is also a regular author in online sites related to political analysis and theory. His current research interests focus on a theoretical and historical study of justice, leading to the publication of a monograph, *A Materialist Theory of Justice: The One, the Many, the Not-Yet* (Rowman and Littlefield, 2019).

Index

"Passim" (literally "scattered") indicates intermittent discussion of a topic over a cluster of pages.

ABOUT PM PRESS

PM Press is an independent, radical publisher of books and media to educate, entertain, and inspire. Founded in 2007 by a small group of people with decades of publishing, media, and organizing experience, PM Press amplifies the voices of radical authors, artists, and activists. Our aim is to deliver bold political ideas and vital stories to all walks of life and arm the dreamers to demand the impossible. We have sold millions of copies of our books, most often one at a time, face to face. We're old enough to know what we're doing and young enough to know what's at stake. Join us to create a better world.

PM Press, PO Box 23912, Oakland, CA 94623, www.pmpress.org
PM Press in Europe, europe@pmpress.org, www.pmpress.org.uk

FRIENDS OF PM PRESS

These are indisputably momentous times—the financial system is melting down globally and the Empire is stumbling. Now more than ever there is a vital need for radical ideas.

Friends of PM allows you to directly help impact, amplify, and revitalize the discourse and actions of radical writers, filmmakers, and artists. It provides us with a stable foundation from which we can build upon our early successes and provides a much-needed subsidy for the materials that can't necessarily pay their own way. You can help make that happen—and receive every new title automatically delivered to your door once a month—by joining as a Friend of PM Press. And, we'll throw in a free T-shirt when you sign up.

Here are your options:

- **$30 a month** Get all books and pamphlets plus 50% discount on all webstore purchases

- **$40 a month** Get all PM Press releases (including CDs and DVDs) plus 50% discount on all webstore purchases

- **$100 a month Superstar**—Everything plus PM merchandise, free downloads, and 50% discount on all webstore purchases

For those who can't afford $30 or more a month, we have **Sustainer Rates** at $15, $10 and $5. Sustainers get a free PM Press T-shirt and a 50% discount on all purchases from our website.

Your Visa or Mastercard will be billed once a month, until you tell us to stop. Or until our efforts succeed in bringing the revolution around. Or the financial meltdown of Capital makes plastic redundant. Whichever comes first.

In, Against, and Beyond Capitalism: The San Francisco Lectures

John Holloway
with a Preface by Andrej Grubačić

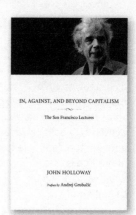

ISBN: 978-1-62963-109-7
$14.95   112 pages

In, Against, and Beyond Capitalism is based on three recent lectures delivered by John Holloway at the California Institute of Integral Studies in San Francisco. The lectures focus on what anticapitalist revolution can mean today—after the historic failure of the idea that the conquest of state power was the key to radical change—and offer a brilliant and engaging introduction to the central themes of Holloway's work.

The lectures take as their central challenge the idea that "We Are the Crisis of Capital and Proud of It." This runs counter to many leftist assumptions that the capitalists are to blame for the crisis, or that crisis is simply the expression of the bankruptcy of the system. The only way to see crisis as the possible threshold to a better world is to understand the failure of capitalism as the face of the push of our creative force. This poses a theoretical challenge. The first lecture focuses on the meaning of "We," the second on the understanding of capital as a system of social cohesion that systematically frustrates our creative force, and the third on the proposal that we are the crisis of this system of cohesion.

"His Marxism is premised on another form of logic, one that affirms movement, instability, and struggle. This is a movement of thought that affirms the richness of life, particularity (non-identity) and 'walking in the opposite direction'; walking, that is, away from exploitation, domination, and classification. Without contradictory thinking in, against, and beyond the capitalist society, capital once again becomes a reified object, a thing, and not a social relation that signifies transformation of a useful and creative activity (doing) into (abstract) labor. Only open dialectics, a right kind of thinking for the wrong kind of world, non-unitary thinking without guarantees, is able to assist us in our contradictory struggle for a world free of contradiction."
—Andrej Grubačić, from his Preface

"Holloway's work is infectiously optimistic."
—Steven Poole, the *Guardian* (UK)

"Holloway's thesis is indeed important and worthy of notice"
—Richard J.F. Day, *Canadian Journal of Cultural Studies*